MY WILD AND
PRECIOUS LIFE

MY WILD AND PRECIOUS LIFE

A Memoir of Africa

SUSANNE RHEAULT

BUSH BABY
PRESS

Published by Bush Baby Press, Lincoln, Massachusetts

Edited and designed by Girl Friday Productions
www.girlfridayproductions.com

Editorial: Alexander Rigby, Laura Whittemore,
Sharon Turner Mulvihill
Design: Paul Barrett

Image credits: cover © Ina Ghaznavi

The Summer Day from *HOUSE OF LIGHT* by Mary
Oliver, published by Beacon Press, Boston
Copyright © 1990 by Mary Oliver, used herewith by
permission of the Charlotte Sheedy Literary Agency, Inc.

ISBN (paperback): 978-0-578-50095-9

*This book is dedicated to my husband Gil,
his optimism, and his generous heart*

THE SUMMER DAY

Who made the world?
Who made the swan, and the black bear?
Who made the grasshopper?
This grasshopper, I mean-
the one who has flung herself out of the grass,
the one who is eating sugar out of my hand,
who is moving her jaws back and forth instead of up and down-
who is gazing around with her enormous and complicated eyes.
Now she lifts her pale forearms and thoroughly washes her face.
Now she snaps her wings open, and floats away.
I don't know exactly what a prayer is.
I do know how to pay attention, how to fall down
into the grass, how to kneel down in the grass,
how to be idle and blessed, how to stroll through the fields,
which is what I have been doing all day.
Tell me, what else should I have done?
Doesn't everything die at last, and too soon?
Tell me, what is it you plan to do
with your one wild and precious life?

—Mary Oliver

CONTENTS

Author's Note xi
Prologue xiii

CHAPTER ONE Life as a Rolling Stone 1
CHAPTER TWO A Separate Path 15
CHAPTER THREE Things Fall Apart 25
CHAPTER FOUR Peter and Zack 29
CHAPTER FIVE Lions and Leave-taking 39
CHAPTER SIX Ethiopia, the Early Years 49
CHAPTER SEVEN Getting in Deeper 65
CHAPTER EIGHT Small Countries at Risk 83
CHAPTER NINE Two Kinds of Migration 103
CHAPTER TEN We Take on Precious as a Project 115
CHAPTER ELEVEN Big Wins and Big Challenges 139
CHAPTER TWELVE Heartaches and Resilience 165
CHAPTER THIRTEEN Corruption Up Close 187
CHAPTER FOURTEEN A Season of Loss 197
CHAPTER FIFTEEN The Roller Coaster 231
CHAPTER SIXTEEN The Future 251

Photos 257
Acknowledgments 265
About the Author 269

AUTHOR'S NOTE

This book is a memoir. It reflects the author's present recollections of experiences over time. Some names and characteristics have been changed, some events have been compressed, and some dialogue has been recreated.

PROLOGUE

Nshupu, Tanzania. The sun beats down on us as my husband, Gil, and I steadily climb the slopes of Mount Meru. The change in altitude makes me short of breath. The village, such as it is, is a warren of footpaths dotted with tiny one-room brick houses. Each house has a small area for planting maize, and the dried stalks rustle in the wind. The soil is gray and dusty. I cannot imagine how anything has grown here. The only color is the sprawling fuchsia bougainvillea, which seems to thrive on neglect and drought. Along the path on either side are cement blocks, which almost look like gravestones. I know from my work that these are the remnants of abandoned efforts by the World Bank three years ago to build a $1.4 billion water project, which has utterly failed. I am sweaty, dusty, and thirsty, and I am beginning to wilt on this "cultural walking tour." I have been working in Africa since 2007 in short consulting stints throughout a number of countries, but this 2011 trip is different. I have managed to lure Gil here on a safari in the hopes that he would fall in love with Tanzania as I have. Now we are together, on the lookout for possible projects in this rural area that could use our skills to the benefit of local people. In somewhat random fashion we are casting about; my usual hyperorganized networking methods have failed. I am hot and ready for this walk to be over so I can retreat to the cooler confines of our lodge room.

At the top of the rise, our guide, Adam, points to a barren enclave of small, gray, concrete buildings surrounded by dirt and a thin hedge of bougainvillea. "This is a new orphanage," he announces. "Nine AIDS orphans live here." *Here?* I think. I see no kids, no color, no signs of life. Gil and I ask if we might see more. Adam takes us inside the largest of the three buildings. There are indeed nine small children playing in one room. The room is utterly bare but for one bunk bed, the walls and floor the same dirty color of gray concrete. I am horrified and peer into the next room. It is the same as the first, one small barred window, one bunk bed. No bedding, no curtains, no rugs, no toys. Not one shred of the detritus of books and stuffed animals that might suggest a child's bedroom in the world I come from. A cramped storeroom with one double mattress is where the two rotating "mamas" sleep.

This is not my first trip to Africa. It is my nineteenth. I have swatted flies in Maasai mud-and-dung huts. I have visited dispensaries with no running water where babies are delivered. I have walked the streets of tiny villages where barefoot kids scratch in the dirt alongside chickens and goats. But this scene stuns me. It is so spare, so gray, so grim.

While I am trying to mask my shock, the kids are doing what kids do, crowding around, clowning for our cameras, saying "Hello, madam" proudly, then on request, singing a hymn, which Gil records on his camera. Like so many Tanzanian hymns, this one requires a lot of hand gestures and choreographed movement. The smallest boy among them, Innocent, is the biggest ham. Planting himself center stage, Innocent puffs out his chest and proudly points to each of the requisite body parts just a beat ahead of all others. The kids then shriek with hilarity to see the playback on Gil's tiny screen while I get Adam's translation of the Swahili lyrics. "Jesus is dead. But I know he lives. Look at my arms, my legs, my hands, my feet. This is how I know he lives."

The children press in on Gil and one another on the lower bunk bed, laughing and teasing. Gil is in a sandwich of wriggling, giggling little bodies. I stand apart at the threshold of the two barren rooms having an out-of-body experience. The contrast is so great, the sheer energy of the kids and the desolation of their circumstances.

Soon it is time to go. The young mama needs to finish getting the kids ready for school, and we are creating havoc. So we stagger out into the bright sunlight and walk back to the lodge in stunned silence. Once Gil and I part ways from Adam, we turn to each other to say the same thing: "We have to do something here." We are just not sure how or what. My experiences in Africa have already irrevocably changed my perspective. This next venture will change my life in ways I could hardly imagine. The foot of the compass of my life will move to another hemisphere. I will live on a knife-edge of highs and lows. Gil and I will be joined at the hip in a small project suddenly made huge. And I will see up close the corrosion poverty creates, and the hope that somehow endures despite all odds.

CHAPTER ONE

Life as a Rolling Stone

My upbringing could not have been more different from that of the children I saw, but I do know something of dislocation. I grew up as a rolling stone, an "army brat." All through my childhood, my parents and two siblings and I moved like Bedouins. We moved eleven times by the time I finished high school: from the flatlands of Kansas to Germany to South Carolina to the Right Bank of Paris.

We never fit in for long. We never had pets except for a loaner poodle named Anatole and a hamster. And my parents, once freed from the dictates of their wealthy families, carved out lives of idiosyncratic adventure. On Sunday morning, we did not go to church; we went rock climbing, my dad teaching my sister and me to rappel off the sheer sides of small cliffs. My dad, Bob Rheault, joined the elite Special Forces, then popularly known as the Green Berets. Although his education at West Point put him in line for increasing leadership roles, he had been weaned on Granddaddy Rheault's stories of self-reliance in the deep Canadian wilderness, living for months with only his sled dogs. Dad found office work confining and dull and lived for his "maneuvers" out in the field. He was not permitted to tell us anything about his mysterious nocturnal disappearances. It wasn't until he had long retired from the army that we found out he was doing war games in places like Afghanistan, Pakistan, India, Laos, and Cambodia.

Dad was on the fast track to a brilliant career. Mom and Dad were deeply in love at nineteen and twenty, their feelings amplified by the strident objections of their fathers, difficult men wrestling with their own failures. Grandpa Young, Mom's father, lost most everything in the Depression. He took out his rage and impotence on his wife and three children. One night when my father's telephone call from Fort Benning to Mom interrupted the sacrosanct cocktail hour, Grandpa ripped the phone off the wall.

Granddaddy Rheault was less grandiose but equally frozen in his view of the world. He boycotted my parents' wedding when Mom refused to convert to Catholicism. Granddaddy grew up as one of thirteen in the small town of Sherbrooke, Québec, Canada. He became a Canadian Mountie, the pride of his adult life. He mapped previously uncharted territories in the northwest provinces alone on a dogsled for six months at a time. His ironclad military discipline enabled him to survive those harsh winters, but he was at sea in Granny's world of Boston Brahman old money. The two of them would have never met: they lived in different places, and in entirely different strata. Then something like fate intervened. During World War I, Granny was working as a nurse's aide in the Grenfell Labrador Commission. Mr. Grenfell received a letter from a Mountie asking to be paired with a pen pal. The two of them wrote each other letters throughout the war. Her letters gave no hint of her world of wealth and privilege. After the war, Granny longed to be out from under the irascible dictates of her very rich father, Pa Bradley. She was thirty years old, almost past the point when her spinsterhood would become a lifelong burden. She reached out to Charles, my grandfather, and invited him to Boston without telling her father. When he took the train to Boston to meet Rosamond, my grandmother, he was stunned to be met by a limousine with a uniformed driver.

Later on, Granddaddy's bedroom in the Rheault mansion said it all. More cell than bedroom, his single bed was made up with an army blanket, the walls decorated with sepia photographs of his troops, his old rifle suspended prominently over his bed. He lived as a kept man, imported, tolerated, and funded to rescue Granny from a life of spinsterhood. He was given a senior job managing a petroleum company for the family, a job for which he was ill-suited and ill-prepared. Even by the time I came along, he still spoke endlessly of his time with the Mounties as his finest years and insisted his family speak French at the table.

I never learned how my parents met, to my regret. But we all knew the family lore of how the early marriage unfolded. Because of World War II, Dad's class at West Point was accelerated to three years from four. He proposed to Mom, asking her to marry him and to then wait for his return from Germany. She was still an art student at Vassar, working as a fashion model in Manhattan. She refused. Unwilling to be married and put on the shelf, she knew that a long separation would erode their passion and connection. She would drop out of Vassar and go to Germany or not marry at all. That was her stance. She would need that strong will as an army wife, as the military machine ran our lives.

Once married despite their fathers' objections, Dad's first orders sent him to Allied-occupied Germany in 1947. There Mom and Dad lived in a Quonset hut close to the Czech border. Not wanting to use the bathroom shared by the men,

Mom took a Walther handgun and went to the Russian side of the forest to relieve herself. She got pregnant too soon (in an unguarded moment, she told me I had been "an accident"). There would be no lavish baby showers for this young mother. She was spat on by Germans in the street, an American and a visible symbol of their subjugation.

Thus the family began, with a sense of adventure and an absolute refusal to play by the rules, an odd stance for a military family. My mother disdained the close confines of army bases, opting to venture out into the community to learn the language and find local foods. A landscape artist and portraitist, my mother would set up her easel in the midst of some small town, easily making new friends who would later show up at our dinner table. When she was in her sixties, she planted marijuana in her carefully tended vegetable garden, only removing it when the garden club came to visit. She didn't smoke; she simply liked to shock her green-thumb friends.

Dad's nonconformity was made manifest in his choice to join Special Forces. He loved being in the field, often subtly refusing to embrace the privileges that his rank offered or allowing his men to manage up. He would not ask his men to do things he was not willing to do. He took up the pack and sprayed Agent Orange in Vietnam as they did, a choice that would lead to fierce struggles with Parkinson's disease later in life.

DAD GOES TO KOREA

When Dad shipped out to war in Korea, the army extruded us "dependents." No home, no schools, no roots, no warm extended family to take us in. We were on our own. First Mom tried Florida with us two girls (ages five and two) in tow. The summer heat and the isolation were too much to bear. When

Mom reached out to her father for help in relocating north, he shot back, "You made your bed, now lie in it!" Mom then appealed to Dad's mother, and she helped us to rent a house in Dover, fifteen minutes from their estate in Westwood, Massachusetts.

Granny's home was surrounded by fifty-two acres of woods, fields, manicured gardens, and barns. Three Irish maids occupied cramped second-floor staff quarters, and a full-time gardener lived in his own antique cottage. Ernest was a diminutive French Canadian transplant like Granddaddy. At first it was fun for me to natter to him in French. But when he regularly began to grab for my small breast buds, I was filled with shame and stopped my visits with him in the garden.

In the huge main house, Westminster chimes echoed in the cool tiled entry, and we were instructed in the correct use of finger bowls at dinner. Granny did her best to make us feel at home, but there were no children within a two-mile radius, and the cousins she invited over lived lives of incomprehensible wealth: horseback riding, sailing, and private schools, huge four-poster frilly beds, bedrooms of their own, pampered pets.

Our lives in our rented bungalow in Dover were quite different. Our house was on the wrong side of the tracks, away from the upscale neighborhoods with huge houses and big stone walls. The ramshackle house next door sold what was billed as antiques but was simply old household junk. The more they sold, the more it seemed to proliferate. The woman of the house, Beverly, was morbidly obese, and in two years I never once saw her get up from her porch chair and try to walk.

But from her chair she designed a fantasy world that carried my sister and me through our own isolation. She spun a tale that there were elves living in her copper hot-water heater and that when it clanked that was them at work. When I came to show her the dime that the tooth fairy had brought me, she presented me with an entire cowgirl outfit that she said the tooth fairy had also brought me! My mom didn't mind the drastic inflation on tooth fairy gifts; I was so taken by the magic emanating from that odd house next door.

When my father returned from Korea, the reunion was less than romantic. My mother had chicken pox and was still angry at having been so alone while he was at war. Finally things thawed between them and my mother continued to school us in basic French vocabulary. Remarkably, the army was going to send us to France to prepare my father to run the French department at West Point. This was not an assignment he had asked for. The army sends you where they want you to go. But Paris after Korea was certainly a beacon. My mother's spirits began to lift as she wandered around the house singing nursery rhymes in French.

PARIS, 1954

Once in Paris, we rented an apartment near the Eiffel Tower. As planned, my sister and I were sent to the local school for American military families: my four-year-old sister, Michelle, in the nursery school, and me in the second grade, at age seven.

We lasted two days. My mother deemed the school mediocre and found us a bilingual equivalent. The Ecole Bilingue sat in the shadow of the Eiffel Tower and was well known to families of diplomats and expats. Once we learned the way to school, my sister and I walked there alone each morning across the Champ de Mars. There, young boys in woolen knickers propelled their huge metal hoops alongside a profusion of flowers, the roses tinged with frost in the early mornings.

After a month of language immersion with other foreign kids, I "graduated" to a French-speaking second grade. There was no preparation. I simply was taken one morning and plopped into an ongoing class. Seeing the multiplication tables on the wall terrified me. I had barely learned to add and subtract and now I had to multiply in French! I put on my requisite *tablier* apron and slid quietly into my wooden *pupitre* with its inkwell in the upper corner, while the kids stared at the young American interloper. All of our work was done using fountain pens in composition books. If an error was made, the book could not be disassembled and the page removed. The splat of ink and errors remained in perpetuity.

Each night I took home two hours of homework to be completed in ink. Dad was stunned at the size of the assignments. Together we set up shop on the dining room table, first trying to figure out how to pump ink into my fountain pen without wearing it. Dad fumbled with the tiny lever as much as I did, but we were a team, a source of enormous comfort to me. One nightly assignment was the *dictée*, a short composition that would be read aloud the next day. Punctuation, accents, spelling, all had to be correct. For days I slid a copy just under my lift-top desk and peered at the correct answers as the teacher read aloud, my heart pounding at the prospect of being exposed. The teacher never called me out. Or more likely, she saw me and took pity. I was suffused with guilt and yet no dire punishment ensued. But I kept myself at a distance lest I risk exposure of my cheating heart.

After the *dictée* quiz, I eagerly watched the clock for the lunch break. In the chilly refectory, my classmates and I drank our tumblers of red wine and water, a simple way to both sedate us and inoculate us to French custom. In the midafternoon we were given a hunk of French bread with two large squares of chocolate stuffed inside. Meantime my sister endured her own private hell in the kindergarten. The confusion of two languages had rendered her utterly mute. Two weeks in, she came home with bald spots where kids had pulled her hair out on the playground. My mother complained to the school administrators with no particular success.

Then one day my sister broke her silence, announcing, "They said hello to me! They said *bonjour!*" As our French became more fluent, we all adapted to our new lives. My father grew out his crewcut, my mother set up her easel and paints along the Seine. Mom, like her mother, Susanne, loved to paint. It was her moveable feast that would sustain her through our many moves. She could create a likeness in minutes, and her pastel portraits of children were in demand wherever we lived. In my house to this day are two side-by-side pieces: a pastel of Mom done by her mother, and a drawing of me made by Mom. Each piece looks like it was done by the same artist, so alike are the lines and contours. Later in life, my sister became an artist too, in graphic design, garden design, and filmmaking.

WEST POINT, 1955–58

After France, the next three years at West Point were a respite of calm and predictability. My dad drove his red MG to a normal job, we got a loaner dog, and my mom had a baby boy, Robert B. Rheault Jr. This new addition I tolerated grudgingly. I was the eldest, and I suddenly realized how deeply my father had wanted a son. The night my brother was born, I heard Dad on the telephone exultant, bragging that now he had a son who could be West Point class of 1980. I knew that no such excitement had greeted my birth. Too early in a new marriage.

West Point was beyond safe, patrolled as it was by a surfeit of MPs, with a speed limit of fifteen miles an hour, and an absolute requirement that we stop and step out of the car to salute if the flag was being raised or lowered. Everything on an army post was regulated and standardized, from the layout of a PX to the symmetry of men on parade. Life there was safe even as it was all about preparation for war. So our lives oscillated between fear and boredom: fear that Dad would get his wish to go back to war someday, and boredom with the enforced waiting. Dad clearly loved the excitement and the fear, and that binary whiplash became my rhythm too. To this day I crave the comfort of well-established routine, but soon enough it starts to chafe.

With the glut of three whole years in one spot, my mother started a small garden in our middle unit of the triplex and trained blue morning glories up the side of the kitchen entrance. I took ballet class and went to Sunday school taught by earnest and handsome young plebes.

But I had missed a step being in Paris. All my peers were riding two-wheeled bikes, and our stint abroad meant I had missed this crucial rite of passage. Mortified, I watched from the sidelines and plotted how to catch up. I persuaded my parents to buy me a two-wheeled bike, and, anxious to get on with it, I walked it up two steep hills past two large triplex units just like ours.

At the top of the hill I positioned myself and my bike in the middle of the road. My mother didn't spot me until my feet reached the pedals (barely) and I crested the first steep hill. As I picked up speed, my hair flew behind me, the rows of army barracks beginning to blur. By then I was on an adrenaline high, my mind empty but for the whoosh of wind in my ears. It was too late to stop until I crashed into the side of our neighbor's brand-new station wagon. I was bloodied but I had made the grade. The neighbors were amazingly gracious, and I was given no more punishment beyond my colorful black eye. I had earned my long-standing nickname, Rocky. I still played with Ginny dolls, but more than anything I wanted to be brave. I didn't always know how to fit in, but I knew how to hang tough. I knew too that my dad was secretly proud of my pluck. He understood the lure of risk. It was his life.

FORT LEAVENWORTH, KANSAS, 1960

I am ten years old when we arrive in Fort Leavenworth, Kansas, after three years at West Point. We will be here for only one year while Dad goes to what he calls "war college." It is hot and still, in an area my father jokingly describes as "a thousand miles equidistant from any place you'd rather be." My parents are young, handsome, and irreverent, and my father's career is still on a steady, optimistic, upward trajectory.

The land around the army post is parched and flat, with only the vast expanse of the nearby military prison to break up the landscape. We are moving into a triplex on the base, a featureless brick-and-cement enclave as remarkably ugly as all of our other army quarters. I must learn to hang on tight to the fast-moving roller coaster that is our life as military camp followers. Like all army brats, I have to learn to fit in fast and not reveal the anxiety that dogs me. What if I can't pull it off here, find a best friend, run with the pack? I cannot tell anyone this, not my younger sister, my parents, my grandparents. I am an army of one.

The moving van begins unloading our furniture. Before the military will pack up a family, you must sign a waiver to indicate you understand that if there is any breakage or loss you will be reimbursed at the rate of ten cents a pound. My mother is standing on the sidewalk visibly anxious to see if the few belongings we really care about will arrive intact. Our mahogany dining room table, gift of a wealthy granny, is then unloaded one broken leg at a time.

Even as my mother begins to weep, I am casing the area. If I have only one year to make friends, I had better start now. I notice a few bikes about my size leaning against the unit next door, and then I see two girls my age roll down the road on roller skates, leggy, tan, and laughing. With its rigidly enforced ten-mile-an-hour speed limit, an army base is the perfect place to roller skate down the middle of the road.

While my father tries to talk my mother down, I am distracted. I want to be friends with those girls. I need friends and have no time to lose. But I cannot appear too anxious either. Already even I know that. Army kids are not exclusionary, but they are tough. We are all toughened by our lives of chronic disruption. So I will bide my time. I know from previous moves that my mother will soon suck it up. In a couple of hours she will be banging nails and hanging up her artwork in the house. She knows not to take any time to agonize about décor. She will have our kitchen and our house set up by suppertime.

This is home for now. This is what we have. That night, tornado warnings propel us all into the small, dank basement. But my father will frame it as another adventure, and we will camouflage our fear with knock-knock jokes in the darkness. We are a thousand miles equidistant from any place we ever called home, but within a week I will be roller skating with the pack. I know how to make friends, to shoehorn myself into a tight space. Here I will go to the sixth grade, wear braces on my teeth (Dad describes my smile as "the front end of a Cadillac"), and persuade my mom to buy me my first training bra (a wholly unnecessary purchase as the net effect is, according to Dad, "two peas under a blanket"). Mom will drive me two hours each way to Kansas City once a month to get my braces tightened. She reads *Jane Eyre* aloud, transporting me away from mouth pain to a world of fiction, my refuge ever since. We wept at the same passages.

This time in the flatlands gives us another year of relative normalcy. Again we flout the rules and get away with it, as Dad has just had another promotion. We learn to answer the phone "Captain Rheault's quarters, Susie speaking." In the cold of winter we attach a rope to the back of the Buick and ski behind the car. The MPs are apoplectic, but they can't find a rule in their book that addresses this infraction.

I am earnestly now trying to maintain the right to my nickname, Rocky. Dad thinks I am beginning to look chunky (a cardinal sin in our family). So every morning at 6:30 sharp I join him in his run out to the looming military prison and back. I feel special to be singled out for solo time with my dad, despite the reasons. After the run we do sit-ups on the living room floor while Mom dishes out cereal. It is clear to me what I must do, how I must be: tough, brave, scrappy, and able to laugh at myself.

THIN ICE AT GRANDMA'S

With an average relocation rate of once every year and a half came new schools, new friends, new languages, new rules. When we were temporarily homeless between assignments (while Dad went on ahead to Kansas, West Point, Paris, Germany, Okinawa, Pennsylvania, North Carolina, Washington, DC, or wherever), our short-term refuge was my maternal grandmother's home in Connecticut. Grandma would drive hours to retrieve us from some military airport. Hungry, disheveled, and disoriented, we clutched our mangy dolls as she drove us home through the dark. Grandma's aging colonial was surrounded by six acres of gardens and fields and a small pond where my brother slipped through the thin ice one winter and nearly drowned.

In a manner of speaking, we all skated on thin ice at Grandma's house. She was generous and loving, but Grandpa scared us to death. He had emphysema, and his phlegmy coughing could be heard throughout the house. He used a nautical air horn to summon my grandmother. We could hear him muttering, then yelling, then the air horn would erupt.

The earsplitting screech would stop us all in our tracks while Grandma (long legged, thin, and tall as a Maasai) would speed to his side. The air horn had been purchased to signal emergencies, but Grandpa used it for anything and everything, even to ask for more Kleenex.

Life at Grandma's house tiptoed around Grandpa's needs. He slept late; she would bring him breakfast on a tray in their bedroom. This allowed us kids to go out onto the back porch with Grandma to join her rain-or-shine routine, the daily singing of the doxology. "Praise God from whom all blessings flow, praise him all ye creatures here below . . ." This was followed by what Grandma called a three-cornered kiss, whereby we would press our small faces into hers for a resounding smooch. We loved the singing and the press of bodies against her thin frame. When I became a teenager and slept late, she would go back outside with me to do a second rendition.

At 6:30 sharp every evening, the family assembled in the living room. All of us dressed up for dinner, and the adults would sip sherry while Grandpa listened to the evening news on the radio. The volume was turned up to maximum, and we kids inevitably got restless. Soon Grandpa would bellow, "Susanne, shut those damn kids up!" Mom's eyes would fill as she scooped us up and took us out of range. We knew that Grandpa's outbursts troubled her more than they did us, so obvious was his impotence. We were glad to go play Chinese checkers in the piano room, freed from listening to stertorous newscasting at earsplitting levels.

One fractious night when dessert was too long in coming to the table, Grandpa took a stack of dessert plates and smashed them all on the floor in a show that left him panting and the rest of us stupefied. Perhaps because we were all there to bear witness, Grandma took a stand. "Ben," she said, "I will not pick up these dishes until you apologize." It took seven days. Finally, on the seventh day he muttered, "Sorry." The dishes were cleaned up. Grandma had made her point.

But while Grandpa slept, Grandma made magic for us. In the evenings after dinner we sat on the patio, watching fireflies. Grandma would read aloud to us from Rudyard Kipling or *The Water Babies*, where Mrs. Doasyouwouldbedoneby had her differences with Mrs. Bedonebyasyoudid. And there were fairies who Grandma said were secretly establishing their houses on the lawn. In the morning she would show us the small mushrooms where they had made their homes.

I was named Susanne after Grandma. The full name was usually used for disciplinary infractions: "Susanne, don't you dare talk to your mother that way!" At the same time, I knew that the legacy I was supposed to fulfill as her namesake needed to be etched with compassion and courage, a stretch to be sure. Both Grandma and Mom were role models of this mix of grace and grit, tough-minded and tenderhearted, stubborn and generous.

CHAPTER TWO

A Separate Path

THE NORTHFIELD YEARS, 1962–1966

As Dad's commitment to Special Forces deepened, we were sent to southern Bavaria for the next three years. We lived in spacious old SS quarters near acres of bucolic pasture, the sound of cowbells a comforting backdrop. Dad did skydives for fun on the weekends. We watched from the yard with Mom. Dad told her that he would be the fifth jumper to exit the airplane. We watched the specks hurtling through the sky before their chutes opened, counting carefully. When the fifth speck exited, we held our breath, waiting for Dad's chute to open. He is exuberant. We are terrified.

At the same time I am trying to fit in again, a fraught undertaking in junior high. I quickly figure out that being an A student means being an outcast, so my grades slump to Cs and Ds. My friend Darlene teaches me how to shoplift, and we steal sweaters from the PX. I learn to smoke cigarettes and create a plumbing crisis by pushing butts down my small bedroom sink. I talk back to my mother, and she worries that the boarding high school for American military kids (two hours away) will further encourage my budding delinquency. Mom swings into action, researching boarding schools in the US that will deter me from a life of crime. Granny Rheault offers to pay for me to attend the Northfield School for Girls in Massachusetts. Mom and Granny were anxious that I not be placed in a school where girls were parading their silver spoons and planning debutante parties. Northfield fit the bill; it was founded by evangelist D. L. Moody expressly "for girls of limited means." I watched the discussion unfold knowing that the decision was not mine to make. At some level I was relieved. I knew I was in over my head. On a recent field trip I'd been at the very back of the bus attempting to "make out" with a boy named Reggie who gave up on me, loudly pronouncing me to all on the bus as a crummy kisser. Humiliated, I knew if I stayed I'd have to up my game. I was twelve. I hoped my mother and my grandmother would send me someplace I could feel at home, even at the price of a nine-month separation.

Once installed in my new dorm at Northfield, I wept as Mom's rental car pulled away. She must have cried too. There would be no visits home or family vacations until I would fly back to Germany nine months later. Granny took me in for vacations. I sought out the kindness of the Irish maids, Nellie and Delia, until I was tactfully asked not to "bother the help."

At Northfield, five hundred homesick girls from all walks of life clung to each other while learning humility and service. At that time, Northfield required four years of Bible study, two focused on the Old Testament and two on the New. In our senior year, one of the main assignments was an essay to answer this question: Is it okay for me to have sexual relations before marriage? There was really only one right answer, but I nonetheless struggled with the essay and the appropriate biblical references. After four years of careful management, we hatched into the sixties twenty years behind our peers, emerging from a safe cocoon to the sexual revolution in full swing.

Six days a week we had church services, prayer meetings, and hymn sings. Ours was not a harsh version of evangelical Christianity. It was a mild form of nondenominational worship overseen by father figures standing at a benevolent distance. The Bible was not to be taken as fact, and we knew that Darwin's theories were for real. The gentle Al Raymond, our choral director, we thought was akin to Jesus Christ incarnate. My brain is still cluttered with the first verses of a hundred hymns direct from the Northfield hymnal. Singing them brings me comfort even now.

"Come labor on!"

"For the beauty of the earth, for the glory of the skies . . ."

"Lift up your hearts, we lift them up to thee, here at thy feet none other may we see."

All of our routines at Northfield were designed to teach us values. Each girl had a daily "domestic duty" to perform: cleaning toilets, scrubbing pots and pans, and preparing meals of a variety of indistinguishable starches. One of my least favorites was called eggs goldenrod. A cream sauce was poured over Wonder Bread and sprinkled with egg yolk particles, all soggy and glutinous.

We dubbed domestic work *dummy.* For dummy we had to wear a uniform: a starched white cotton bonnet, a pastel-colored double-breasted smock, and of course our *sturdies,* regulation Oxford shoes and socks. Northfield didn't make for a lot of fashion competitiveness. In our dorm, in a small room beneath the staircase, lived our Domestic Work Supervisor, Gladys Severance, known as Sev. Sev had skin the color of putty, a body the shape of a pear, fingers stained yellow from nicotine, and a chronic phlegmy cough. As steam from the huge cooking pots had us sweating into the soup, she would shriek above the sound of running water: "How could you be so stupid? Didn't your mother teach you anything?" To invoke the absentee mothers was the ultimate cruelty, we missed them so. I missed my mom and my family with a dull ongoing ache. We could not talk by phone while they were in Germany; letters had to suffice, and they were slow in coming. My own mother's kitchen in no way resembled this industrial place of stainless steel. She was an accomplished French cook and never made white sauce. Instead she made chocolate mousse, vinaigrette, soufflé, and to hear her derided in this fashion was bitter indeed. There had been rough edges between us, as with any budding adolescent girl and her mother. But the prolonged separation certainly softened those edges, and I felt her support from afar.

Mostly I leaned on the girls who surrounded me in our dorm. We lived in a three-story Victorian house. Girls from all four years in high school lived together. We idolized the older girls until gradually we became them and gave guidance and comfort to the young homesick freshmen. We taught each other what we thought were the finer points of sex and romance, reading out loud from select passages in *Lady Chatterley's Lover*.

Because we were so gender segregated, the only way we were going to learn about how men and women should relate to one another was through forays into romantic fiction while Johnny Mathis crooned on the tiny record player. Northfield had a sibling boys' school five miles away, the Mount Hermon School. We were not allowed contact with anyone at Mount Hermon except on Saturdays and by careful prearrangement. We could go on a "date" with a Mount Hermon boy but only if he had the foresight to post a letter through the US mail that would arrive at Northfield no later than Wednesday afternoon. The letter would have to be shown to a house mother to verify that indeed we had an invitation, and thus we could go to a football game or watch a movie with a designated young man.

Ultimately the survival of the fittest in this game were the guys who had enough planning skills to get their letters in the mail, the slightly geeky guys, not the roguish nonconforming handsome ones. For those of us with the dubious privilege of going on a date, there was the phenomenon known as Recitation Parking Lot. This was the spot where dates would conclude and from which buses would take us back to Northfield. An interval of about ten or fifteen minutes in the dark of the parking lot allowed us to practice our kissing and necking skills. These moments of fierce and often feigned affection were our only tutorial. We were glad for the waiting buses, more eager to debrief our dates with one another than to stay in a mad clutch with a guy.

As part of our tutelage on how to be ladylike, we also had to take a nonacademic course called Body Mechanics. One of its highlights was the lesson on how to get into a low-slung sports car while wearing a straight skirt and high heels. This of course had to be accomplished without any compromising lifting up of the skirt. And once that was mastered, the supreme challenge in body mechanics was the ability to cross over from the driver's seat to the passenger seat in a car with a stick shift in the middle.

The summer I came "home" to Germany from my freshman year at Northfield was awkward. I didn't know my place anymore; friends had all scattered to other schools and other bases. I had put on ten pounds. My mother was horrified; I saw it etched on her face as soon as I disembarked from the plane. She could not even get me home before sketching out the parameters of a diet for me. Dutifully I gave up desserts, began exercising, watching her carefully for signs of approval. She was lavish with her praise as soon the scales showed a turn in the right direction. It was such a cardinal sin in my family to be anything other than slender.

In addition to rendering me unforgivably chunky, my year-long immersion at Northfield had begun to amplify my parents' values of service. It was baked into every routine of life at Northfield: "dummy work," community service clubs, and a steady diet of do-unto-others Christianity. Since I was never a competitive athlete, I signed up for community service as my extracurricular activity. We knitted blankets for children in hospitals and taught Sunday school in the dirt-poor towns just over the line in New Hampshire. My first day as a Sunday school teacher in the moldy basement of the Hillsborough church found me clueless and without any teaching materials. One young boy about five was weeping when he arrived. It was the day that his pet pig would be slaughtered.

A SOCIAL WORKER?

One day that long summer after my freshman year at Northfield, I careened into the living room and announced to my parents, "I have figured out what I want to be after college. I'd like to be a social worker!" My dad stared across the room at me dumbfounded.

"Why on earth would you want to do something like that?" he asked, while my mother looked on, clearly uncomfortable.

"I want to help people."

"Help people? Then you might choose a profession where you can really make a difference! You can do better."

I fled the room, my eyes filling. I never forgot the exchange. My mother, on the other hand, was fond of saying, "You can write your own ticket. You are really smart." There was no ticket that she prescribed; it was understood that I would figure it out. I never forgot those messages either. And eight years of boarding school and college in the company of women helped solidify my initial wish to do good.

As a psych major in college, I volunteered compulsively: a settlement house in Roxbury, a day center for schizophrenics, a counseling center for women seeking abortion (then illegal in Massachusetts), an inpatient psychiatric unit. Mass Mental Inpatient was close to Simmons College but a world away for the women sequestered there. The squat brick building was set back from the road, its windows barred, its walls covered with ivy. Inside, unforgiving fluorescent lights bleached the linoleum floors and the spirits of everyone marking time in the day room.

My friend Betsy and I had been assigned to run the inpatient beauty salon two afternoons a week, a mildly terrifying assignment. A fashionable hairdo is a morale boost for a woman in any circumstance, and this was especially so for our clients. We began to hope for patients who were actively hallucinating so that they would not register the mediocre results of our efforts. Remarkably they tolerated our ineptitude, choosing instead to relax and chat in the ways that ladies do when someone is gently washing their hair. I began to see the impact of psychiatric hospitalization from the inside out.

My next volunteer assignment was with the Veterans Administration Day Treatment Center in downtown Boston. Schizophrenic World War II veterans, still quite psychotic despite heavy doses of Haldol and Thorazine, spent their days playing pool, in group therapy, or on trips to the North End for pizza and to Fenway Park. At age twenty, I led ten to fifteen of these patients at a time on their field trips. I led and they followed in single file like imprinted ducks, so numbed by their medications that no one ever stepped off the sidewalk without my okay.

A diminutive patient named Manny truly lived in his own world. On our outings he would scamper from one telephone pole to the next, vibrating his hands as he pretended to charge them with electricity. His shoulders would then relax and we could continue. If we got too far from the next telephone pole he became visibly anxious, and so we scurried from one source of electricity to another to keep his agitation at bay. Once when a red light prevented us from getting to the next telephone pole, Manny turned and simply recharged his fingers on the wall of a bank. Clearly not his preference, but an acceptable emergency substitute.

Although the VA was swarming with prestigious psychiatrists in white coats, many day-to-day activities with the patients were left up to me and other young interns. I offered art therapy and, against prevailing advice, asked the patients to draw what was going on in their hallucinations. With crayons and construction paper they laid out the parameters of their waking nightmares: monsters, bloodied bodies all swarming around arid galaxies. These volunteer assignments made real the suffering behind the dry textbooks.

Soon I did indeed go to social-work school. Ironically it was my experiences there that squashed my fantasies of actually becoming a social worker. My first year in class I got into arguments about penis envy with Freud's granddaughter, Professor Sophie Freud Lowenstein. I was showing off for my classmates, but I had met an immovable object. Dr. Lowenstein was stereotypically Germanic, and in her thick accent she conceded no possibility for adaptation of her grandfather's contributions. She determined the content of our core curriculum, and all of it was grounded in psychodynamic Freudian theory.

My field placement was at Mass General Hospital in Pediatrics. There my job was to try to comfort parents whose children were near death in a vegetative state or comatose. At twenty-two and childless, I was clueless. I knew it, and so did my clients.

I was miserable in my fieldwork and chafing at our coursework. My supervisors were all single, middle-aged women who sat at the bottom end of the hierarchy and lived simply on meager salaries. They were long suffering, always deferring to big men in white coats. I began to realize I was no more successful as a real social worker than I was at trying to fix my parents' disintegrating marriage. Gradually I let go as my fantasy turned sour. Just before the start of the second year of graduate school I abruptly decided to drop out. Dropping out of anything was not in the lexicon of our family. I met with Dr. Lowenstein to tell her of my decision a few months before school was to open. She was furious. In her strong German accent she leveled me.

"How could you make this decision so late in the year? Vat are you thinking? I am very disappointed in you."

CHAPTER THREE

Things Fall Apart

DAD GOES TO JAIL

I sat mute, listening to Dr. Lowenstein berate me. I had never really broken the rules. Not at Northfield, where there were so many rules to break, and not during college. But I was on a roll now. I fled into an engagement with my college sweetheart as a bulwark against the sudden disintegration of my own family. It began the summer of 1969 when we all crash-landed into a bad dream. Dad was in jail in Vietnam and threatened with court martial.

The *Washington Post* later wrote:

> Robert B. Rheault, a charismatic Army colonel who could scale mountains, dive to the ocean floor and speak flawless French, arrived for his second tour of duty in Vietnam in May 1969, when the war was at its raging peak. He had the job that had been his destiny, commander of the Green Berets, the elite Special Forces

unit that often operated outside the standard
Army chain of command.
      Within a month, Col. Rheault (pronounced
Roe) was embroiled in a case that spread to the
highest levels of the Pentagon, White House,
CIA and Congress and brought a premature
end to his promising military career. The Green
Beret murder case, which was splashed across
magazine covers and in headlines for weeks,
became one of the most puzzling, disturb-
ing and tragic episodes of the war, but it has
largely been forgotten in the decades since.

The case put Dad and our family on the front of the *New York
Times* and *Life* magazine for three solid months. Journalists
encamped on the Vineyard for the Chappaquiddick case were
elated to get a twofer, showing up unannounced at our door,
cameras rolling. Our family was on TV and Dad was in jail.
It was surreal. By autumn the charges were dropped but the
damage was done. Dad's brilliant career ground to a halt,
he resigned from the army, and life as we knew it was over.
Grandma Susanne died. Mom was inconsolable, and she in
turn came close to death from undiagnosed Crohn's disease
and septicemia. After three weeks in the ICU she came home
gaunt and fragile. Dad sought comfort in a series of affairs,
effectively ending his marriage to Mom. My graduate school
plans had tanked, and I too had an affair, ruining my own still-
new marriage. It was as though the scaffolding of my life was
made of mud and twigs. All was coming down around my ears.
      Dad's new marriage was hard to take on board. Susan was
just six years my senior, still eager for kids of her own. Mom
was emotionally shipwrecked, and I tried to use my neophyte
social-work skills to ease her pain, to no avail. I encouraged her
to see a psychologist and to take the antidepressant medication

he prescribed. She was recalcitrant. I dubbed it "resistance" with my newly acquired clinical superiority. It wasn't resistance. The psychologist was later found to be sexually abusing his clients. Eventually Mom rebuilt her life and her battered self-esteem while I soldiered on in pursuit of a clinical degree I myself could believe in.

Three years later it dawned on me that half a master's degree was useless. I needed to finish my social-work degree. I tiptoed past Dr. Lowenstein's office to avoid her for that last year, then decided next to get a doctorate in counseling psychology.

I FIND A PATH

I soaked up the coursework, the readings, and the research. No longer was I force-fed Freudian theory. I got to read rigorous outcome studies. Classroom discussions were evidence based. I thrived and felt smart. Now I felt I could write my own ticket. Both parents were right. I dreamed of becoming a college professor.

I knew that I was never going to be a good psychotherapist. Too directive, too impatient, too unskilled to know how to provide measured and useful insight. But I also saw the real-world work of my professors: unremitting pressure to publish, endless office hours counseling students, and the same courses taught over and over. When a corporate trainer friend was sidelined with what was thought to be a brain tumor, she asked me to fill in. I taught communication skills to engineers and I loved it. Groups of middle-aged male engineers were hugely tolerant of my inexperience in business. We laughed, we did role plays, and I madly improvised class by class.

I also ran employee assistance programs where I could intervene and get help to someone in the midst of a life crisis.

There was a scientist who was spending a lot of time on the roof of his building readying himself to jump after a drunk driver killed his twelve-year-old daughter. We got him off the roof and into treatment. This chance to help people and to do it rapidly was exhilarating.

Like most of my peers in the counseling doctoral program, I sampled multiple forms of therapy. It was an era of lavish self-absorption, and I was no exception . . . gestalt therapy, transactional analysis therapy, past-life regression therapy. Scream therapy was the only one I skipped. I ultimately landed in a small ongoing group therapy where we lounged on huge pillows and toyed with stuffed animals. Over that year I always sat next to Peter Gardner, jealously guarding my special seat. Peter exuded a gentle acceptance and humor. He was a musician, a therapist, a photographer, and the father of four. His demographics did not favor us as a couple. I fell in love anyway. Soon I had moved in with Peter and his two teenage boys, and we rattled around a huge Victorian on Centre Street in Newton. I finished my dissertation while learning at age thirty how to be a stepparent.

PhD in hand, I went to work for McBer, a consulting firm pioneered by the legendary Dr. David McClelland. McClelland had developed seminal work on the achievement motive and leadership. His research had been validated the world around. I got the equivalent of a post doc working with global Fortune 500 companies. While the travel was brutal, the work was fascinating. I could palpably see the difference that some of our workshops made in the behavior of the managers who attended and the organizations they led. Finally, I had found my own way, complete with an idiosyncratic home life.

CHAPTER FOUR

Peter and Zack

With a sixteen-year age difference, two ex-wives, and four children of his own between the ages of nine and twenty, Peter was not the mate my mother would've chosen for me. I was enthralled by his gentle spirit and his creativity, by the calm that he could create out of chaos. But his age was a concern. As we approached our wedding, I obsessively recited a mantra of how our age differences would play out in the future. "I am thirty and he is forty-six. When I'm forty he will be fifty-six, when I'm sixty he'll be seventy-six, when I'm seventy he will be eighty-six." None of that felt real or offered any comfort. We were in love and we could weather anything together. It was the together part that made this calculus manageable. Peter's youngest girl, Amanda, age nine, lived with her mother in New Hampshire, and his oldest daughter, Debbie, was on her own in Texas. The boys, Chris and Matt, were in the early phases of adolescent experiments with various controlled substances. I was a marginally effective stepmother, at my best when I could introduce kids to cross-country skiing, hiking, and crafts.

After the boys graduated from high school we bought our wonderful too-big, too-old Concord house. It faced the sunrise, and on Sunday afternoon, parades of canoeists would float below the house on the Sudbury River. Peter bought me a grandfather clock that marked the time with Westminster chimes, just like the one my grandmother had. We papered over the repairs the house really needed. And I happily puttered about in the first home I had ever owned.

I FORGOT TO HAVE A BABY

Then an unexpected malaise crept in. It was as if my brain had been colonized by some cliché; the "I forgot to do something important" yearning for a baby began to show up. This was never the plan. I had changed careers from social work to corporate work, gotten a counseling PhD, helped to parent and to launch Peter's kids. I never liked going to baby showers, never wished to see myself pregnant and ungainly. I didn't even like babies, preferring the company of little people who could read and ride bikes. So the ache arrived unplanned.

Peter, always pliant and generous with me, did not accede as readily as I had hoped when I brought up the idea of children of our own. Of course not. His four children were just out of the nest, and he had in his sights the last of the college tuition payments. We had just bought a house well beyond our means.

Peter stalled for time, hoping that my latest obsession would ebb. Instead my fantasy simply amplified, untethered from reality. My obsession knew no bounds. I wanted to be the real deal, not the stand-in stepmom who could never get it quite right. We were living in my dream-come-true house and it needed to be populated by a dream-come-true baby, preferably a blond, blue-eyed little girl who would make paper dolls with me and play dress-up in my heels. We would live happily ever after in our picture-postcard house and at last I would grow roots.

I did have a child, but I did not grow roots. My father always dubbed life's difficulties as a chance to "grow character." For the next eighteen years I surely grew my character. Zack's birth was difficult, but it was not until nursery school that we realized there were any concerns. After only a week, his teacher asked me to come in for a conference. Zack was throwing blocks at other children, hiding under the desks, and running into the street.

Raising Zack

In what was a preview of coming attractions throughout his schooling, I sat in the tiny school desk chair weeping as his teachers recited the litany of his lapses. I was an older mom of a child with "special needs." How I hated that facile euphemism. I would never belong as one of the younger families with perfect children. There was a pharmacopeia of medication, much of it still "off label," playing roulette with my son's maturing brain. There was ongoing and futile debate as to his correct diagnosis: Attention deficit disorder with hyperactivity? Oppositional defiant disorder? And the last one, my favorite: pervasive development disorder not otherwise specified (PDDNOS). By age three we had to lock the doors of the house so he would not run into the street, and we gated the kitchen so he could bang on the pots and pans with abandon but not run amok inside the house.

These realities intensified my endemic sense of isolation. Concord, Massachusetts, is an affluent town where the bulk of the new moms were in their thirties, at home with children and nannies. I was an older working mom of a kid no one wanted to invite for playdates. And then suddenly, at age forty-four, I was a widow.

WE LEARN TO LIVE WITHOUT PETER

It was a sparkling spring Sunday afternoon. I took three-year-old Zack to the Children's Museum so that Peter could do some home repairs undisturbed. A few hours later we returned in high spirits anxious to share with Peter how well things had gone. Zack ran around the back of the house at full tilt and then came running back to me. "Why is Daddy going nighty night?" he asked. What do you mean? I ran back with Zack to find Peter splayed out on the ground near the basement door, his body still, his eyes wide open. I had never seen a dead body before, but I knew I was looking at one. I grabbed Zack and brought him into the house screaming for our au pair to take him and dialing 911 at the same time. They asked me if I knew how to do CPR. I had taken a course when I was pregnant with Zack but could not remember a single move. The hospital was less than a quarter mile from our house and the ambulance came screaming around the corner in minutes. "He's dead, isn't he?" I asked the young EMT. His response was careful: "We will do everything we can." I knew he could not pronounce him dead on the spot. I asked if I could travel with him in the ambulance, and then came the telling piece of advice. "Take your time, call your family, and get someone to drive you over. We will take care of him."

Hearing the ambulance, a neighbor rushed over and offered to drive me to the hospital. Trembling violently, I could not get my seat belt buckled, and refused to leave the drive-way. I finally muscled the snap into place. When we pulled up to the emergency room entrance they escorted me to a tiny windowless cinder block room and asked if I wanted a priest or minister to join me. I crumpled, put my head between my knees, breathing in the stale air in the now crowded space, suddenly walking the landscape of the moon. Shock carried me through the huge memorial service and the early phases of casseroles and condolence letters. And then the days shortened and the dead weight of mourning settled in. Zack would run into the yard, throw himself on the ground, and intone, "I died. I died." And when he wasn't reenacting his father's death, he was dogging my steps, asking over and over, "Mummy, why did Daddy's heart stop beating? Is your heart going to stop?" My carefully rehearsed answers to his questions helped to calm us both down. "Mommy's heart is very strong," I would say. "I am not going to die for a very, very long time." I hoped this was true even as my husband's death had annihilated all the future plans we had created together. Once again, I was watching life happen in the cheery living rooms of other houses. Each night when Zack was safely asleep with a sitter on duty, I would power walk through our neighborhood, breathing in the crisp night air, muttering to myself, and imploring the heavens for some sign of Peter. A shooting star would do nicely, I thought, some evidence that his spirit was present. I never saw a single shooting star that long, cold winter.

Through one snowstorm to the next, I shoveled and shoveled in a quiet frenzy. I would not let myself be buried in a white catacomb of grief. Huge drifts accumulated on the deck outside the kitchen. Terrified that the weight of it all would pull the deck right off our old house, I shoveled. I shoveled for my sanity, for my son, for some future I could not yet imagine and did not want to. I shoveled the driveway until the shovel bit the asphalt, and I slept under a cloud of barbiturates. My beloved old house began to betray me, pipes freezing and bursting under the window seat, carpenter ants nesting in damp crevices.

Months later Zack and I emerged from our winter's hibernation blinking like moles. Buoyed by the kindness of close friends and strangers alike, we had begun to grasp the parameters of Peter's absence. Still, our mere physical presence sparked fear in others. We were the living proof of how capricious life is. They too could face tragedy some sunny day, the scaffolding of their lives collapsing without warning. Zack and I were their living reminders. People could take a deep breath when we left a social gathering to go home.

Spring sunlight revealed a host of home repairs too-long delayed, so I called on my friend and Peter's, Gil, to come help. Ceiling tiles had begun to fall around our ears in Zack's playroom. Gil showed up with his tool belt slung around his waist, and with easy assurance swung his hammer and began to restore order. I took a few deep breaths. Winter had at last given way to spring, and I was through the first year of widowhood. All the how-to books say that the first year is the most difficult. It is the firsts: the first Christmas, the first wedding anniversary, the first birthdays, the litany of celebrations and rituals that mark family life that must be endured and, finally, redefined. Somehow, I had come through this year bruised but intact, and so had Zack. I still had a small shrine to Peter in my dressing room, but the glimpses of his smiling face in picture frames no longer socked me in the gut. I attended the Young Widows and Widowers group, actually going to three sessions, a record for someone who prefers to lead meetings, not attend them. But when one of the members announced that after fourteen months she still kept her husband's toothbrush, I decided it was time for me to leave. I would not have my life be over at forty-four. I had a soul mate, I had been loved, and I refused to believe that the door had been shut on this as a possibility ever again.

GIL COMES INTO THE PICTURE

Gil and I had been as close as girlfriends for seven years before Peter died, with offices next door to one another in Human Resources at Digital Equipment. We talked about everything, everything but the sweet sexual tension that animated our conversations but would never be made manifest. Peter and Gil too had been very close. Androgynous men of the sixties, they were both good cooks, sensitive listeners, attentive parents, and avid photographers. In rare weekend getaways when they would leave the demands of wives and children, Gil and Peter drove off to photography workshops where clear-skinned young women would pose nude draped around garden statues, looking vacantly into some middle distance. Then upon their return, well into the dead of night, Peter and Gil would blockade themselves in the basement darkroom. In perhaps the only moments that were for them preserved from intrusions of family, they would burrow contentedly into their separate reality.

Three years after Peter's death I married the only man that I could imagine being with. It was messy. Gil was only a few years into a marriage with a woman Peter and I had introduced him to. The divorce was swift and acrimonious, driving a wedge between the camps. My mother grilled Gil the first time she met him. What were his intentions? Was he financially solvent? How was his health? There was nothing subtle about her mother-bear inquisition. Mom did not want to see me widowed again, reduced, bereft, moving through life as though underwater. Some of my own close friends were equally cautious. I had spent two years bearing down on the work of mourning. They don't call it grief work for nothing. It is work, work to remember, relive, release. But my friends were spared this as a twenty-four-hour-a-day job, and some of them were not ready to let Peter go and see me with another partner.

But I was reborn. I had a second chance. Years ago, on a long road trip, Peter had casually mentioned that I should remarry if something happened to him. It was an idle offer and one that didn't sustain our conversation for more than a paragraph. But it lodged in my consciousness and helped give me permission for a second try.

Taking a best friend as a lover is special. There is the romance and the excitement without the anxiety and the unknown. After seven years of working as colleagues in adjacent offices, I knew this man deeply: his strongly held values, his compassion, his daily acts of kindness. I also saw his fierce competitiveness and his anger in the face of social injustice.

Zack knew him too, his virtual godfather, his "uncle Gil." And so with grace and forbearance, Gil not only married me but also took up the job of parenting Zack in earnest.

Months before we married, Gil and I took Zack and his buddy Mark to the Audubon farm. Parents in the chauffeur business know that kids in the back seat will talk with such candor it is as though the adults in the front are completely deaf. Mark turned to Zack and said, "This car smells like dog." Zack's reply: "Yeah, we had a dog but she died. My dad died too." Gil and I froze, listening closely from the front seat. "So who's that guy?" Mark asked, pointing to Gil. "Is he your pretend dad?" Without missing a beat, Zack said, "No, that's my new dad." Gil and I resumed breathing and drove on.

And so it was that Gil was now fully enrolled, not as a stepfather but as a new dad. This was no small deal. There were the endless school conferences, indecipherable Individual Educational Plans, special summer camps, tutors, years of searching for schools, endless road trips to the Adirondacks, Pennsylvania, Georgia, Illinois, Gil at the wheel, Zack and I playing back seat car bingo, shrieking when one of us spotted an elusive Corvette. There was one school after another. The parent groups in these places were clubs I never wanted to join, the adults often as socially awkward as their progeny. After all, I was a PhD psychologist. I knew way too much from my reading, and I did not want to listen to parents and others who knew less. Mostly I did not want to join their desperation or to share my own.

One particularly grim boarding school I sent my son to at age fifteen was situated in the flatlands of Illinois, sandwiched between an FBI lab, an evangelical church, and a shopping mall. Given my own history of dislocation, I desperately wanted to find a secondary school that was close to home. With fifty-two colleges and universities in the Boston area, how was it possible that not one secondary school would fit? Our educational consultant assured me that the quality of teaching would be worth the distance. I was not so sure. It was impossible to reconcile what the educational "experts" were telling me and what my intuition told me. The dorm "counselors" looked like prison guards, huge muscle-bound men, many of whom had not even finished high school. I always boycotted the parent meetings there. Instead Zack and I would barricade ourselves in my crummy motel room and watch as many movies as we could. I let him have junk food while I would nurse a bottle of cheap white wine and eat vending-machine pretzels. As a young adult, he had become something of an expert on film, perhaps the silver lining of all those long misspent afternoons.

I still worried that Zack would be playing video games in our basement at the age of thirty, but his suspensions from school slowed down, and his jumping-bean restlessness started to subside. Later he would show courage and a budding work ethic as we took on volunteer work halfway around the world.

CHAPTER FIVE

Lions and Leave-taking

COMING OF AGE IN AFRICA

I stand with Zack, now a tall sixteen-year-old, as we prepare for our first walk with the lion cubs we have come to Zimbabwe to work with. I wanted him to have exposure to other countries, as I had. And I wanted us to work for it, not be pampered as tourists. That is how we find ourselves standing in an open field next to a large wire enclosure. Unlike the teddy-bear-cute cubs being bottle-fed in the brochure, the six lion cubs inside are huge, easily 250 to 300 pounds. They pace the enclosure perimeter with increasing agitation. The male cubs have only a hint of a mane sprouting on their necks, but their paws are the size of dinner plates. They push toward the exit gate, eyeing us, sniffing the air, hip checking one another like bumper cars. At age two they display all the grace and raw power that marks the species. I am dumbstruck, my mouth hanging open, my heart pounding. Once we have our initial safety briefing, the gate will be opened and we will be surrounded. I look over at

Zack. His eyes are wide but he seems fully attentive, not anxious like me.

We have together chosen this month-long volunteer assignment among other options I had unearthed in Africa: teaching computer skills, caring for orphans, tutoring English, working to save the white rhinoceros. I wanted Zack to see beyond our silver-spoon American life, to get a more global perspective, to see how others live, and to go on an adventure that was not preprogrammed for "special needs" kids. Zack, who loves all furry things (especially our two house cats) lobbied for this assignment.

Antelope Park is an oasis in Robert Mugabe's unraveling Zimbabwe. Andrew Connolly, the owner, was working on a bold experiment: raising lions in captivity but readying them for release. Previous attempts at releasing lions had never worked. They were released as singletons, and lions must always hunt as a pride. Unlike the faster, solitary cheetah, lions make up for speed with surprise and teamwork. They must remain as a pride, ready to hunt. I was eager to go to Africa for the first time. So after all the packing and preparation and inoculations, here we were.

Two African trainers and a white Zimbabwean go through a set of safety guidelines. Their delivery is serious and deliberate. Gone is the lighthearted humor. They watch our faces closely to make sure we are taking it in. Their rules include staying in the group, the "pride" of humans. By instinct, lions will go after an animal that has strayed from the herd. And never, never run, the trainers stress. Stand tall and "make yourself big" by holding up a big stick between your hands. Lastly, these lions will check you out and remember you individually. If you display fear, anxiety, and poor judgment, they will remember that the next time they see you, and you will be at risk to be "taken down."

I listen to these rules with my own anxiety ratcheting up by the minute. How could they not smell the fear emanating from my every pore? This is day one of the thirty-day assignment. How am I going to manage? Ironically, it is Zack's even gaze and demeanor that calm me down. I certainly did not want to embarrass him any more than the bare fact of my being his mother seemed to do.

Soon the lions will be released, and we will go with them on the first of many walks. In order to prepare them for the wild, the lions need to be out of their enclosures as much as possible to run, to chase animals in the park, and to gradually develop the skills to bring down prey. Once the briefing concludes, the trainers tell us to stand well away from the enclosure gate. The gate opens and the cubs come spilling out together and run up the hill. My anxiety subsides somewhat as I see their behavior, like huge kittens released from a box. Over and over they pounce on one another, rolling in the dust in a heap. At first the cubs ignore the new pride of people, anxious as they are to escape the confines of their enclosure. But we are a novelty, and gradually they grow curious. Our African trainers watch the lions watching us. I see how subtly and masterfully they keep this crew of rowdy cubs in check, a word here or there, an upheld stick. They carry no weapons and don't need to. The cubs seem to respect the boundaries set by their longtime caretakers. But we are blatant newbies and therefore ripe for some testing. One female, in a quick turnaround, goes from sniffing the grasses to staring at me. Her look, in a split second, goes from neutral to laser focused. Her eyes widen, her head drops, and her huge yellow-brown eyes don't blink. This is the "naughty look" that I had heard about. At the same time, she lowers into a crouch and begins to inch forward, her paws extended before her. Jumbali, the African trainer, is watching too. But first he must see if I can do what I have been taught to do. I stand up straight to my full five feet four, hold my big stick overhead between my two hands, stare back, and shout, "No!" I can barely breathe. Then remarkably, the lion breaks her gaze, and wanders off to join her sisters as if to say, "Just kidding." This was test number one, and I seem to have passed.

We spend a month with four prides of such cubs, taking them out every dawn and dusk, cleaning their enclosures, delivering food, carefully logging their behavior, sweeping the park perimeter for snares, and building miles of wire fencing. We work seven days a week with two half days off for sleeping past dawn and taking showers, begging the kitchen for extra food, and trying to cadge extra blankets. It is wintertime in Zimbabwe, and at the altitude of 4,500 feet it is penetratingly cold at night. The volunteers are a motley crew of British gap-year kids, Zack, me, and, thankfully, two other women near my age. Romances flare and sputter among the young crowd, and after two weeks of living on the awkward social periphery, Zack finally figures a way in. I am relieved and I am sticking to my plan of keeping a distance from him. He does not need to be visibly mothered in any way. I tell the staff not to put us on any of the same work details and look on from a safe distance, hoping he will find his way, and he does.

For the first weeks at Antelope Park, I am preoccupied with doing my job and staying safe. Connolly, who runs Antelope Park, is a grizzled third-generation white Zimbabwean, missing his right arm from the elbow down, gone to a lion's dinner years back. No volunteers have as yet sacrificed body parts, but the mere sight of this man instantly tamps down any nascent hubris among us. As the weeks progress, my insulated gaze grows beyond my own immediate concerns and begins to take in the Africans, their customs, and what is happening in their country. Antelope Park is a fenced, thousand-acre wildlife safari destination. It houses not only the lion rehabilitation program, but herds of zebra, antelope, eland, giraffe, impala, and gazelle. The lodge, its kitchen, dining area, and now-empty thatched-roof guest cottages look out over the river. Some forty staff work with the lions, provide park security, run the kitchen and the laundry. The volunteers stay in old staff quarters, and the African staff walk ten kilometers home each night past the park entrance. There, I learn, they are frisked and threatened with job loss if they try to bring home any extra food, clothing, or gear. Zimbabwe is in free fall now. Inflation is running at 300 percent, so a loaf of bread costs a twelve-inch tower of bills. These jobs at Antelope Park are a rare godsend, with plentiful food, uniforms, and some measure of job security, even as the safari guest traffic has dwindled to near zero.

As our month progresses, we volunteers gradually form friendships with the African trainers and staff. The ladies in the laundry laugh with me as I try to learn to say hello in their two competing tribal dialects, Shona and Ndebele. It is our steady routine, my mangled pronunciation and their good-natured hilarity. By African standards we volunteers are impossibly spoiled, indulged, overfed, and paying for the privilege to scoop lion poop and photograph ourselves posing with the cubs. We will get to go home and brag about our brave exploits. They will stay on, and if they are lucky keep their jobs for another batch of wide-eyed volunteers while all around them Zimbabwe plummets into irreversible economic decline. We have come for the lions, but it is the people I cannot forget.

It is only as we get ready to go home that the desperation and poverty of the staff begin to show. A trainer appropriately named Lovemore was a favorite of all the volunteers. A big bear of a man with a huge belly laugh, Lovemore had five children. Three weeks after we arrived, his six-year-old daughter died suddenly at home. When we asked what had provoked this, he said he had no idea. We were stupefied. Sudden death without medical care or a diagnosis? How is this possible? In subtle and not-so-subtle ways, they let us know that they cannot afford to send their children to school, that they do not have enough to eat at home, and that they hope we will leave behind some of our excess clothing and money. This is always done sotto voce and out of sight of the park managers. It will cost the staff their jobs if they are discovered. Most of us come home with our suitcases empty but for the African baskets and souvenirs we have acquired. The rest of our clothes are left behind with the staff.

The whole experience is indelible in ways I could not have predicted. It is not the lions I remember when I get home, it is the African staff, their generosity of spirit and their courage in the face of fear. This is how my love affair with Africa began. Maybe it is ever so for rich Americans. Go to see the animals and fall in love with the people.

The trip was also the first sign that my son, Zack, had life skills I had never seen before. At Antelope Park, Zack never missed a work duty, ever. And he wasn't wearing a watch! And by the end of our one month he was telling jokes and hanging out with the pack. I was delighted and eager to share our adventures with my mother.

OUR PAINFUL REENTRY

After a month in Zimbabwe, Zack and I return from Africa weary but jubilant. We have stories to tell and tourist trinkets to distribute, but first we each need a hot shower and a good night's sleep. Gil grabs my hand and pulls me aside. Don't unpack, he says. We have to leave for your mother's. Now. Exhausted and uncomprehending, I resist. Why now? Can't we get a shower and rest?

Gil blurts it out. Mom has a rare and aggressive cancer of the gallbladder. During our month away she had insisted that we not be told. She did not want to spoil our great adventure for which she had been a vocal cheerleader. Instead, the party line we got was routine gallbladder surgery with an uneventful recovery. The truth was that a hidden cancer had metastasized. When we left home for Zimbabwe, Mom had been gardening, painting, golfing, and keeping up her usual nonstop pace. In one month everything changed.

I don't want to accept this news. Must we leave this minute? Yes. My two siblings have gathered and they are waiting. My sister, Meesh, has flown from Colorado, where her own son is in the hospital with serious GI bleeding. There is no time to waste. I am the oldest, the go-between, the one who spends the most time with Mom. We tell Zack only that his beloved Nana has been sick and wants to see us. He contorts his long body into sleep in the back seat of the car, insulated temporarily from impending loss.

Living alone at seventy-nine, my mother could exhaust many of her age contemporaries, preferring the company of people ten to twenty years younger who could keep up with her. She was generous to a fault, once buying and delivering a dishwasher to a harried neighbor and never revealing its origin. In her sixties she cross-country skied across a huge tidal saltwater pond, alone, of course. In her late seventies she bicycled to church, fifteen miles round-trip. She loved to thumb her nose at convention. When a housing development across the street installed an ugly stone entrance, we had to convince her not to go out with spray paint at night. Our Thanksgiving visits were peppered with long walks she had carefully planned to trespass on wealthy people's estates while our turkey overcooked in the oven.

After the divorce from Dad, Mom took up residence on Martha's Vineyard. In those days the winter months were especially grim. No restaurants, no movies, no adult education, no theater, no upscale activities for retirees, just a lot of AA meetings and a closed social system made up of islanders with generations behind them. But she crafted a life there, lonely but self-reliant. Once when a huge snowstorm took out the power, she phoned to report that she was cooking food on the wood-stove and that soon she would get on her cross-country skis and go down the road five miles to see friends. My mom was a force of nature, upbeat and indefatigable, an army wife with class and stamina, an artist, a green thumb, an environmental activist, and a politically incorrect peacenik.

Zack and I had planned our triumphant return knowing that Mom would delight in every graphic detail of our adventures. We make our way from Woods Hole to Martha's Vineyard. Gil and I have built a house next door and we know this drive by heart. As we barrel down the highway, Gil whispers how sick she is, pulling back the fiction Mom had insisted on while we were in Africa. She knew that if we knew the facts, we would have come to her side, and she did not want us to miss any wild exploits.

In only a month's time my mother has become diminished, growing fearful, her skin like parchment. Her cancer is rare, uncommonly aggressive, and has no recommended treatment protocol. All that can be offered in the way of care is chemo as a palliative. Mom will have none of it. She tells us three adult kids that she will not seek treatment. She wants out on her own terms, she wants to go before the pain gets bad, and she wants us to help her. Numbly, naïvely, we agree.

She begins to put her affairs in order, I begin to think about her eulogy, and my brother researches what options she has for her own deliverance. It is the middle of the summer on Martha's Vineyard. Sunny days, clear skies, cool nights. Mom's garden begins to overrun with weeds. Hospice nurses begin to administer daily pain medications. I begin to grieve her the day she starts this pharmaceutical barrage. In only twenty-four hours she becomes fuzzy, querulous, and forgetful. I am used to talking to her in-depth about the news and the books we are both reading, about politics and the environment. She can tell a complex dirty joke complete with foreign accents, the punch line delivered with a flourish. I have heard her rendition of the French-English lessons joke thirty times, and still it makes me laugh. "Oui, teacher, perhaps zey will go pipi in the piano!" Her edgy intelligence and sense of humor is blunted now with fentanyl and oxycodone. I realize belatedly that she is in much more pain then she will let on. I see her disappearing by the day. I start to compulsively run back and forth from my house to hers to check on her. I cancel work calls, fearful that she will slip away alone and unnoticed while I am only next door. Her vaunted Scrabble skills deteriorate. We are losing her by degrees. I want to see this as a temporary regression so I can say a real goodbye. I want to tell her it was she all along who stitched the family together move after move, that she has been brave and steadfast, that she was the port in the storm. I want to ask, Did she really take a gun out across the Russian border in 1947? And when did she meet Dad? Did she really put a baby lamb in our bathtub when we were in Regensburg? I want to tell our old family stories together to reminisce with her before she is gone. For a few nights we make margaritas in the blender and she gets tiddly and gay. I hang onto this glimpse of who she used to be. I am not ready, and increasingly she is.

Six weeks later, when the three kids and spouses are again assembled at the house, Mom tells us she is ready to go. She wants to go within two days, and she is adamant. We are in shock but we made her a promise.

We cannot now dicker to keep her one more day, one more week. We say our tearful goodbyes while she is steeling herself and slipping from us moment by moment. Turning inward, she will no longer meet our eyes. Two days later we keep the overnight vigil by her bed while a cold snap brings in nor'easter rain. By morning she is gone. The sky has turned a dark gray. There are big whitecaps in the lagoon, and this preview of winter echoes our bleak hearts. Two undertakers in ill-fitting black suits zip her now-tiny frame into a brown bag, wheel the pallet outside into the drizzle and up the hill to the hearse. We are sleep-deprived, scared, and bereft, and the enormity of her loss settles in. Once Mom's body has been taken, I walk around the house wrapped in a blanket, weeping. I am eight years old and I want my mom. I go into her bedroom and steal her sheepskin slippers. They fit my size nines and they will warm my cold feet. Once again I have grief work to do and I am not ready. Who is? I bend to it, remembering the sign that used to be in Peter's therapy room: "The only way out is through." Ambivalent grief is the worst, when powerful memories of the loved one are both positive and negative. I know this from my studies. And now I am living it. While Mom had been loving and supportive, as she aged she was intermittently harshly critical of my parenting. I rarely heard the comments directly. They were funneled through my sister and brother. It was as though only one child could be the temporary favorite, and this merry-go-round made for tensions between us three. With Mom's death we mended the fissures and reconnected, though we each mourned a different mom, I think.

CHAPTER SIX

Ethiopia, the Early Years

ED SIGNS ME UP

It takes a year after Mom's death to mend, and to dust off dreams deferred. Slowly the images come back: the open savannahs, the acacia trees stark against an orange sun, the openhearted warmth of the Africans, the urgent public-health needs. I hoped that what I knew about leadership and change might be put to use in some of the HIV-prevention efforts that were trying to stem the tide.

Once I set my sights on a return to Africa, the networking to get me there was easier than I could have imagined. The first person I called was Bill Bean, a colleague of Gil's and a veteran of volunteer work in Africa. When I told him I was looking to volunteer and to use my management consulting skills, he erupted with enthusiasm. "This is a fabulous idea. You do have a lot to offer, and I will introduce you to Ed Wood, who is the Clinton Foundation CEO and a great guy." The Clinton Foundation's Health Access Initiative was working in seventy-five countries to try to stem the epidemic of AIDS then ravaging the developing world. The staff of bright young expats and regional experts worked at a furious pace, eschewing any hint of the bureaucracy that slowed some of the larger international development agencies. Ed was gruff and gracious on the phone, and we set up a lunch meeting for the following week, the same day I was to meet with the CEO of a financial-services firm around the corner. What a study in contrasts. In my first meeting I am in a sumptuous glass corporate fishbowl looking toward Boston Harbor. Then I descend fifty-two flights for a conversation about Africa and the AIDS epidemic in the Cottonwood Restaurant, crowded and noisy.

This psychic whiplash will color the rest of my life: my New England life of predictable privilege, and my African life of warmth and chaos.

The Clinton staff nicknamed Ed "silverback," like an older male gorilla. He is senior to them all by decades, a grizzled eminence with a great sense of humor and a deep affection for his African colleagues. He asks me to tell him a bit about who I am and what I do. I give him the executive summary of my practice in coaching and change management. His face lights up, and he leans across the table and says, "How soon can you leave for Ethiopia?" Just this week a request had come to Ed to find an American female coach. Dr. Betru heads up the AIDS office for all of Ethiopia and thinks that a coach might help him deal with his team and the ubiquitous American donors. I scurry to get ready in the next weeks, full of nervous anticipation.

Arriving in Ethiopia

It is New Year's Day, 2007. I have flown seventeen hours on Ethiopian Air from Washington, DC, to Addis Ababa, arriving at nine o'clock at night. My body has no idea what time it is. I stagger off the plane, stand in an interminable line waiting for a visa written out in longhand, retrieve my suitcase (thanking the travel gods), and proceed to the exit. At the gate, crowds of people push up against the glass partition, frantically waving arms and signs. Anxiously I look to see my name or the Clinton Foundation logo appear on some placard, and I see none. I stand, rooted to the spot, frozen and trying to blink back tears. I feel like a five-year-old lost in a street parade. The parade is not in my country, and I don't understand the language being used.

Ed told me that my willingness to travel on New Year's Eve and miss the festivities in the US demonstrates my interest and my commitment. What Ed didn't know is that I'm usually in my pajamas watching the ball drop on TV. And what I long for more than anything right now is to be in my pajamas in bed with Gil.

Suddenly a short, handsome, young Ethiopian man comes toward me calling, "Sussie?" At first I wonder how he could pick me out of the crowd. Then I look around. There are only a handful of other white faces, and none of them are blonde or female. So much for anonymity. Fikadu introduces himself, flashes me a wide grin, grabs my bag, and off we go to his "taxi." Once we leave the brightly lit airport lobby, the parking lot is completely black. No lights mark the exterior, and Fikadu peers into the darkness to find his car. The air is cool and dry and smells faintly of exhaust and woodsmoke. Fikadu's cab looks like all the other cabs in Addis, bright blue and beat-up. Instead of a gas cap, a black garbage bag is stuffed into the tank.

I climb in, groping for a seat belt. No such luck. Furthermore, I do not seem to be able to quite close my passenger door. Fikadu needs to lean across me and slam it shut. Thus ensconced, he starts up the motor and, the car belching black smoke, we sputter out of the airport parking lot.

Addis is a city of almost eight million people. It houses the UN, the African Union, many embassies, a university, and an

ever-increasing number of high-rise hotels. But at night, far
from the main thoroughfare, Addis appears to be simply a
sprawl of shanties. Streetlights are poor or nonexistent, so cars
and pedestrians simply play a game of chicken. While I am
taking all of this in, Fikadu keeps up a cheerful patter in heavily accented English. "Welcome to Addis!" he exclaims. "Now
you seven years younger!" The Ethiopian calendar is seven
years behind ours. I feel rather that I have gained seven years
in the last seventeen hours of flight time, but Fikadu's enthusiasm is undimmed. "How my friend Beel doing?" he asks. "He
so nice guy!" Fikadu waxes on about Bill at such length that I
begin to feel like a lousy substitute. But I am so disoriented, so
jet-lagged, so utterly overcome by the strangeness of my new
environment that I cannot join the Bill fan club, not now. As
we put-put through the city, the air inside the taxi begins to
feel a little close and smells of gasoline. I try to open my window and find there is no handle. "No problem," says Fikadu. He
takes the handle off his door and hands it to me so that I can
lower my window. At one point during the ride, my door simply swings open. Fikadu hears my sharp intake of breath and
without missing a beat, reaches across me and slams it shut. I
again reach for my phantom seat belt.

After what seems like an interminable ride, we are at last
at the outside gates of the Hilton Hotel. Before we can enter we
must submit to an inspection of the car's interior, and mirrors
on long sticks are used to check for explosives under the car.
(On my third trip to Ethiopia, a bomb in a minibus explodes
just across the street from the Hilton, killing twelve. But this
night I do not know these risks and simply long to get horizon-
tal in a bath and then a bed.)

Once through the car inspection and the metal detector, I
am in the lobby of a Tower of Babel. The hotel is teeming with
Africans, Europeans, adoptive families holding tiny Ethiopian
babies, backpacking tourists, evangelicals in sensible footwear,

and UN officials in elegant African regalia. Four harried desk clerks check people in with such genuine warmth that I am stunned. This welcome will characterize my every interaction with Ethiopians for the next several years. Chambermaids, street sweepers, waiters, guards, secretaries, and shopkeepers. People living just this side of desperation will smile with their eyes and ask me if I am happy here in Ethiopia. This connection will fuel me as I learn to metabolize some of Africa's heartbreaking realities and come to a truce with the dissonance that moving back and forth from the US will provoke. By the time I stagger up to my room (last renovated in 1960), I cannot wait to fall into bed and hope that pharmaceuticals will help me sleep. There is a schedule next to the bed that outlines the cast of luminaries I am scheduled to meet. I set it aside; it is too late, and there is too much information.

The breakfast meeting at 8:00 the next morning is more than a wake-up call. This is my first encounter with the senior staff at the Clinton Foundation. I am seated at the breakfast table with Dr. Yigeremu, CHAI country director and revered physician, and several senior Clinton staffers. In the interim between the first lunch with Ed Wood and my arrival in Addis Ababa, fantasies about what I could deliver had inflated considerably on the Ethiopian side. Certainly I would be there to offer coaching to Dr. Betru, but my role had morphed into something much bigger. The minister of health, Dr. Tedros, decided to undertake a complete, top-to-bottom business process reengineering (BPR) of his entire infrastructure: laboratories, hospitals and clinics, doctors, nurses, scientists, administrators, community health workers. Dr. Tedros was always ahead of his time, a visionary leader quite a cut above the corporate clients I had left at home.

Dr. Yigeremu: "Do you know this BPR?" he asks with the inimitable Ethiopian rolling *R*.

Me, cautiously: "Yes, I know a bit about how it is done."

Doug, a senior Clinton staffer: "Well, Dr. Tedros wants to improve the efficiency and effectiveness of all the departments in the Ministry."

Me, almost choking on my jet-fuel coffee: "All? How many people is that, ballpark?"

Dr. Yigeremu: "Only fifteen hundred."

Me, swallowing hard: "Here is the dilemma. You need several full-time BPR experts living here. I am not an expert, and I am coming only intermittently!"

I have been in the country twelve hours. Business process reengineering is an exhaustingly layered and complex change methodology. I thought I was coming to offer some coaching, and now I am trying tactfully to backpedal from an assignment I know I can't deliver. I can see the disappointment on the faces of the others around the table. But I have to be realistic about what it is I am offering.

The Clinton Foundation is held in high esteem in Ethiopia, and this goodwill carries me through the morning meetings, though I am busily paring down expectations as I go. By afternoon I am finally in front of Dr. Betru, my assigned client. I have been told that he has a bright future but a blunt style and that he needs to do more to develop a followership. That's it. There are no more pieces of data for me to go on except what I can discern on my own.

To get to Betru's office I must negotiate a Byzantine series of ancient elevators. I cannot read the signs in Amharic, this lovely script with 138 letters in the alphabet. I am so obviously lost. The elevator in the Clinton building broke and dropped ten stories only a month ago. My heart is racing from too much caffeine plus imposter anxiety, and this factoid does not help.

Dr. Betru runs the HIV/AIDS Prevention and Control Office for all of Ethiopia. He is a small, handsome man with a fierce intensity and a broad smile. He dives right into the business at hand. At least this is familiar choreography, conducting interviews and collapsing my findings into palatable bits: strengths, areas for development, future career thoughts. He is open and completely receptive, so much so that I wonder, Is this because I am a white woman with a PhD? But his face is so unguarded, I doubt he could fake this. He is on fire to move up the career ladder, and he sees corrective feedback as crucial step one. A year later he emails me this tender letter:

> *HI SUSIE,*
> *Imagine how very great you are?? Really you are so great. You are my mother who has been culturing and molding me I am always remember you,*
> *Your effort showing result. I am managing quitely everything now.*
> *Your SON,*
> *Betru*

My US corporate clients don't usually talk to me like this, hold my hand, exhort God to bless me and my entire family. They don't invite me home to meet their revered and aging parents. Here in Addis I am not a vendor, a service provider, or even a traditional consultant. Here, relationships are the bedrock, the place to start, the place to which you return. No relationship, no work, no results, period. Not that this isn't true at home. But in the US I can work for years with a client and still the relationship can be purely a transaction, nothing heartfelt.

Soon it is the weekend. I am exhausted from having lived the week in translation but eager to see this remarkable city. A senior Clinton staffer suggests that for a small stipend, his driver, Tariku, would take me to see some of the churches, the Mercato (the biggest outdoor market in all of Africa), and finally to a special dinner at his parents' home.

MY WEEKEND WITH TARIKU

Tariku comes to collect me at 8:00 a.m., and the entrance to the Hilton is mobbed by UN SUVs, jeeps headed on safari loaded with duffels on top, a few battered Mercedes for local dignitaries, and blue-and-white taxis careening around the corner. Smartly uniformed Hilton doormen try to contain the chaos as the hotel entrance disgorges middle-aged women wearing plastic nametags, blue-black men in bright robes from other African countries, Arabs in long white robes and red-and-white checkered head scarves, and NGO (non-governmental organization) workers in sensible shoes.

I clamber into the front seat of Tariku's blue taxi with its broken window handles, blue velvet seats, and blue velour dashboard. Once I gratefully fasten my seat belt, Tariku accelerates past the guards at the gate and into traffic, his car belching gray-black exhaust into the sunny blue skies. Tariku motors along at a typical breakneck pace through Saturday morning traffic in Addis, past squares built by occupying fascists a number of years ago, past Addis Ababa University teeming with students, past the locked and manicured gardens of the UN, and past government ministries looking worn and gray, signage faded, windows grimy with pollution, not a shrub or a plant to alleviate the facade. And as always, past the many, many homeless who have spent a long night on the dirty streets. We pass what Tariku tells me is the American embassy. No flags, no plants, no gardens, no signs whatsoever except one that prohibits photographs. There are three layers of concrete barricades and a thirty-foot stone wall with an iron gate that opens and closes swiftly. Lots of men with guns.

As we climb steadily out of the city to the hills beyond, the roads are clogged with churchgoers, swathed in all-white cotton scarves and robes. Many people amble in the streets, where taxis and buses come within inches of them. A mere ten minutes and we begin to come out of the city slums and store-fronts and head up a road bordered by eucalyptus trees and red clay. Legions of donkeys clot the road, nearly buried under their burdens of wood, leaves, and branches (all brought down the hill for cooking fires). The eucalyptus trees are so stripped of bark and branches that they stand roots exposed, thin blue-green fingers holding the trunks aloft.

Our car climbs higher and higher, narrowly missing many women, men, and donkeys, and soon we are in another world. The landscape looks like California as it must have been years ago. Rolling hills and pasture as far as the eye can see, tiny farms, juniper and eucalyptus trees. This is the dry season, so the fields are the color of the wheat being harvested. We are at about 7,500 feet, the air is cool and dry, and I feel light-headed. We stop to visit one of the many orthodox Christian churches. Wood or stone, most are octagonal in shape. Fierce-looking priests in long robes and distinctive round hats with flat tops let us in after I pay a fee and we remove our shoes.

The church interior mirrors the social order it supports: a side for women, throne seats for former emperors, and a sacred space in the middle for high priests who sit behind velvet curtains. Ethiopians can spend up to three hours daily in church, and the church portico is loaded with women standing in prayer, bobbing and kissing the church walls. They are not permitted inside except during services.

Because I am a *farengi*, or white person, I shell out more money to get in than they see in a month. The high priest unlocks the sanctuary for us, and I enter with Tariku. Once there, we are treated to numbing detail about the origin of relatively contemporary stained-glass windows and crypts. Tariku listens, rapt, kisses walls and floors, and eagerly translates for me stories of what he calls "God magic," stories of miracles said to have happened within the church walls. I cannot imagine a benevolent and intercessory God who would save so few while millions suffer daily in ways I cannot imagine. But this is my young driver's world, and I am taking my cues from him.

Back at the front of the church, Tariku suggests it would be appropriate to give alms to the poor. I take what remains (a hundred-birr note worth about $3.60) and change it into one hundred single-birr notes at the church entrance office. I am trying to be subtle with my now-large wad of bills, but in a moment we are swarmed, old women wrapped in colorful scarves, barefoot kids, men with canes and missing limbs. In a matter of seconds I am the center of a scene I never wanted to create. The priest quietly admonishes the people to form a line, and immediately they do, squatting by the side of the road, a line that snakes well up the hill toward the village. I give Tariku the money to disburse, and he does so, following the priest's suggestion that one birr be given to two people to share. I am floored. What will six cents matter? (Tariku later tells me that one birr will buy four loaves of bread!) It takes Tariku half an hour to give out the money while I stand with the priest at the bottom of the hill. There is a quiet chorus of *"Igzerstaling!"* (May God be with you) that many take up. Eventually we get in the car and drive slowly away while kids who didn't make the handout run alongside. Tariku feels better. I am nursing chagrin, guilt, embarrassment, but Tariku beams and says, "Good job!"

To get to Tariku's house we must negotiate a pitch-dark stone alley, which he illuminates with his cell phone. Once there I am greeted like royalty by Tariku's parents. His mother, wreathed in white robes, is squatting on the floor next to a tiny charcoal brazier roasting coffee beans for the special coffee ceremony. His father, a handsome, slender man with a regal bearing, fixes me with one of those light-up-the-face smiles, and I am shown a seat. The room I am in is no bigger than eight by ten, smaller than my hotel room by half. It has four upholstered chairs, a coffee table, a wooden dish cupboard, and in the corner a TV. One bare ceiling bulb lights the space, which is decorated with stuffed teddy bears affixed to the wall along with some plastic flowers and several pictures of a very blond Jesus Christ. The mud floor is scattered with clipped grass, part of the coffee ceremony to come. The meal is served: injera, of course. This is Lent, and Tariku's mother apologizes for the lack of meat in our meal. I am beyond relieved that this is the case. Butcher shops in Addis Ababa are a scary sight. Huge carcasses hang in the hot midday sun, covered with flies, and yet Ethiopians and some tourists are fond of having carpaccio, chopped raw beef or goat, a local delicacy extolled in the *New York Times* travel section.

I am careful to clean my plate as Tariku's mother looks on. She tries to give me more while she will take no food whatsoever until I am gone. She is busy with the preparation of the coffee ceremony, and the small room fills with smoke and the aroma of the roasting beans. As is the custom, the beans are passed under the nose of the honored guest to savor the smell, then they are ground by mortar and pestle. Water is poured through the beans into tiny cups and sweetened liberally with raw sugar. I have never tasted coffee like it, fresh, sweet, not a hint of bitterness.

The next day Tariku takes me to the Mercato, the largest open-air market in all of Africa. The scene is overwhelming, people hawking their wares, donkeys, goats, cars, and thousands of people. Smells of food, exhaust, smoke, incense, and donkey shit give way to bins of chickpeas, lentils, teff flour, and spices so aromatic the air is filled with scent. I wander in Tariku's wake, dizzy with the sensory overload.

I spot a very old woman in traditional garb selling armloads of rosemary and lavender. *Picture perfect,* I think. Through Tariku I ask permission to take her photo. Immediately she asks for money. He offers her ten birr (about $1.20). She counters, asking twenty, and I offer it up. Behind us a crowd has gathered, and they get into a lively exchange and commentary. "She wants twenty birr for a photo. That is too much!" Back and forth they go. I now simply want to snap the photo and vaporize from the scene. She is in shadow crouched near a car. I don't have the temerity to ask her to move into the sunshine for a better shot. So here is the JPEG I have for posterity: tiny brown lady, crouching near car fender clutching her twenty-birr note close to her face, grinning like she has just won the lottery. Not quite the *National Geographic* shot I had hoped for.

TEAM BUILDING IN NAZARETH

Back in Addis on Monday, Betru tells me he has a new senior team of leaders, but he is not yet happy with their performance or their ability to work together effectively. I have done a lot of team building in the US and hope that some of what I have done there will be applicable in Ethiopia. I agree to return in five weeks to run the session.

The two-day meeting is to be held two hours outside of Addis Ababa in a place called Nazareth. With its biblical association I fantasize a lovely, remote, rural area free from the hustle and bustle of the city, a place where people can get a perspective on their work absent the intrusions of the day-to-day. Not quite. My clients are all employees of the Ethiopian civil service, and as such their salaries range from $200 to $300 a month. If they choose to go off-site for a meeting then they are given an additional stipend of $20 a day. So this is why we have repaired to Nazareth, for an extra $40 each, not for its bucolic peace and quiet.

Nazareth, or Adama as it is known on the map, is a city of three hundred thousand and is the epicenter of the Ethiopian AIDS epidemic, situated as it is at the intersection of all the major trucking routes. It has a huge transient influx, with the attendant prostitution and virulent disease. Nazareth is ringed by huge factories that tan animal hides and make soap. We pass through some stunning countryside while playing chicken with hundreds of semis on a two-lane road. So many people are killed every year by the ubiquitous Isuzu trucks on this very road that the vehicles are nicknamed "al-Qaeda" by the locals. I am in a soup of adrenaline- and caffeine-fueled anxiety. But I'm also feeling more alive than I have in a long time. I am on an adventure, I am intrepid and terrified in equal measure, but I am here to do good.

We pull into the city at dusk as the heat abates and the city residents throng into the streets by the thousands. All the commerce takes place in the road, illegally. People spread out their wares in the dirt: clothing, shoes, food, and electronics. They scatter if the police show up to fine them. Cars, donkeys, stray dogs, and horse-drawn buggies go at full tilt through the crowds. I don't see another white face for days.

Finally we peel off to drive into the gates of the spectacularly misnamed Palace Garden Hotel. That first night I tuck my netting in tightly and try to sleep in a fetal position so as to not touch the brown bed net. Close to the hotel I hear the local band that night, and the amplified Muslim call to prayer before dawn. Dinner is the same as breakfast, lunch, and dinner everywhere in Ethiopia: injera. Injera is made from a grain called teff, fermented and cooked into a pancake the color of putty. It is then topped with various other foods cooked to the same shade of gray. Potatoes, lentils, green beans, hard-boiled eggs, and a sliver of meat the consistency of leather, all swimming in a soup of orange cooking oil. I crave a stiff drink with which to wash this down, but none seems in evidence and I am hardly going to draw attention to myself by asking for one.

After a long wakeful night and a breakfast of more injera, the team and I are assembled at a table in the hotel dining room. Dr. Betru opens the session very formally and previews the many small miracles that he hopes I will engineer. I am mildly dizzy in the heat. The ten attendees sit upright at full attention at their places, and the room is utterly still but for the sounds of the local rooster in the yard.

I begin by trying to make an agreement with the room that they will interrupt if my English is not understood. They nod yes, and I know no one will. Eventually I find that one guy, a handsome man named Mercuria, will blink a lot if he doesn't understand, then I can backtrack and replay. I must also omit the buzzwords that are in common use at home: bottom line, hitting it out of the park, moving the ball up the field. Over time I have laboriously learned these military and sports analogies to talk with my largely male clients. Now I must self-censor this corporate lingo.

I am also trying to memorize and learn to pronounce the wonderful names: Freheywot, Meskele, Hassan, Alemu. The agenda is not unusual for an initial US team-building session. Go over a self-assessment, clarify goals and roles, revisit the vision and values, and begin to give each other feedback about mutual support needs. As the day progresses, things get looser, there is more laughter and more jokes, and I invite them to do as many of the complex discussions as possible in their own language, Amharic. When they speak in Amharic I rely on body language, the occasional brief translation, and the odd sprinkling of English words: *accountability, performance, objectives* (all apparently with no Amharic equivalent) to gauge their progress. *If these words don't even exist in their language,* I wonder, *are we are imposing some Western standard that will not stick?*

After the preliminaries, Betru starts by telling the group he has leadership weaknesses that he is working on and asks for feedback, positive and negative.

We can hear a pin drop, there is a prolonged pause, and then the lone woman on the team, Freheywot, the head of finance, starts to speak. Freheywot is a stunning woman in bright colors and red lipstick. Then she does what is never done. She takes on her boss, who she felt had made a wrong decision without consulting his team. To Betru's credit, he listens respectfully and does not pull rank.

Remarkably, this is the way the next day and a half proceeds. Having broken the mold, the team is energized by the truth telling that ensues. Each member of the team gives and receives candid feedback about how they can do their jobs better. I don't know if this candor and honesty will stick once we get back to Addis Ababa, but for the time being it seems to be a welcome exercise. Only one more injera supper, one more night in my dingy little room, another epic trip dodging trucks on the highway, and I will be able to return to what seems now like the utter lap of luxury, my well-worn room at the Hilton Hotel.

CHAPTER SEVEN

Getting in Deeper

OUTBREAKS AND NEAR MISSES

This sixth trip to Ethiopia two years later has meant the usual warm welcome from old friends and total strangers, the usual assault on the senses: Remarkable beauty juxtaposed against ubiquitous grinding poverty. Cascading fuchsia bougainvillea and pastel-colored storefronts concealing acres of tin shacks and open sewers. My work has begun to take the shape of ten days in Africa every six to eight weeks. The travel is grueling, but it has begun to solidify into a predictable pattern. I know the sixteen-hour route on Ethiopian Air. Africa's pull for me has not abated; it has intensified. I am greeted like a rock star by clients and colleagues. We hug (the Ethiopians greet me and one another like the French, alternating three kisses). Earnest inquiries after my family and my health always come before business.

Much has changed. The food crisis shows up here in very stark fashion. Teff, the staple of every Ethiopian meal, has tripled in price in only three months. As elsewhere in the third world, this seems to be an outcome of a perfect storm of causal factors: fuel costs, drought, speculation, and now hoarding. Thousands face starvation after seven years of steady economic growth. A dead homeless man is discovered down the street from the Clinton Foundation's office. Drought too threatens the harvest and creates lengthy power outages. I am spared, as the Hilton generators roar into service many times each day.

In Addis a mysterious disease quietly stalks a few very poor neighborhoods. It starts with painful leg swelling, progresses quickly to respiratory shutdown, coughing up blood, and death, all within twelve to twenty-four hours. My second client group (a CDC-like agency) swings into action running studies, initially suspecting an infectious process. Careful epidemiological work unearths the culprit: locally produced and adulterated cooking oil, the kind sold in poor neighborhoods to families who bring a plastic jug to be filled. In a made-for-TV moment, my clients decipher the problem, arrest the distributors, and avert a large-scale health disaster in a city that can hardly bear another. They are relieved and proud, and so am I.

All in all, the week unfolds as it usually does. I facilitate many team meetings big and small in a cacophony of Amharic and mangled English. Participants exhort each other to make their presentations more "crispy," and they laugh good-naturedly at my horrible pronunciation of basic phrases in Amharic. Very strong, sweet Ethiopian macchiato coffee is served every two hours in every gathering, and I am on a jittery high. We joke about how Starbucks tastes to them like "brown water."

One night the roads leading to my hotel have been all blocked. A bomb has been detonated across the street from the Hilton, exploding a minibus loaded with passengers, killing twelve. Body parts are propelled into the adjacent park, and a severed head and hand show up not far from the Hilton entrance. I hear of these sights but, fortunately, do not actually see them.

There are no announcements in the hotel, no safety briefings, no acknowledgment whatsoever. The suspicion is that rebel groups from Eritrea have engineered this event. Only a small Al Jazeera internet posting informs the Clinton staff of this. In the cocoon of the Hilton compound, life goes on oblivious. Children splash in the pool. Waiters set up for a wedding reception. UNESCO meetings drone on. An international conference on manufacturing quality condoms still takes place. Somehow this disregard helps me to burrow into a form of denial as well.

DEEPER INTO AFRICA

Once I earn my stripes in Ethiopia I am invited over time to replicate the work in Tanzania, Malawi, Lesotho, and Swaziland. I am thrilled to see more of Africa, but the back-and-forth trips get tougher, longer, more taxing. The visit to Ruangwa in southern Tanzania is a prime example.

I am dancing in a conga line in an old barn, the African midwives and me. It is hot, my rubber sandals are clunky, and the dance steps are quick and graceful. The women all around me are dressed in long, colorful *kitenge* dresses, skirts that hug ample bottoms and flare to the hem, tight matching bodices, and wrapped head scarves. Birds fly into the building through rafters and open eaves, blue sky visible at each end. The older woman just in front of me has slowed her pace, lifted her skirts a bit, and is exaggerating the steps so I can follow. Hips and skirts sway, the footwork takes more concentration than I can muster. All around me brown faces smile indulgently. I am sweaty but mildly euphoric.

We're on our lunch break in a maternal health meeting in rural Ruangwa. I am the only white face here. We have assembled seventy-five carefully chosen village leaders who will draft a plan to get more pregnant women to deliver their babies in health centers. We're trying to stem the tide of mother-to-child HIV infection, and three teams of thirty have only two days to draft ninety-day implementation plans. Remarkably, the midwives have joined us even with the knowledge that if we are successful, their small enterprises will dwindle. The meeting started as all meetings do in Africa, late. A few stultifying speeches, a prayer, and best of all, some a cappella singing of hymns.

I flash to the memory of the well-appointed US corporate conference rooms I have come from. Over-air-conditioned and pristine, they all look alike. Food is lavish and plentiful, and I do not have to carry my own toilet paper to an open-air latrine, which may or may not have an operative door. There is no singing or praying at these business meetings, and there certainly is no dancing.

I am a little worse for wear after three days. Ruangwa has no restaurant, only a seedy bar with an appended patio where there are exactly three things on the menu: chapati, tea, and chicken soup. The chickens who will be commandeered for the soup race around the perimeter of the patio, and a gang of homeless boys gathers outside the grass kitchen hut to wash dishes in exchange for a meal. I try not to think about how well our dishes are being washed. We have now had six chicken-soup meals since my arrival, and the soup is remarkably good. The broth is dense and flavorful, and the single scrawny leg that floats in it is tough but tasty. I am not starving here in Ruangwa, but I am still recovering from last night's events.

My Ethiopian colleague, Henok, and I are staying in what is reputed to be the "best" guesthouse in town, named the Mayai (the Egg) for no discernible reason. My tiny bedroom has a bed so close to the wall it can be accessed only on one side. To my surprise, it has its own bathroom, a toilet with no seat and a shower hose but no shower stall. Mercifully, the mosque two doors down amplifies only an abbreviated version of the early morning call to prayer, so it is possible to hear it and then fall back to sleep.

Two a.m. in Ruangwa means barking dogs and errant roosters, Africa's everywhere chorus. I am sleeping soundly with the help of pharmaceuticals to overcome my chronic jet lag. Suddenly I am jolted from sleep by a banging on my door so loud it is as though the flimsy door will collapse. Loud male voices yelling in Swahili. I freeze, hoping they are drunks banging on the wrong door. The pounding continues, amplifies, I yell for them to stop, and finally I get an answer in English. "Open your door," one bellows. "We are police!"

In Tanzania the police are notoriously corrupt, and so this is not particularly reassuring news. First of all, how do I know they are actually police, and second of all this cannot be good that they are coming to get me in the dead of night. Eventually I capitulate, throw on a bathrobe, and open the door, half asleep and terrified. Two huge uniformed men are standing there. And they have guns. To my relief, I see they have also extracted Henok from his room next door. They can take us away together. His face looks as ashen as mine. The police then inform us that we have failed to sign the guest registry book and we must do so now. They produce the book, we write in our home address and names, and they leave. Later we learn the guesthouse was trying to withhold the 5 percent occupancy tax by failing to register guests. So this is the solution that has been devised by the local government to ascertain how many guests are actually staying in the guesthouses in town! I go back to bed and try to sleep before the call to prayer will wake me once again. Once we are back in session the next day, the evening's bizarre events recede. They will make good war stories. The police will not come for us again, and we can stay focused on the AIDS prevention work that brought us here to begin with.

RETURNING FROM AFRICA

I will travel home to the US from Tanzania after my late-night adventures in Ruangwa. It is the week before Thanksgiving. The heat has bumped up to a humidity level that leaves all of us on the team limp and enervated. The only relief comes when we drive from point to point in our Clinton Foundation air-conditioned SUV. The drivers turn up the air-conditioning so high that we are nearly refrigerated as they blast at top speed through small villages, scattering chickens and children. But I cannot spend each day in an air-conditioned SUV. And I hate to parade our conspicuous privilege. I am ready for a break after three weeks. Every item of clothing I have brought is now a dull gray, and for the time being our project seems to be progressing without our weekly presence.

So it is time to come home, see friends and family, and enjoy my favorite holiday, a feast without the need for gifts: Thanksgiving. The trip home involves an hour drive to the airport, two hours standing in line, twelve hours in the air from Dar es Salaam to Amsterdam, another eight hours to Boston. Gil picks me up at Logan Airport. I am delighted to be back with him. But I am spent, stiff, sweaty, and dislocated. My high spirits last through the ride home, a hot shower, and a glass of wine, then exhaustion, jet lag, and the reentry set in.

I am always mildly euphoric with my first shower at home. I stand under gallons of rushing hot and potable water. It is a miraculous luxury. My bathroom is huge, and it is clean. I can put my toothbrush under the tap and my head too, taking in huge gulps of cold, clean water. And as I give myself over to small pleasures now made huge, I am at the same time suffused with images of Africa. In my mind's eye I see the countless villages of one-room mud-and-wattle houses, the women as beasts of burden carrying babies, water cans, firewood. At one level my reentry unfolds as any return trip would: laundry to do, bills to pay, junk mail to sort, plants to resuscitate, emails and voice mails to answer. I pick up the thread of life but always with a heightened awareness of what I have left behind. This grinding poverty is not scenic or colorful. It is a brown-and-gray palette of suffering whose parameters I see more and more each trip I make. I cannot easily reconcile these images with my life. My house with its air-conditioning and hum of appliances, our two-car garage with electric door opener, grocery stores with raspberries in winter, and my own closet with enough shoes and shirts to clothe a small village. I am unsettled by the contrasts made all the more extreme as Americans approach their season of excess: the Thanksgiving overeating, the drumbeat of ads for Christmas consumerism, and the hordes of Black Friday shoppers trampling anyone in their way. The contrasts are acute and yet somehow undiscussable. Who wants a lecture over pecan pie about another famine in Ethiopia?

I don't know how to talk about my experiences, and many people don't know quite how to ask. When people ask, "How was your trip?" I am stymied into silence. The only answer is "Fine," but I have not been on a sightseeing tour, a vacation, a getaway, a project that I can easily condense into a palatable executive summary. I have been on an adventure, a mission. I have found a calling, and it is much more than a series of trips. But it is a calling I have still not figured out. For now I am oscillating back and forth from the US to Africa about every six to eight weeks. This will not be a sustainable scenario year after year. The travel is too wearing, and the worlds are too different.

I am also a bystander at the Clinton Foundation itself. I am one of a kind as an organizational development consultant when others represent distinct technical specialties: medical professionals, researchers, analysts. I am decades older than most of CHAI's employees, scary-smart twentysomethings from Ivy League schools. CHAI is for many an idealistic two-to-three-year stop-off on the way to business school. I never share my exact age. Already I know I am way older than their faraway mothers, women they miss and reflexively disparage in equal measure.

But my age also has benefits. For some young employees I become an older mentor and coach, and we can jointly do great work. I can easily establish rapport with older male African professionals in the Ministry, men who are politely but mildly insulted to be called on by consultants twenty to thirty years their junior. In Africa, age means wisdom, whereas in the US it means obsolescence.

Over time I strengthen ties with younger colleagues, American and African alike. We mix their local and technical savvy with my experience as a psychologist and consultant, and it works. We come up with solutions and ideas that seem quite brilliant, at least to us. At night we laugh and tell stories over meals of mediocre food and cheap booze. I get attached to them even as they eventually leave CHAI or get reassigned. I still miss many who left years ago. Repeatedly I too go home to the US and they stay on. So, I am peripheral, a familiar if painful reality.

Virtually everything about my parallel lives stands in stark contrast. The brown and gray colors of New England's approaching winter, and the riot of color that is springtime in Africa. The chilly interpersonal distance New Englanders preserve, and the Africans' unguarded affections. Our huge houses and cars sealed tight from the elements, and life in Africa lived outdoors and on foot. The more I come and go, the less articulate I can be about why I am compelled to return. Slowly my picture postcards of Africa are changing. From safaris in the Serengeti to clinics with blood-spattered walls and almost no medical equipment, houses so grim they barely deserve the name, corruption so endemic that it is routine. And yet, the work is seductive. The promise of saving lives at its most elemental, the adventure, the gracious appreciation for my efforts. The business consulting I resume when I come home begins to lose its luster. I dress up, drive downtown, park in forty-dollars-a-day garages, sit in impeccable glass office towers overlooking the city, and try to tune back into the conversations I have left behind. "How soon can we take this company public? Why did I not make partner this year? How can I move up in the company faster? Why wasn't I given a larger bonus? How do we get this team to take more accountability?"

When I am asked by my clients over coffee breaks about my work in Africa, I talk too much and too long. My listeners' eyes glaze over; some wistfully say that someday they too will be in a place to "give back." But I must remember that here I am being paid handsomely to pay attention to their agendas. I must sort out my dichotomous existence on my own nickel. This is tricky for the extrovert that I am. I find I can talk with people who have actually been to Africa. They understand experientially the painful ambivalence that being there provokes, the pull toward the Africans themselves, and the sheer day-to-day difficulties that being there presents.

Maybe it is the generosity and good nature of my clients in Africa, but they make me feel like a hero. As a consultant in the US I'm always challenged to come up with the next best thing, and chided when an idea may be a few years old. In Africa my clients are so thrilled that I have come so far to help them that they never second-guess my suggestions. Dr. Yigeremu calls me a rock star, and I am oxidized by the feedback. It is all about the relationship, and the relationships are remarkably intimate despite the long absences between my visits. I treasure every connection, knowing that in five or ten years' time they will still be as strong.

One example is my sweet connection with Hareg, the indefatigable nurse who heads the rural program for Tigray. She supports, hires, and trains all the medical staff in this far-flung rural area. She has an ample figure, a generous heart, and a warm smile. I am drawn to her from the start. After a day in her company she greets me with a hug and says, "Hello, darling." On my next trip home after work in Tigray, I am marking time until my midnight flight leaves. Hareg and I agree to have a farewell dinner together, just the two of us. She takes me to a tiny, well-hidden place with plastic tables. This will clearly not be a preferred hangout for expats, but I have choices other than raw goat, so I am happy. Hareg offers a prayer before our meal. We bow our heads and she talks for two or three minutes in Tigrinya. She concludes, looks up, and grins. "This was a very short one!" she proclaims. Hareg, like so many from Ethiopia, is a deeply observant orthodox Christian and was raised and educated by missionaries.

Plates piled high with food arrive, and the owner hovers to make sure we are happy (the two dinners cost about three dollars). Hareg has injera, and I have chicken and rice. We talk from the heart about our lives, our kids, the losses, the learnings, the heartaches, the things that matter. I tell her about the husband I lost, she tells me about the husband she almost lost (Ethiopia is a hard place to have deep vein thrombosis). She invites my family to come and be guests in her home. At the end of our meal she smiles at me with her eyes and says she prays for my safe return and that God blesses me and my whole family. I breathe in her blessing and hold it close as I get ready to come back to the cold places.

THANKSGIVING IN BAHIR DAR

Two years into my Ethiopian assignment I impulsively agreed to spend Thanksgiving week in Ethiopia. Rumor had it that I might get to meet again with Dr. Tedros, the minister of health, always gracious and full of bold ideas. I did not bargain for the backwash of homesickness that was to ensue. This was, after all, my twelfth trip to Ethiopia and I knew the drill. But after the usual grueling night flight to Addis Ababa, cheery emails with "Happy Thanksgiving" in the subject line begin flooding my inbox, and I find myself pining for family and for the annual rituals, even for foods I don't especially like, like cranberry sauce and creamed onions. I am fine so long as I can remain thoroughly anchored in the compelling daily realities of Africa, but need to distance myself from reminders of the holiday at home. So, when the chance comes to travel to Bahir Dar and visit our teams at work in the rural clinic there, I leap at the opportunity.

Bahir Dar is a small city perched alongside huge Lake Tana, gateway to tourist destinations of ancient monasteries and famous stone churches. Broad, tidy boulevards are lined with palm trees, and in the center median are flowering orange flame trees and huge, colorful hibiscus. Bright blue three-wheeled taxis careen up and down the street, just missing donkey carts and herds of goats. Children mass in the early morning for school in uniforms of lavender, turquoise, and red. The sky is a brilliant blue, and the air is clean and clear. I breathe it in deeply. After Addis, it is a relief.

I meet the local health coordinator, Ramrin, who efficiently organizes Clinton Foundation activities in twenty-five health centers in the region. We pile in the car with Henok, my colleague from Addis. The driver puts in a CD of music, and soon we are barreling out of the city to the sounds of Jennifer Lopez. Within minutes we are outside city limits and in utterly rural

Ethiopia. But for the asphalt road we are on, the countryside is timeless, expansive, unchanged, and unmarred by any signs of modernity. Fields of maize, wheat, and teff are being harvested; herds of skinny cattle are being tended by tiny barefoot boys. Baobab trees dot the fields picked clean of all underbrush for cooking fires. The mountains are lavender in the distance. As everywhere in Africa, the road belongs to pedestrians and livestock. Our car straddles the center line to avoid them, moving back to the right-hand lane only when oncoming trucks bear down on us. I wish I did not know that Ethiopia leads Africa in traffic fatalities. More people are killed here by cars than by malaria. By Ethiopian life-expectancy standards I am at fifty-nine an elder matriarch, and I pray this morning to get to live to a ripe, old American age.

The sun is high and warm here in Bahir Dar, and most of the walkers on the hot asphalt road are barefoot. Women balancing impossible loads of firewood on their heads and babies on their backs, children unaccompanied, and old, turbaned men carrying walking sticks. The access to the clinic is an unmarked dirt road in a village of mud houses, each with a tiny vegetable plot. Our purpose today is to meet with the team leaders who have been part of our Fast Track initiative geared at preventing mother-to-child transmission of AIDS. Crucial to this effort is outreach to expectant mothers and getting them in for early testing, treatment, and prenatal care. Our team is proud and energized. In merely fifty days they have tested and treated over eight hundred women, an increase of 225 percent. They are visibly energized. This excitement is obvious well before I hear the translation from Amharic.

Then I am offered a tour of the clinic and ask to see the delivery room. We go down the dark hallway. Ramrin knocks and strides right in with me in his wake. I register in slow motion the scene that greets us. The floor is awash with blood, as is the simple birthing chair. On a bed in the corner is a new mother with her infant not thirty minutes old. The mother is in street clothes; her baby is wrapped in the mother's head shawl. Surrounding the bed is a gaggle of very old women clad in black. Appalled that I have barged in at such a moment, I offer congratulations for translation. All present reciprocate with wide smiles. This bond is as old as time and as universal. I ask the sex of the baby. It is a son, another cause for joy. More smiles. He is named Arafat by this Muslim family. Now emboldened, I ask to see the tiny raisin face, and his mother peels back her shawl. Arafat lets out a howl. We all smile again. Childbirth in Africa is dangerous business, and life has prevailed. I murmur a few things said to all postpartum moms, then walk gingerly across the sticky floor to leave.

My host is anxious to show me more, so we proceed down the hall lined with patients waiting to be seen. Barefoot, squatting on the floor, nursing babies, some look at me with vacant eyes and some return smiles warmly. Malaria, AIDS, and TB are the primary presenting problems, and I give a wide berth to a man coughing vociferously. The next room we enter unceremoniously is the family planning room, once again interrupting a patient procedure. (Privacy, one of those things I consider an inalienable right, here is almost unknown.) The woman lying on a cot has just been given a contraceptive implant, which will be good for three years. She has had eleven pregnancies and lost five children. She looks too old to be of childbearing age, but then a lifetime of poverty and continual pregnancy takes its toll. She tells me she is happy to receive this help and says she will tell all her daughters to do the same. After the clinic tour we make our way back through the queues of preternaturally quiet patients and the sheep grazing in the clinic yard and head back into town. Henok, Ramrin, and I have a Thanksgiving lunch of fish fried to the consistency of a Frisbee. It is surely a time to give thanks for all I have, all I have left behind, and all I will come home to.

I have stitched heartfelt connections across Africa over five years and twenty-five trips. I know how to start over in some new, far-flung location, how to set up camp, however briefly, but I am beginning to weary of my yo-yo existence. I sorely miss my husband, Gil, on these excursions. He is there to pack me up and send me off and patiently paste me back together upon my return.

But what if he could go with me? Quietly, privately, I begin to nurse a fantasy. It goes like this. What if Gil and I could live in a rural community in Tanzania where we could work on community projects at the local level, where we could have a small but visible impact, where the friends we made we could keep? What if we didn't have to live in some expat gilded cage surrounded by cut glass and razor wire? What if we didn't have to stay in sketchy hotels and guesthouses trying to learn a different language each trip? What if Gil could share in the challenges, the setbacks, and the small victories?

But Gil has not even been to Africa. First I have to get him here. The idea is so audacious that it barely shows up in my journal. Off to the edge of the page in pencil it is there: "Live in Africa?" There it is with a question mark. I cannot even make it a declarative statement, so radical is this idea.

But the idea incubates and matures even as I start projects in Lesotho, Swaziland, and Malawi. I will dodge lightning in Swaziland, bombs in Dar es Salaam, and guns in Lesotho before Gil and I settle in Nshupu, Tanzania. In Nshupu there will be no murders in hotel parking lots or large-scale drama for the big screen. Instead there we will feel like small-town heroes as we raise money and hopes for orphaned kids with neither. We will see the best and the worst of humanity in this village of subsistence farmers: integrity and sacrifice, violence and extortion. In this late-life roller coaster, we will be hugely stretched. We will learn a little Swahili, our Tanzanian friends will try to interpret for us the cultural chasm, and we will still be looking in at their lives through scratched plate glass. But first I have some miles to travel, teams to teach, sessions to run. The Tanzania fantasy will have to incubate for another three years before I can make it real.

PACKING FOR AFRICA

Although I have packed for Africa many times, I have learned enough to make me slightly more anxious each time I go. This time I am going to Malawi. It is the month of October, a time of drought and heat fondly dubbed "suicide month," a fact I wish I did not know. I start weeks in advance making lists and amassing piles of things I know I must not forget.

My headlamp—for the inevitable nights with power outages.

Malarone for malaria prevention.

Imodium, antibiotics, antinausea meds—a small hedge against the seemingly inevitable GI distress.

Hand sanitizer in dozens of small bottles. Everyone in Africa shakes hands. It is rude not to.

Bandages, Benadryl, dental floss, vitamins, and various products that promise to "strengthen my immune system" for the seventeen-hour flight and the guy in row 22 who coughs for the whole trip.

Long skirts and blouses to cover my shoulders so I don't offend Muslim sensibilities in the rural reaches.

And of course, SPF 70 sunblock, as my pasty-white coloring can fry in the equatorial sun.

I check and recheck my list and my preparedness. If I forget any of these things there is no handy CVS to go to for their replacement. I will simply do without. I put together my assemblage of stuff knowing that I am equipped to handle only the most basic and predictable discomforts. But I'm flooded with the what-if fears. What if I have a toothache, need a root canal, have appendicitis? What if I am in a car crash? What if my luggage is lost, stolen, rifled through, and I must travel equatorial Africa in my New England woolens? What if I lose my phone, my laptop, my lifeline to the world I left behind? The what-ifs escalate. They dog me. I wake in the middle of the night, heart pounding, sweating under my down comforter.

Not all the litany of what-ifs come from my overactive imagination. The worst come from real stories that have beset other NGO workers. The young girl raped in India, the nurse shot to death in a Lesotho hotel parking lot (the same hotel I will occupy in three weeks' time), the doctor butchered in his own kitchen with his newly purchased steak knives, the nurses in Malawi cowering in a locked bathroom while men with machetes stripped their house bare, the seventy-five-year-old female volunteer mugged in Addis Ababa in front of a high-end hotel. These stories run in an endless loop of horrors in my head. I do not share them with friends and family, so they fester and metastasize. Already enough people think I am nuts to do this work, so I need not fuel that conclusion any further with this information. I sit with my fears, try to keep them at bay as my departure dates get closer.

While some friends and family might feel that these trips are a flirtation with danger, I know that my father is the one person who deeply understands. He and I do not talk about it, but I know that he has felt the regular pull from the safe confines of home to adventures that call for risk and service. In my own way I am still trying to join him, to be brave, to earn the nickname he gave me, Rocky.

I remember the late-night phone calls when I was young, watching Dad's face light up when it was time to lace his combat boots and leave for midnight maneuvers. No part of our predictable domestic life could ever compete with that excitement. I could hear him and his buddies whistling and joking in the dark street below as they strode quickly away from wives and kids to the German airstrip.

While my dad was going off those nights to rehearse war games, I get to do something even better: work to save lives. There would be no such drama doing this work in New England. So while the continual oscillation between the two worlds is difficult to manage, it is so dramatic that I feel like I'm starring in my own movie, my self-importance fueled by the vocal admiration of my young African colleagues and clients.

And yet this movie set is no picnic. I have a long-standing GI disorder, and this worsens with the lack of sanitation in all of the countries I visit. Hardly the stuff of Hollywood movies. I regularly suffer epic bouts of food poisoning. I come home wasted and bloated, unable to eat a sensible diet for weeks. The third bout of food poisoning in Ethiopia hit me just as I was going through passport control on my way home. Three times I ran from the line to the nearest bathroom to throw up. Finally I managed to get through and go at a dead run to the gate.

This was Ethiopian Air, and I had anted up an extra three hundred dollars to fly business class, a bit of a misnomer on this aging airline. But the seats were big and the lovely costumed stewardesses were kind. After boarding, and throwing up again in the airplane toilet, I have the luck to sit next to an emergency room MD who sees my state and offers to take me under his wing for the sixteen-hour flight. "I can even put you on an IV if needed," he reassures me. He opens up the pharmacopeia in his backpack and gives me antinausea tabs and antibiotics. He and a group of other medical professionals have been in the far reaches of Ethiopia for three months. Once I recover, twelve hours into the flight, he urges me to get tested for TB and to be dewormed if I am going to spend any further time in the country. Too weak to ask for details about what it means to get dewormed, I simply nod and thank him for the information. Pasted together, I am ready to make another trip six weeks later.

Although the comings and goings are physically challenging for me, the work itself actually benefits from the on-and-off pattern. I am training local facilitators to run grassroots team-based interventions we dub Fast Track. The trainings and the meetings themselves are short but fast. The follow-up for ninety days can and should be done by the local teams. I come and do a week or so of twelve-hour days, then the teams learn to fly on their own. I train teams in Ethiopia, Malawi, Tanzania, Lesotho, and Swaziland. My Ethiopian buddy, Henok, gets really good at the work and goes with me. In every country we must run the sessions in the local language, which he does not know, but his African presence is deeply reassuring. Impossibly I fall in love with every team I train. They work their hearts out, we laugh and joke. The women take me shopping, their mothers sew me long dresses in the local fabrics, we all go out drinking and dancing at night. But the grant money runs out, and too often the teams must be laid off. Or they become so capable they no longer need me. I head to the next destination and I mourn the friends I made and then lost in the previous country.

This was my life as an army brat, a life I recapitulated as a consultant, and now I am doing it again in Africa. A life of intense work and connection, then leave-taking and loss. Working in the tiny and vulnerable countries of Swaziland and Lesotho only intensifies this emotional yo-yo.

CHAPTER EIGHT

Small Countries at Risk

SWAZILAND

Swaziland is a surprise along any dimension you can name. Most people need to look it up on the map. I was no exception. There it sits, this country of only 1 million people, a small blip of a spot landlocked within South Africa and backing up to Mozambique to the east. It is breathtakingly beautiful. Rolling hills and mountains dotted with odd-shaped granite outcroppings, abundant trees, flowers, and birds, long vistas of green valleys. And its main city, Mbabane, is a wonder. Streetlights! Sidewalks! Asphalt roads and four-lane highways, shopping malls, fast-food chains, KFC, a snazzy hotel with a casino, a few very green golf courses, and a movie theater. This is not the Africa I know. I am floored. Of course I don't know South Africa either, so I am not used to this juxtaposition of wealth and privilege right alongside some devastating demographics. Swaziland, like nearby Lesotho, is in free fall, life expectancy plummeting to thirty-four years from fifty-five, and with the world's highest prevalence of HIV, AIDS, and TB. Though there are many agencies big and small working to improve the odds, the infection rate is soaring. I walk around thinking this: every fourth person I see is HIV-positive.

As if it were not already bad enough to have the world's worst AIDS prevalence, Swaziland also has the most deaths per million from lightning. Lightning storms in Swaziland last for hours at a time, striking a landscape littered with huge granite outcroppings with great drama and regularity. This week's Swazi *Times* headlines brought home the tragic realities:

Schoolgirl killed by lightning, 22 injured.

A random perusal of other headlines from the Swazi *Times* yields more stories that bring home this parallel universe that I am visiting. The headlines are pasted to electric poles, so the morning trip to town is an invitation to whiplash:

Rabid Dog Bites Pregnant Women near the Half
Price Shop
Jericho Gang Bites Ear off Young Boy. "The
devil was in him," They Say
MP Found Hiding in King's Wife's Bed

The king has fourteen wives and fourteen girlfriends at last count, so it is perhaps hard to keep track of them all. His father lived to age eighty-eight and had seventy wives, so this forty-four-year-old has a legacy to live up to. Polygamy and promiscuity are modeled throughout this small country, so imagine how effective the Bush-era campaigns of "Abstinence and Fidelity" were!

The Clinton Foundation driver assigned to me has been dubbed Warren because his given name has twelve consonants plus the click sound. He accepts this diminution of his name but not without some very quiet resentment, I think. I ask for tutelage in how to say hello, how are you, and thank you, the basic niceties so essential in any setting. I assiduously take notes, and each time I clamber into his car, Warren quizzes me. He frowns, repeats the lesson, and I try once again. It is not as though the new words are hugely difficult, but they are rattling around in a brain already taxed with my early efforts at Swahili, Chichewa, and Amharic. I am spread too thin and these lessons make that manifest as much as anything.

The Ematjeni B and B, where I spend the week, has been chosen for me as a special introduction to the country because of its location and panoramic views. It is in character and price point quite outside the frugal Clinton norms, and no one from the foundation has yet stayed there. This is my first trip to Swaziland, so this upgraded accommodation is designed to sweeten the pot, I think. The two-room suite is pristine. Even the toilet paper rolls have white lace covers. I feel as though I have somehow landed in a 1980s *Ladies' Home Journal.* The garden below my room is ablaze with zinnias, dahlias, roses, daisies, cosmos, marigolds, lilies, hibiscus, and birds of paradise. African staff are on hand to do laundry, cook meals, scrub floors, nurse babies, and stand like lawn statues watering English flower beds.

A quarter of the population here is dying. Forty-two percent of pregnant women are HIV-positive. I am told that every native Swazi family goes to at least one funeral every weekend. A quarter of the staff at this guesthouse must also be impacted. The apparent lack of curiosity on the subject stuns me. Or maybe it is just denial. In fact, it is denial writ large that becomes the cornerstone of my own introductory hypothesis about what is happening here.

The project I am here to support is breathtakingly ambitious. The newest concept on the AIDS landscape to be tested in this five-year effort is "treatment as prevention." In other words, if everyone who tests positive is put onto antiretroviral therapy, then the transmission of the virus can be arrested. This makes sense. This proposal is to be jointly run by the Clinton Foundation and the Dutch group Stop AIDS Now, and it seeks to put 95 percent of eligible patients on ARVs by the year 2014. The proposal is dubbed "the Dream." And that it is. I want to join in that audacious optimism and roll up my sleeves, but what little I know (and I am no public-health expert) has me awash in doubts and questions. I couch my nascent skepticism in curiosity to try to understand why things are so bad in this tiny, beautiful country. Swazis are not quite forthcoming, even with other Africans, never mind white expats. But my endless questions yield this picture.

Swaziland is an absolute monarchy. The king gives speeches about the importance of being tested for AIDS, but no one listens. The king was tested several years back and never disclosed the results. His own lavish polygamy is the standard to aspire to.

From the king on down to his lowliest subjects, multiple concurrent sexual partners is normative. Chiefs, MPs, church leaders are regularly exposed for this. Newspaper headlines blare "MP has 14-year-old girlfriend" and the like. Transactional sex is hugely common and works like this: Young girls who drop out of school work in the Chinese-run textile mills for barely a living wage. They seek a sugar daddy for the rent, a sugar daddy for the cell phone, a sugar daddy for clothes. Should the young girl have the audacity to ask the sugar daddy to use a condom, she will rapidly lose his affections and his support. Or it is Christmastime and a family has no money for presents. A young girl will be told by her parents to go get the gifts. There is never overt discussion of how the gifts will be bought. It is understood.

There it is in plain sight. Transactional sex, sex fueled by older men, is at the core of the issue here. How on earth will this fact be named when all who display it are the religious and government leaders in the country? Despite these grim statistics, we push forward.

The planning for the first Fast Track in Swaziland has been exhaustive, as we are targeting to double the number of men and adolescents who get tested for HIV (two notoriously tough groups to recruit). We will do this Fast Track in a very rural lowland *inkundla* comprising eleven thousand people and some twenty chiefdoms. Complex, overlapping, and occasionally competing networks must be tapped and a fragile consensus crafted before we can proceed. After an hour on well-maintained asphalt roads out of Mbabane, we turn onto dirt roads that make up the rural Africa I am familiar with. It is springtime here, the streams and rivers are running high. We ford a few and fishtail along in the red mud.

Finally we arrive at the venue, and as we draw near I blurt out tactlessly, "We're not meeting *here*, are we?" Our meeting space is a cavernous, utterly empty, tin-roofed concrete building. Its glass windowpanes are long gone, as is a third of its roof. The chilly wind blasts through the gaping window and roof holes. If it rains (and it surely will), our participants and their numerous flip charts will be inundated. I have run these kinds of meetings in schools, in grass huts all over Africa, but this is an all-new low. There is of course no power source and no toilet either. A hundred or so community members are there to greet us, and at least as many plastic chairs also show up on a truck.

Having ill-advisedly drunk tea at 5:00 a.m., the no-toilet discovery is especially of concern to me. Across the meadow where goats and cattle graze, I see a small brick structure that must be the community latrine. I grab some Kleenex and make a beeline, willing myself some invisibility that my white skin will never afford. Tiptoeing in my sandals (another regrettable fashion choice) through the cow patties, I arrive at the latrine. It has no door, and, moreover, its construction is a huge challenge for me in the long skirts I must wear. Instead of the usual bear-paw hole-in-the-ground design, this latrine features a brick chimney-like structure three feet high and two feet across. I study it for a while in some dismay, clamber on top, and pray that I don't slip in my long skirts and fall in. I decide to opt for fluid restriction and dehydration for the next day.

Eventually our meeting convenes with the usual prayer and a cappella hymn. The singing always gives me goose bumps. The sound fills the huge space, resonant and melodic. The senior sponsor then opens the meeting in Siswati while Henok and I say a silent prayer that he is actually talking about our focal topic. Working in the local language is essential for buy-in, but for us it is a high-wire act. We rely a lot on body language and our local staff who whisper summaries to us when they can.

The meeting begins with our too-large crowd (we invited sixty, and eight-five have shown up) sitting in neat rows, hands folded, politely waiting for what usually happens in these gatherings, a long string of speeches. Instead we mix it up, and, in a peculiarly American touch, use an "icebreaker" to engage the crowd. Soon all eighty-five attendees are on their feet and hooked to one another in pairs with simple household string. They are instructed to disentangle themselves without actually untying the knots on their wrists. The room erupts in laughter and hooting as the pairs work to free themselves, putting themselves into impossible contortions. We have done this exercise in countless countries and languages, and it always has the same result. People relax, laugh uproariously, and see that this meeting will not be business as usual. Soon our fledgling facilitators assemble their teams and get to work brainstorming ideas and covering the walls near them with a blizzard of Post-it notes. The participants are engaged, animated, and crowding around one another. Henok and I start to breathe easy, but it is too soon for that. Through the huge hole in the roof I see the sky darkening. Sure enough, a storm is coming and it is fast upon us, early raindrops making a din on the tin roof. People scurry to rescue flip charts as the wind picks up and collapses our food tent just outside. The senior community spokesperson tells us that we can't wait it out. Everyone scurries home in the downpour, grateful that at least we do not have lightning to contend with.

The next morning, miraculously, all the attendees have returned and they are dressed for the weather. Wearing coats and hats, wrapped in thick blankets, they are undeterred by the muddy floor and collapsed food tent. We are all dressed for the bitter cold, which of course brings out the bright hot sun. The participants resume their animated discussions. By afternoon the teams are presenting their proposals to the assembled senior sponsors and get the enthusiastic endorsement we hope for. The only glitch is a guy who pronounces that the Clinton Foundation is going to provide a goat as well as thirteen cow heads for men's meetings. But we have not promised goats and cow heads, and we must demur, lest we set a precedent and put ourselves in the meat business throughout the country.

The next trip to Swaziland, I am awash in ambivalence. Odds too great, HIV prevalence too high, people too guarded, culture too opaque, too many NGOs fighting like cats in a bag, no leaders talking candidly and forcefully about what needs to change. Overlay that on a society where polygamy has been practiced for centuries and an economy in collapse, and I wrestle with low-grade but recurrent fears of futility.

But this second trip yields a sea change in this remote rural area of Mhlangatane. I do not know if this rekindled hope will transcend the grim realities, but for now it is a heady mix. It is winter in July in Swaziland, and I have brought my parka. I'm delighted to see that spring is arriving. Flame trees are beginning to bloom, magnolias have blossomed, and even the jacaranda trees are beginning to flower.

But the peaceable kingdom here still struggles with its demons. The government (which employs 40 percent of the population) has run out of money to pay salaries while the king remains one of the most lavishly paid monarchs in the world. Then there is the under-the-radar network of traditional healers. These healers have been around for centuries. In some countries they have been brought into the fold. But in Swaziland, they are untouchable, undiscussable. They charge much more than the government clinics, often asking for a cow in return for their assurances that they can eradicate the virus. No one engages or confronts them.

Everyone straddles that contradiction, the reliance on both witchcraft and Jesus Christ. Big-time Christianity is in evidence everywhere. There is the Jehovah's Witnesses megachurch that could pass in any Houston suburb. It is a monstrous glass-and-steel building with an electronic billboard out front inviting all to join. There are the Luxury Atonement Villas. (If I fail to atone, do I still merit them, I wonder?) There is a huge sign outside the airport that proclaims, "We love you best. But Jesus loves you more." Near the Arrive Alive Driving School are signs that warn of an imminent Judgment Day. It seems that Judgment Day is already upon this beautiful small country. Epidemiologists predict that the country will soon cease to exist if the epidemic is not arrested. I want to be part of the solution, this dream. And to do so I must join all in a hope for redemption, grace, and a few miracles in the bargain.

The weather too is a bizarre reverberation of climate changes elsewhere. The electrical storms here, already so fierce and epic, become more so. The capital of Swaziland loses power for two days, and the internet in my B and B is out for the foreseeable future. I am here this time first to run refresher training for the seven Swazi Fast Track facilitators I have trained: Bongani, Sicelo, Thokozane, Menzi, Thikona, Zakeh, and Sizakele. Our first Fast Track with them last month was a near-disaster: rainstorms, huge holes in the roof, washed-out roads, grouchy nurses, and false promises of Clinton Foundation largesse pledged by political hopefuls running for office and trying to hijack our event for their campaigns. I fear that none of our usual ambitious goals will be met. Yet remarkably, we are on track to test as many as two or three thousand people within ninety days! Another NGO is rumored to be recruiting one of our newly minted facilitators to initiate Fast Track in their shop. Our seven trainees know that their efforts are starting to yield results. Nonetheless they show up for the refresher training subdued, serious, polite, and careful. In other countries the welcome is warmer, and that warmth spans long separations between visits. I wonder, Do I have to start all over here? What is the deal? I have become accustomed, nay reliant, on a hero's welcome: in Ethiopia I was greeted like long-lost family, each visit concluding with a ceremonial thank-you dinner and gift. In Tanzania we went out dancing together. In Lesotho the staff had a traditional local dress sewn for me. This welcome helps to compensate for the hard parts: the interminable air travel, the chronic jet lag, the bad food, the loneliness and dislocation. Now in Swaziland, would I have to draw only on my own intrinsic desire to do good? Would that be enough? Appalled at my own neediness, I feel my zeal for the work dwindle in the heat and what feels like indifference. But this is only a polite distance—a distance, by the way, quite normal in chilly New England. Fortunately for me, my trainees' reserve melts, and by afternoon we are laughing and sharing jokes. But the aftertaste of my own needs and vulnerability lingers and is bitter to contemplate.

The two-day session will take place in the Mhlangatane district in the far northern highlands area, two hours' drive. At 6:00 a.m. we are assembled outside the Clinton Foundation offices, bleary-eyed and nervous as thoroughbreds at the starting gate. Fast Tracks live up to their moniker. They are indeed fast and must run like clockwork to elicit the best ideas in a compressed time frame. Late starts and infrastructure problems (life as usual in Africa) can pose real challenges. Now, not even on the road yet, we face our first. The power in the city has been out since yesterday's storms, and we cannot get into our offices. Every shred of what we need to run the Fast Track is on the other side of a locked door: flip charts, paper, tape, food, etc. Our frantic phone calls go unanswered. As the minutes tick by in the chill of early morning, I fret that eighty people will show up and we won't be there. But the Swazis are resourceful, and soon Menzi, our most agile facilitator, has squeezed into the office through an open bathroom window, and we are on our way with all our necessary equipment. So much for fancy security systems, a good lesson on several counts.

The Mhlangatane area is remote and arid and is home to thousands of acres of sugarcane fields. Here men come to work the fields, staying three to six months for backbreaking work in the hot sun. There are no city lights or bars here. But there is the local brew and the very poor local girls. So the girls are bedded and bragged about like football scores. Some girls are pregnant as young as thirteen or fourteen, at risk not only from HIV but from the dangers of early pregnancy.

Few people in this region get tested for HIV, as the clinics are ill-equipped and far-flung. If a married woman wants to be tested, she must get her husband's permission. If she tests positive, the assumption is that she has acquired the virus from her own infidelities, not from her husband. In fact, the prevalent belief in this area is that men cannot spread the virus, only women. Traditionalists still hold much sway here. They have been unwilling to import toilets, as they are thought to house evil spirits. Many old beliefs die hard.

We hold our meeting in the local church. The small building sits on a rise, a basic concrete box with a simple wooden cross at the entrance and a corrugated tin roof. Cows and goats graze around the perimeter, and just down the hill some four hundred primary students are singing their lessons in school. Here the views of fields and mountains are long, and the sky is big. Bright green fields of sugarcane in the distance contrast with the parched brown grasses around us. The participants are early, sitting under shade trees near the church. When eighty people enter the small church, the din is huge, and the sun beating on the tin roof soon makes the heat unbearable. So we do what Africans have been doing for centuries, go outside to meet under the trees. The teams are large (up to thirty each) and vocal, but our facilitators (now veterans at their second Fast Track) are facile. I shuttle between the three teams to offer support as unobtrusively as possible. Everyone seems engaged and animated. As the schoolchildren are released for the day, they file past, slowing to stare curiously at the meetings taking place. In their khaki uniforms, many are barefoot, and all of them are very skinny. Many will walk as far as ten kilometers to get home, and their sole meal for the day will have been the maize porridge the school had provided at midmorning.

Within a day and a half, the teams have come up with a raft of great plans. In addition to going door-to-door to recruit for HIV testing, the young adults will sponsor a sports day where mobile testing will take place. The men will recruit one another in an exclusively male domain, the cattle dip tanks. There they will participate in their traditional roast of a cow head and once again bring the testing to the site.

On Fast Track day two we all assemble, sweating, in the packed church to present our plans to a panel of seven senior sponsors. One is a radio personality who will take to the airwaves with the messages from the teams. Another is a local member of Parliament. He is easily three hundred pounds, dressed in his traditional garb: a beaded necklace, an off-the-shoulder red-and-white cape, a skirt, and an animal skin tied around his waist. He is an imposing figure, and it is his season to campaign for reelection. In a fortuitous win-win, he agrees to provide refreshments for each event. The applause is thunderous. Eventually, blissfully, we can conclude and get out of the sauna building. A hymn and a prayer are offered. Then suddenly all eighty participants are running out of the building in a stampede. Curious as to what has provoked the exodus at this pace, I ask for translation. Juice and biscuits were on offer just outside. Hunger trumps all. Soon I will be back in the US, where too much food has created an epidemic of obesity. But for now, here, minor refreshments will fuel these all-volunteer teams to work miracles.

LESOTHO

Since early rumors of our success in Swaziland reached nearby Lesotho, I find myself traveling there three months later. It is clear and dry here in Maseru, the capital city. The skies are indescribably bright and blue. I can spend much of the day out of doors if I choose, without so much as a thought for malarial mosquitoes. It is a refreshing change after Boston's long deep freeze. That is the good part. The tough part is that I am soon checked into a hotel room with bars on my windows, a view of the parking lot, and a fence on the perimeter of the property. I am a prisoner in this expat cage. I have now heard one too many horror stories of muggings and murder in this small city. Just last month a young Peace Corps volunteer was shot dead only two blocks from here.

This trip I am wrestling with a toxic mix of low-grade fear, loneliness, dislocation, and existential questions. Although I took what Ed dubs the "old person's route" here, staying over in London for a night, the trip from Boston to Lesotho was exhausting, and within an hour and a half of my arrival I was giving a presentation to an assembly of forty people. By the end of that first day, for the first time ever in three and a half years, I begin to mutter to myself, "I can't do this anymore." It feels weird to say that. Somehow it is freeing to simply say it. It reminds me that I have a choice. Then I imagine really just staying home and giving up Africa, and my eyes fill. But I cannot live this way forever.

The night I was scheduled to go back to Tanzania from Lesotho, our trip was abruptly canceled. An outbreak of cholera had begun to escalate in the rural area where we were headed. We will not go to rural Lindi and convene community meetings. Large gatherings of people are prohibited while officials try to contain the outbreak. Cholera can kill someone within a day. The painless watery diarrhea and vomiting create dehydration that must be very quickly reversed. So our planned intervention around maternal and child health was a good idea at the outset, but not now. So be it. I will stay on another week in Lesotho.

This turn of events give me the mixed blessing of a weekend alone, which serves to amplify my isolation. I made a foray out of the hotel in the morning to buy sunscreen, but I will not venture out after dark. Instead I take my Kindle to the near-empty hotel restaurant. This expat hangout virtually empties on the weekend while people drive a mere fifty minutes to access another existence, South Africa. Shopping, fine restaurants, and a whole westernized world. Tiny Lesotho, landlocked as it is within this reality, is its own beautiful and sad story. The country is about the size of Maryland, has only 1.7 million people, and sits on the precipice of despair. A third of the population is HIV-positive, the life expectancy has slipped to age thirty-four, and the agricultural sector has collapsed from climate change, soil erosion, heavy rainfall, and too many people too sick to farm.

The country and its landscape are so unlike any other part of Africa. Often referred to as the rooftop of Africa, the country has the highest average elevation of any country in the world. While I sit at five thousand feet in Maseru, once you get to the periphery of this very small capital, you can see why it's unique. The landscape seems like a cross between Montana, New Zealand, and the lower Everest Valley. It snows a lot here in winter and gets very cold. The valley floor once showcased a large agricultural economy but is now a residue of short grasses and canyons where the soil has eroded. It is sparsely populated and very beautiful now in the height of its summer season. Come winter, all turns brown and gray, and the mountains are etched in white. No buildings here have central heat. The Clinton Foundation staff become quite friendly with their electric blankets, they tell me. I am lucky to be here in the sunshine.

After my weekend break I set about training another batch of facilitators. They are eager and quick on the uptake. In a refreshing departure from the usual hierarchy, one of the drivers is invited to work on our team. He is smart, fast, and well connected in the villages we will touch.

BASUTO FASHION STATEMENT

The next week I am in Maphile, Lesotho, to launch another community meeting. I am standing in my underwear in the only bathroom that adjoins our big meeting space. It is tiny, and the door will not lock. I hope none of our fifty meeting attendees will need to get in. But Matsepo is with me, and she will see to some measure of privacy here. Matsepo is one of our newly trained facilitators, eager and bright. It is indeed Matsepo who has insisted that I use the bathroom to change clothes. The mother of one of the foundation staff has made me a traditional Lesotho *seshoeshoe* (pronounced "seshwayshway") dress, and all the Africa staff want me to wear it the moment it has been delivered to our meeting venue. This *seshoeshoe* style is very different from any other traditional African dress and is quite prescribed. The skirt is three-quarter length with deep pockets and a sash. The top is short-sleeved with complex insets and embroidery. The *seshoeshoe* fabric comes in only a few colors: blue, brown, or red, and the patterns are very small and geometric. This amazing outfit has been produced for me in only twenty-four hours, and the Lesotho women on our team were insistent that I wear it for the meeting. So this is why Matsepo and I are squished together in this tiny bathroom. She's helping me to get the tight top over my head and working with a recalcitrant zipper.

I am self-conscious; my skin seems so white, so mottled, so unattractive. But there is something so sweet, so universal, so regressive about changing clothes in a bathroom with a girlfriend, and I am happy for Matsepo's attentions. She is beautiful and I like to look at her close up. Her skin is flawless, an even caffè-mocha color. She has dusted her eyelids with a touch of lavender, and her very full lips are bright with red lipstick. She is wearing her own *seshoeshoe* with a matching handkerchief and large gold hoop earrings. Matsepo has taken liberties with the traditional design. She wears a gold silk sash around her waist, and that same gold silk is inset into each pleat of her skirt. The pattern of her dress is the mirror image of my own although the color is different. This pleases me as she fusses with my buttons and sash. There is no mirror here. I depend wholly on her eye as she tugs and turns and carefully adjusts my dress.

"Susie," she breathes. "You look beautiful!" I know this is not quite true. I just hope I don't look ridiculous. I know from having turned up in Tanzania in a fancy locally made dress that it was seen there as a gesture of respect, a joining. I hope that will be true here in Lesotho; I just don't know.

Eventually Matsepo deems me ready for prime time, and I leave the bathroom carrying my Western pants and top in a plastic bag and try to move unobtrusively to the back of the room. The people of Lesotho are less gregarious than Tanzanians, but as I walk in, those gathered take in my *seshoeshoe*, and I get big smiles. I pause, pivot, and show them the handiwork on the reverse as though I am on the runway. More smiling, laughter. There is a moment of innocent connection. It cuts across culture, race, age, class.

Fabric and tailoring: $25

Fashion statement feedback: priceless

BOMBS IN DAR

The work in Lesotho is much like it has been in other countries: introduce the basic concepts of the Fast Track method, train a team of facilitators, convene many community meetings to build readiness, run the two-day plenary, and galvanize the teams to work toward specific measurable goals. It works here too, and I can exit stage right and support the teams remotely.

I am ready, past ready, to leave Lesotho. We have had some successful community meetings in the far mountains, but I am spent and impatient to rejoin Gil in Tanzania, where I have organized a safari for the two of us. I am wildly eager to see him and to relax into being a pampered tourist.

I wake up in my Lesotho hotel room very early, already packed, anxious to leave, and laboriously log onto the very slow internet connection for one last look at emails before my trip. My inbox is jammed with a glut of alarming emails. Explosions have rocked Dar es Salaam, closing the airport and its access road. Antiballistic missiles and every kind of bomb have been detonated, and the debris extends for a good ten kilometers around the airport. The Clinton Foundation safety officer writes that I should reroute myself. Reroute myself to where? How? I must pass through Dar to rendezvous with Gil in Kilimanjaro.

It is midnight in the US. Phone calls to South African Air yield no information and no options. I get ready to go to the Lesotho airport anyway. Maybe this is just a bad dream and the situation will be soon resolved. I cannot bear to extend my stay in this hotel another night and to miss Gil. This trip to the airport, I'm going in the back seat of what is called Perfect Taxi. No Clinton Foundation drivers are available, so I am told that this should be my plan B.

Many taxis in Maseru are dangerous for their riders. The Clinton office will fax a license plate number to the hotel desk so I can verify that the guy who shows up is the guy who is supposed to show up. At the appointed time, a skinny young man in a bucket hat appears, the license plate checks out, I take a deep breath, put my luggage in the trunk, and off we go chug-chugging through Maseru's morning rush hour. I leave before the hotel has served breakfast. It is just as well that I have no caffeine coursing through my veins, I am nervous enough. While my Clinton team has done good work this week, I have not been able to shake the images of the nurse killed in my hotel parking lot and the Peace Corps volunteer murdered across the street.

The Perfect Taxi fuel gauge looks like it is close to empty, and we have a forty-minute drive to the airport. The driver tells me we need to stop for petrol. Sounds like a good idea. The third gas station actually has fuel, and off we go. No one at Maseru's tiny airport has any knowledge of the Tanzanian airport explosions, nor can they reroute me through another city. I am beyond anxious to leave Lesotho, though I am not sure where I can get to from there. I swallow hard and get on my originally scheduled plane for Johannesburg, hoping that once I get there I will figure out what to do next. Our plane is tiny with great views of Lesotho's high mountain ranges, steep canyons, gorges, and green valleys. At some point during the flight I remember that I have acquired a small stash of Xanax for just these moments, when traveling solo through Africa provokes anxiety well above my usual escalated baseline. I pop a Xanax and experience no wave of calm. In fact the Xanax turns out to have been a dubious idea when I must run the length of two terminals in Johannesburg to get to my gate and feel an overwhelming desire to stop and take a nap.

Not one person at any of the airline desks or boarding gates in Johannesburg knows anything about the situation in Tanzania. This is surreal. Even a pilot sitting at the gate with his BlackBerry cannot find any information when I inquire, so I go ahead and board my plane for Dar es Salaam. We will fly somewhere, I just don't know where. Once we are buckled in and taxiing down the runway, the pilot comes on the intercom to say that indeed there have been many explosions around the Dar airport, that it is still closed, but that they have decided to get airborne and hope for the best.

Another opportunity for existential surrender. I hope that my luggage is actually below me in the cargo hold, and I wish that a second hit of Xanax would do a whit of good. But it won't. I will simply fly the friendly skies northward and try to cultivate a stance of Buddhist detachment. They are showing a movie of Bruce Willis and Morgan Freeman in a comedy thriller. Lots of gunfire but lots of laughs. This helps.

Three and a half hours into the flight, the pilot comes on and announces, "Good news! The airport in Dar has just opened after having been closed for over twenty-four hours." We land in a scene of pandemonium, with stranded passengers and newly arrived passengers mobbed and jockeying for space.

I stand in an interminable line at passport control, fetch my luggage (sweet relief), and proceed to the exit.

Throngs of people are yelling and holding signs. I see my name and the smiling face of Mr. George, my favorite CHAI driver. I have never been so happy to see him. We clamber into his SUV, lock the doors, and head out into traffic, bizarre even by Dar standards. Then he tells me the story of what has actually been going on. The night before, bombs went off for a period of about six hours from a military depot only a few kilometers from the airport. The explosions involved heavy artillery, including antiballistic missiles, tank artillery shells, and many rounds of ammunition. Some bombs landed ten kilometers from the area before they detonated. At last count twenty-seven were dead, four hundred wounded, and four thousand made homeless, now being housed in the sports stadium (just like Hurricane Katrina victims in New Orleans, though with less food and water, I am sure.)

The government issues a statement saying that the cause of the explosions was too much heat in the munitions storage area. I email my dad for his opinion. He has had plenty of experience with explosives in two wars. He writes back that the explanation is impossible and urges me to stay clear of the area. His emails are usually terse and understated, but I hear a note of worry. The government's explanation is specious and he is concerned for my safety.

For the time being I retreat to the quiet, manicured grounds of the Southern Sun Hotel, an oasis of calm and denial far from the airport and the panic. The hotel lobby is sparkling, and porters in faux colonial-era costumes greet me like long-lost family. Wealthy African families sip fancy fruit drinks by the pool, their children all in party dresses. Dutch and German NGO officials sit at tables piled high with paper and speak in urgent but quiet tones. Traffic is muffled beyond the hotel's high walls, and the only anomalous sound is an occasional shriek from the domesticated peacocks that parade around the property.

My hotel room is virtually refrigerated with air-conditioning, has a sparkling clean bathroom, and has not one but two beds. I sip my welcome glass of chilled South African wine and truly begin to relax. There may be bombs still unexploded fifteen kilometers away, but for the time being I feel safe. I will have a day to recoup, then I will fly to Arusha and rendezvous with my dear husband. We will see Africa the way most white, well-to-do tourists do, from the vantage point of a well-equipped safari SUV, far from the urban desperation I have just fled.

CHAPTER NINE

Two Kinds of Migration

ON SAFARI

At last Gil and I are reunited in Arusha. He listens to hours of my stories, my fears in Lesotho, the bombs in Dar, the cholera in southern Tanzania. He listens steadily, intently, and without interruption. It is this gift at the core of our marriage that enables me to loosen the spring-loaded tension in my solar plexus. Once my stories are told I can fully join him in this next adventure, our safari into the Serengeti.

Our guide, Patrick, stands about my height. He shows up after every breakfast in a crisp, newly ironed pair of chinos. His skin is very dark, his teeth movie-star white, his head shaved. Patrick's enthusiasm for every aspect of the wildlife we will see is genuine. With his contagious sense of humor, he says that he loves his "office" (the Serengeti) and that he learns new things there every day.

We are here fervently hoping that we will see the migration. It all depends on the rains, a radically diminished blessing in recent years. Global warming has caused a huge lake in the Ngorongoro Crater to recede by two thirds, and Lake Manyara has receded as well. Yet those of us who are causing this unfolding climate disaster want to stand openmouthed before an event we hope can fit into our carefully planned travel schedules. Our travel agent this year gave us the appropriate disclaimers, but we nonetheless quietly hope that somehow we will beat the odds and see the migration. Yet in twelve hours of driving we have seen naught but a few errant wildebeest, so I am busy privately talking down my disappointment. The next morning we set out early, and within half an hour we see four lions asleep, lavishly snoring in the shade, their bellies distended from a recent kill.

Then as we progress up the valley floor in a cloud of dust and flies, we begin to see large numbers of zebra with their brown-striped young in tow. Skittish with the lion family just behind them, the adult zebra bark to alert the others and keep them moving. Soon we spot zebra everywhere, as far as the eye can see. On the valley floor, running on the dirt strip just ahead of our jeep, dotting the horizon, their stripes no longer visible in the distance. I wonder aloud about where the wildebeest are, and Patrick explains that the zebra head up the migration. They have teeth in both upper and lower jaws and can handle the long grasses. The wildebeest come later as the beneficiaries of the zebra mowing services.

Gradually we begin to see the follow-on herds of wildebeest. Many have young, small beige carbon copies. All legs, the youngsters can run as fast as their mothers. Not all the wildebeest are running like they do on *Animal Planet* specials. Some are resting in the shade of the very few acacia trees. But all are headed steadily southwest, it is clear. Out come our cameras. We think we are seeing the peak but we have no idea. Over the next half an hour the valley floor becomes black with moving wildebeest now running in front, behind, alongside our vehicle, urging one another forward with their distinctive honking grunts. We realize that this is it, the actual core of the migration, and it is so truly awesome as to give all-new meaning to the word. Mouths agape, we forget for a while to take pictures. There is no shot that can capture this 360-degree press of life. It predates us and our twenty-first-century gear by millions of years, and it has to be purely experienced, not framed in a viewfinder.

The rest of our safari offers up other sights we have only seen on nature programs: mating lions, leaping leopards, sleeping cheetahs, and birds of prey so huge that a large monkey is the kill of choice. We sip vodka and lukewarm tonic outside our tents while watching sunsets worthy of a *National Geographic* spread. We stand beneath night skies so clear, so thick with stars that we soon retreat inside, dizzy and light-headed. We sleep deeply in our tented camps where there is not one sound of motorized anything, no air traffic, no TV, no hair dryers. Utter stillness. That is, until the hyenas come to camp after midnight and begin their eerie whooping calls.

While our sightings of animals and stars are as breathtaking as advertised, it is the deepening connection with Patrick and other Tanzanians that moves me. In between game sightings on the long drives through the Serengeti's endless expanses, Patrick patiently instructs me in crucial Tanzanian call-and-response exchanges. Tanzanians are scrupulously polite, and these ritual greetings form the backbone of any and every exchange. Tourists are taught to say the simple word *jambo*. It means "hi," but Tanzanians rarely use that phrase in speaking with one another. Instead they follow the predictable back-and-forth sequence that is an absolutely necessary preface to any other conversation.

Good morning. *Habari za asubuhi.*
How are you? *Habari gani?*
I am fine, thank you, and you? *Nzuri sana, na wewe?*

How are the children? The work? The farm? And so on. The payoff for these basic language lessons is huge and immediate. Every single time I make that extra effort, there ensues a pause, then surprise, then delight, then affirmation. "You speak Swahili?" the other person will exclaim. I demur with a phrase it took me days to learn. *"Nafahamu Kiswahili ki dogo ki dogo, lakini sivisuri sana!"* (I understand Swahili a little bit, but not very well.) Then more laughter and smiles, and the ice is totally broken. Day by day under Patrick's tutelage my vocabulary expands, and each night I try out my new words on the local staff. Patrick grins in the background like a proud parent, and his colleagues gently tease him about his language lessons. As our trip continues, I get imperceptibly better. The Tanzanians can radiate welcome so remarkably that I shamelessly chase it like a kid looking for a good grade.

I have asked Patrick to teach me to say "It is wonderful" (*Inapendeza sana*). And another phrase, "I really appreciate your kindness." Patrick's kindness to us and to others is indeed reflexive and genuine. When we had a broken main spring on the road leading out of the Ngorongoro Crater, another guide stopped to help and gave us some rubber tubing that Patrick used to jury-rig a repair. The next day the very same guy ran into his own car troubles, and Patrick was able to return the favor. He was ebullient that he could reciprocate.

As our safari ends and we are negotiating the smelly chaos that is Arusha traffic, I begin to feel a sense of loss. We've spent seven days together, all day, every day. I will miss Patrick hugely and I tell him so. He is pensive for the next hour or so and then asks, ever so gingerly, would we like to come to his house and meet his family? This, he tells us, must be kept a secret. His safari company prohibits him from sharing personal stories, giving out his email contact information, or in any way trying to evoke the sympathies of his guests. At all costs, safari guests are to be cocooned and protected from the harsh realities that make up real life for Tanzanians. Patrick scrupulously follows these guidelines, lest he lose his spot in the queue for further trips, or worse yet, lose his job. Our tented camps and lodges cost more per night than many Tanzanians earn per year, and we must not be made to feel discomfort with that dissonance. Patrick's invitation flouts those rules. We agree and are touched by the invitation and the trust it implies. We then leave the teeming city center's asphalt streets and head down a crowded dirt thoroughfare for several miles. Not one white face or safari vehicle in this dense warren of simple storefronts, mud and concrete houses, and tin-roofed huts. We pass the Black Man's Hair Saloon, the Bolts and Nuts Hardware Store, the Fancy Electronics Shop, the Wimpy Restaurant, the Maryland Butchery, the Real Nice Dress Shop, and countless other nameless small enterprises. The street is thick with pedestrians, some in their Sunday best coming home after services, and some in the only clothes they have.

We are ready for some of the mean houses we have seen, but Patrick's home is an oasis born of his hard work. Behind a wall and a locked gate is his small gray concrete house surrounded by banana trees, a mango tree and avocado tree, bougainvillea, and a small garden. Patrick honks his horn twice, and his entire family tumbles out to greet us. Warm handshakes, huge smiles. *"Karibu, karibu sana,"* they all say many times. "You are so very welcome here." Patrick's wife, Maggie, and his three children usher us inside. The entrance is narrow with a few small rooms curtained off. We pass the kitchen, a closet-size room with only three buckets and a cutting board. We are then guided into the living room, a tiny room so crammed with overstuffed furniture that the only space that remains is between our knees and a coffee table laden with pink and red plastic flowers. On the wall are a calendar and a print of a blond Jesus with his disciples. Each chair back has an embroidered scarf reading "Hallelujah."

Patrick gathers his brood in the small room, lines them up by age, and tells us, "Now I present you the true history of my family." Then one by one he extols the virtues and accomplishments of each. First his wife, Maggie. "She is my first wife and my only wife," he begins. He goes on to say how he treasures her, that she has borne him five children, manages the house, garden, kids, chickens, and an embroidery business while he's off guiding safaris. This is of course all in English for our benefit. Her English is nonexistent but she gets the gist, smiles shyly, starts to sweat, and dabs her forehead with a handkerchief. I am floored to hear his public proclamations of love and respect for her. This is unusual in this male-dominated society. I am moved, and so is she.

Patrick goes on to introduce and brag about each child one by one in ordinal position, the two girls and one boy present. The three children are all achieving in school, their smiles blossoming as each in turn is proudly acknowledged. In Africa 80 percent of girls never finish secondary school. Not so for this family. Patrick will see to that, putting his shoulder to the wheel and leaving home three weeks out of four in high season to pay school fees.

Soon we are offered the "homecoming soup" Maggie fixes for Patrick the first day he comes home from a safari. She offers a lengthy prayer in Swahili with blessings for our health, our children, our travels, and we all taste the soup made from green bananas and beef. It is delicious. Patrick's youngest, Sam, sixteen, studies us intently and, each time I catch his eye, offers a shy grin. He looks like his father and wears a large beaded Christian cross around his neck.

After the soup and then mangoes sweeter than I have ever tasted, we all go out to the back garden to admire the tree from which they were picked. There is also a prolific avocado tree and a small banana grove. Tiny three-day-old chicks peck for seeds in the earth. All too soon they will be full grown and

Patrick will be eyeing them with a meal in mind. Maggie will have none of it, he tells us, laughing. "She makes me go supermarket buy chicken!" he says. "Too big heart."

Soon it is time to go. We snap some family portraits in the yard and then begin a series of tender and protracted goodbyes. Maggie and the girls clasp our hands over and over saying, *"Karibu tena"* (Welcome and come again). None of us can quite let go and I don't want to. I have been welcomed without reservation, without guile, without expectation of reciprocity. In my tightfisted WASP world I have no experience with this, and I keenly feel the loss even as we back the car out of the yard and onto the road to our lodge.

After our visit with Patrick and his family, we head for the Ngare Sero Lodge to spend a week in suspended animation. This is not my usual MO, to go someplace without a plan, just a hope. But I am hoping that some project will drop out of the sky that will enable Gil and me to spend more time in Tanzania and do something of use while here. Repeated email outreach to the plethora of NGOs in the area has yielded nothing. I'm hoping that something might show up, and if nothing does, we will be in a place of real beauty and serenity. Little known on the crowded safari access circuit, the lodge sits on the slopes of Mount Meru. The name Ngare Sero means "sparkling waters" in the Maasai language.

LIFE AT NGARE SERO AND NSHUPU

Once the bastion of the German colonial presence on Mount Meru, the lodge now protects 55 acres of old-growth forest, lakes, waterfalls, and 250 species of birds. The main lodge building still has its original tin roof, now faded to a faint shade of red. The veranda faces Mount Kilimanjaro, and each evening at sunset, hornbills and cranes fly so low overhead that the noise of their wings and calls quite drowns out conversation. To add to the evening's entertainment, two species of monkeys, colobus and Sykes, do their acrobatics in the trees just below. All around the property are vibrant bougainvillea in orange, red, fuchsia, and pink. Poinsettia plants, dahlias, ginger flowers, birds of paradise, and hibiscus dot the gardens. Just below the lodge is a huge lake and a trout farm.

The lodge owners are Brits who long ago settled in Tanzania and now run the hotel with relaxed indifference. Instead it is the staff of Tanzanians who greet guests, feed them, answer their endless questions, and exude a warmth and welcome that no whites could ever match. Our language lessons continue, and we feel once again welcomed like long-lost family.

Like many Tanzanian lodges, Ngare Sero offers to take its guests on a guided "cultural tour" of the nearby villages. Usually Gil and I prefer to explore on our own, but the warren of footpaths surrounding the lodge is so complex that we worry about finding our way back. So instead we plan to go out with Adam, the hotel reservations clerk, and arrange to meet him in the morning. Within our first twelve hours at the lodge we are on this outing with Adam.

Adam's age is indeterminate. He has a bit of a baby face, and a soft belly, the legacy of the office, not the farm. While Adam's demeanor at the lodge is subdued and careful, the minute we leave the grounds, he becomes more open and animated. His English is good, so while we trudge up and down the dusty village footpaths we learn a lot about the village and about Adam's own life. While the lodge grounds have huge trees, lawns, and gardens, the village plots on its perimeter are gray and sparse. When the rains come, and they are late again this year, maize will be planted. For now, the only color in evidence is from small banana trees and flowering bougainvillea.

Adam says that when he was a boy, all the slopes of Mount Meru were planted in coffee. Dense green bushes held the erosion and yielded well. But when the coffee market tanked fifteen years ago, everyone chopped down their mature trees to plant maize. Now of course coffee is once again very lucrative. But it takes many years to bring coffee plants to maturity, and these poor families cannot wait years to yield a cash crop. Maize won't make them rich, but it can feed their families. Coffee farms flourish in Arusha, but these are owned and managed by large foreign companies.

We walk the paths of Nshupu village, scattering chickens and greeting children as we go. The houses are basic brick or cement with one or two rooms. Dotting the entire hillside as well are half-built small brick houses, walls built on a bed of stones. Adam shows us the one that is his, now in progress for three years. He saves money to buy bricks, hires a mason, then brick by brick, a wall is added. The work is then suspended until he gets some more cash set aside. These houses will have no indoor plumbing, so this incremental approach will work so long as he keeps at it. Many of these partially built homes look like they will never be finished. One monument after another of hope over experience.

As we walk, we learn about Adam's childhood in Nshupu. Adam's father died young. His mother took a job cooking at the lodge and gave Adam's entire care over to a childless older couple next door. This couple raised, fed, and clothed Adam and ultimately gave him a plot of land on which to build his own brick house. He speaks of them with much affection, and I nurse my private questions. How come Adam's mother could not care for him at all? Were her hours at the hotel too demanding, or was there something else? Adam takes us to her home to meet her. His older sister, a schoolteacher from Dar es Salaam, is visiting. We get them to pose for a family portrait. Adam's mother's eyes are vacant, her demeanor subdued and distracted. She does not smile for her picture. She has retired from her cooking job and lives well enough in a two-room house that sometimes has electricity, all thanks to Adam.

I leave her house puzzled. There is a network of mutual obligation that binds Tanzanians together, transcending family ties. A former guide once told us that if you so much as learned of a neighbor's neediness, sick child, or some such, then you are obligated to help in some fashion, with food, money, or care. People withhold sharing bad news with others lest it activate this built-in necessity to help. On the contrary, we Americans so prize our autonomy and individualism. We may feel concern or sympathy for a neighbor's misfortune, and this may prompt offers of help. But that help may be a trip to the grocery store, not a lifetime of raising another woman's son.

After visiting Adam's mother, we stop by the government-run primary school. There the class sizes of eighty or more reinforce a long tradition of rote learning and brutal conformity. There is no room for anything else. Most of the classes are indoors, but there are two huge open pavilions. In one, an enormous vat of maize is being prepared for lunch over an open wood fire. Children must bring their own water and food to school. I wonder how it works for those kids who have not contributed to the communal pot?

In another open pavilion some sixty pubescent girls are rehearsing their singing troupe. They are lined up single file, the line snaking up into complex figure eights. They are all wearing their blue uniforms, turned drab with the blowing dust. In a sea of tall skinny girls in dusty blue uniforms the teacher is a huge yellow bird in her bright dress. She is an imposing, big-busted figure, and her singing voice booms. She calls out the first line, the girls reply in unison, and everyone begins to move, to sway, and to sing together. The sound is loud and rhythmic, and two girls tap out the beat on big drums. The footwork is not complex but it must be coordinated. Left, right, left, right. The lineup is so close that missteps mean small collisions. Reluctantly we continue on our way.

For years now I have longed to have Gil join me in my wild and challenging adventures in Africa. He has been a steadfast cheerleader and supporter, listening patiently when upon my return I spill out my stories of small successes, lost luggage, food poisoning, jet lag, dislocation, and always the exhilaration of unexpected heartfelt connections. Gil and I have both spent too many years, I think, working for corporate America to make money for those who already have too much. I long to turn back the clock and take the path not chosen. After all, my first graduate degree was in social work, and one of Gil's early jobs was as a primary school teacher and principal.

This trip to Tanzania, I have seen Gil truly open to the possibilities. We have walked dirt roads into small villages, followed like pied pipers by laughing children. We have been welcomed into Africans' homes and lives as though we were returning family. We have learned and practiced a bit of Swahili and seen African faces register surprise, then warmth, then openhearted welcome. This is our third week in Tanzania together, and I can see that something in Gil has shifted. Ordinarily he has trouble learning a new language, but his Swahili seems to be progressing at a rapid rate. He basks, as I do, in the delight and approval this provokes in the Tanzanian staff at the lodge. California boy that he is, he is quite at home in the dry heat and stark beauty of this part of Africa. I don't want to say anything to jinx it, but as we wander back down the hill to the lodge after visiting the grim orphanage on our walking tour, it is clear that the discussion is about what *we* will do, not what *I* will do.

I don't say anything as yet, but the use of the plural pronoun is deeply reassuring to me. Over the past four years, I have made seventeen trips to Africa, and I miss him acutely every time I go. Gil has an unerring ability to connect with people from all walks of life, and I know that the Africans I work with would take to him immediately. I hate doing work without him, and I hate the cultural dislocation and anomie that dogs me every time I come home. And it does not get better with time. In the ensuing week, as we tentatively explore the notion of going to work to help this orphanage and coming back to Tanzania, my heart is full. Gil is a soul mate and a partner in all things, so the possibility that we may return here together on some regular basis lifts my spirits hugely.

CHAPTER TEN

We Take on Precious as a Project

The evening after the cultural tour we are sitting on the lodge veranda watching the nightly sunset parade of nesting birds, and monkeys swinging through the canopy of tall trees. Less than eager to mingle with the usual safarigoers, we have installed ourselves at the extreme perimeter of the porch so as not to invite casual conversation. But I cannot help but overhear talk at the opposite end. A woman is speaking very enthusiastically, very loudly about a project she is working on. She has platinum hair, a deep, phlegmy laugh, and a relentless extroverted enthusiasm. *Either I will really like her or she will drive me nuts,* I think. Since there is no tuning her out, I begin to listen. She tells her captive audience that she and her husband started a small NGO in Nshupu six years ago. They have founded a preschool, and started a vocational training program for unwed mothers. They have built a classroom for the primary school, raised money for scholarships, and are housing five orphaned teenage boys. I am now paying very close attention. When she finishes her pitch and stands up, I call out, "I couldn't help but overhear what you're up to. I might be able to help."

"Fabulous!" she booms. "I'm Ann. I already know about you! You're the lady from the Clinton Foundation, aren't you?"

My heart sinks a bit. The Clinton Foundation confines its work to other areas in Tanzania, and besides, I have not one shred of influence over where their funds are disbursed. I hasten to tell her this; she is clearly disappointed but recovers nicely. I say that I have experience in Africa to leverage, but no money to speak of. But a spark of mutual interest has been lit, and we agree to meet in half an hour with husbands in tow to talk further.

I had seen Ann's husband earlier and made some unflattering assumptions about him. Robert, a corporate attorney from Chicago, had his BlackBerry scrolling all afternoon, while he ordered one gin and tonic after another.

But as the evening unfolds, we hear more and more about what this couple has made happen in the previous six years. They had led with their hearts and wallets and hung in through tough learnings, disappointments, and small-scale successes. They were making a palpable difference in a number of young lives. And this is what we want to do for the nine kids we saw earlier that day at the orphanage. With an expansive generosity, Ann and Robert then begin to pull us under their wing, to show us the ropes, and to offer a partnership so that we might work in conjunction with their existing NGO. The next day we hike back up the hill to the orphanage to meet its founder, William Modest.

By the time we arrive, the children have left for school, so the orphanage is quite desolate. Three gray concrete buildings cluster around a dusty yard with not one blade of grass. One building serves as a kindergarten. It has mud floors, high windows barred with chicken wire, and a large antique chalkboard at one end. It has a dirty tarp on the floor where the children can sit. The "kitchen" and storeroom sit adjacent. The storeroom is empty but for one small burlap bag of maize. The kitchen has a two-burner cooktop and a few buckets, nothing else. Like most houses nearby there is no electricity or running water. There is one grim freestanding outhouse, and that is it. It is as impossibly sparse as I remembered it from the day before.

Ann accompanies Gil and me, and we arrive a few minutes before William. We have set a meeting time of 9:00, but no one here wears a wristwatch, so time is always an approximation. Soon William appears, a bit out of breath, and greets us with a firm handshake and a broad smile. William is very dark skinned. His teeth are very white, his hair closely shaved. His English is fluid and gently accented. His last name, Modest, seems quite apt, yet at the same time he seems animated by his dream of doing better by children whose chances have run out.

Ann carries a notebook and scribbles his answers to her barrage of questions. How long has the orphanage been in place? Who owns the land? What is the rent they pay? Where do they get water? How did each of the children come to be here? What is the status of their health? What are the duties of the young mama that we saw the other day? William answers her questions directly and without a hint of defensiveness. He tells us his life story and we hear the dedication that has brought him and these children to this place.

William grew up in Kenya as one of five. When he was fifteen, his single mother died of AIDS in his arms. It was up to him to care for his younger siblings, and he depended on the kindness of neighbors for food, housing, and schooling. He never had a home again, bouncing from one house to another in that small village. William described that he made a vow early on that he would dedicate his life to caring for children in the same circumstances. He and his wife, Sarah, were local schoolteachers, and when their church kept finding orphaned kids alone and homeless, he impulsively quit his job to start the Precious Orphanage. The church helped to pay the nominal rent for this primitive site and every so often would provide a sack of rice. William planted an acre of land with green beans for export, but aside from that there was no "business plan" for how this little orphanage was actually going to survive. God would provide.

So here it is. My long-nurtured half-baked fantasy suddenly made manifest within twenty-four hours of showing up in this small village. We need look no further for a project that needs us. This is it. We have never run an orphanage, we don't speak Swahili, and we have never done any fund-raising. We wanted an adventure, we wanted to do some good in Africa, and so we jump in with both feet. With stunning naïveté, we join the legions of other white safarigoers who start projects with open hearts and wallets. I am convinced that somehow my experience crisscrossing the continent will inoculate us from making the most egregious mistakes, but that is not true. We will spend the next years on a roller coaster of hope and hard learnings. We will be mildly euphoric with a sense of renewed purpose in life, and we will be regularly humbled by the undertow of desperation that poverty engenders.

And for now we have just twelve days remaining on the continent to get started and see what we can make happen for the kids.

Shopping at Tengeru

Armed now with the serendipitous offer of support from an established NGO, we tell William we are ready to help in some way and ask him what his needs are. "We need beds," he tells us. There are only two bunk beds for nine children: one for the five boys and one for the four girls. In Tanzania you don't just go to a store and buy a bed. You go to a *fundi*, a craftsperson, and get it built. With guidance from Adam at the lodge, a *fundi* is located, an estimate is made, and, ebullient, we march up the hill again to share the good news with William. Beds will be built! We are already feeling like local heroes.

Proudly we announce to William our gift in the works, and to our dismay, his face falls. "I am very sorry," he says. "We cannot accept your gift of beds. We have run out of food. That is most important." Dumbfounded, we pivot, take our small fortune of $120 in Tanzanian shillings, pile into our rented jeep, and go with Adam to the food markets.

Tengeru is the closest open-air market, two acres sectioned off into areas for food, used clothes, fabric, tools, tires, housewares. Half a city block of nothing but used black school shoes and rubber flip-flops. Under a huge tarp, vendors sell tomatoes, onions, rice, maize, carrots, bananas, avocados, plantain, eggplant, beans, lentils, potatoes, yams, ginger, and garlic. Goat meat hangs on huge hooks with a skim of buzzing flies. Potatoes are fried in massive vats of boiling oil. Live chickens protest from their confining baskets, music blares from multiple boom boxes, and vendors yell out come-ons. It is hot and I feel painfully conspicuous.

Here we are studied and watched closely. I have a death grip on my purse and Adam has our cash. But Gil has a camera around his neck, a Nikon worth more than these vendors will see in their lives of hard work. This was the height of naïveté, we realize. A man comes up to Gil and says, "There are bad people here and they will steal your camera." His expression is so fierce that he looks like the likely first candidate for such a theft. Gil abandons all pretense of taking any photographs, tucks the camera under his arm, and we watch Adam try to negotiate a price for a kilo of beans. Adam thoroughly understands how this verbal ping-pong works, but we can tell by his expression that this is not going well. He is being offered an inflated price because we are there and it is clearly our money. Adam moves on to another vendor to get a better price and tells them we are buying food for an orphanage. The second vendor calls out curse words to the first woman, saying, "God will remember your selfishness."

The air is thick with tension now, and we belatedly realize that we should have never set foot in the market. We decide to retreat to the jeep and wait for Adam to do all the shopping. An hour later we see him and a young boy with an enormous pushcart laden with food. Adam has bought food for a month. Maize, rice, beans, carrots, onions, tea, sugar, tomatoes, eggplant, and fruits. He is weary but proud of the sheer volume he has acquired.

For the second time this day we go up the hill to the orphanage, this time with the jeep loaded to the rooftop with sacks of food. The children see the jeep arrive, and their faces register first anxiety, then surprise, then delight. Food! Lots of it! They start clapping and grinning. I have never gone hungry for more than a day and that was usually while going on some stupid grapefruit diet. I do not know what it is like not to know where my next meal is coming from. We have signed up to help these kids and we realize how basic the situation is. Before we will set about building beds, bathrooms, and classrooms, we must first feed the children.

THE DOG THAT CAUGHT THE CAR

In a matter of only two days we found what we were looking for, a project that clearly needs us in Tanzania, a viable way to make it happen with the help of an established NGO, and some new friends. All my trips to Africa over the past four years have been an exercise in self-reliance. Even as I have vivid adventures, I pine for Gil and count the days until I will see him again. Now that we are in the soup together, my life at home seems to abruptly recede, so much so that I must exert special effort to pull it into view. My clients, my house, my daily routine seem like an album of sepia photographs while Africa is a riot of heat and color.

It will ever be thus, Africa's sensory overload and challenges eclipsing my tidy, predictable life in New England. Gil and I will bask in the warmth and welcome of the Tanzanians, the unguarded affections of the children at Precious. We will stand slack-jawed at the night skies and migrating birds, pick lemons and avocados from our own trees, feed bush babies at close range on our veranda. We will learn enough Swahili to be polite and to buy food. We will impress foreign visitors with our stores of local knowledge, and we will begin to believe that we understand the life of the village that surrounds us. But our lives of affluence and privilege will blind us to evil as well, evil that is the corollary of desperate poverty.

For now, though, we are embarked on the adventure of seeing how much money we can raise to make good on our promise to the children at Precious. Our efforts are naïve but well intended, and remarkably, within only three months we raise four thousand dollars. We have a fund-raising event at the house, my sister designs a beautiful brochure, we blitz our friends and colleagues with stories and photographs. And as if by magic, donations began to come in. First William and Sarah are able to buy beds, mattresses, and perhaps most importantly, bed nets for the kids (three of the nine have already had malaria). Friends and family sign up to sponsor the nine children individually at seven hundred dollars a year. Donors send enough money for a new chicken coop, new bathrooms, fencing for the orphanage, and eventually new desks for the small kindergarten.

Gil and I are deeply moved. Each gift to the kids feels like a gift to us personally. People tell us that it is indeed their trust in us as project sponsors that fuels their willingness to donate. If you give money to Oxfam, you don't know if you are buying a copier or feeding children. William can tell us to the shilling how each donation is spent. We follow up each donation with personal thank-yous and photographs of the kids enjoying new shoes, new clothes, new bedding. The oldest boy, Baraka, holds up an egg from the new chicken coop and smiles into the camera.

While in the US, we are in steady email communication with William, and this is also deeply reassuring. In careful English, he writes "Hello. I hope you're doing good. I wish to inform you that today we purchased bed nets for all nine beds. We spent 5,000 shillings for each and now have 10,000 shillings left over. God Bless you!" William negotiates with the *fundis* (the tradesmen) who will do the work and then supervises every second of construction. He knows what we do not, that construction materials will too often disappear from a site, and cement bags will be shorted. The *fundis* are dismayed to have supervision this close but what can they do? William works alongside them to speed progress, hefting cement bags and bricks.

Within a month of our sending money to Tanzania, William is sending us photographs of completed projects. We in turn crow about the successes and email updates and photographs to our donors. This kind of feedback loop energizes everyone. Our donors feel like they are part of something tangible and valuable. The kids look better and happier in every photograph we see. William tells us that God is working through us, and we are on a "helpers' high."

The Precious project becomes an integral part of who we are. Each day some hours are spent in correspondence, or planning for fund-raising. A good day is when we get emails from

Africa. While I am still embarked on projects for the Clinton Foundation in Swaziland and Lesotho, increasingly Tanzania becomes a more singular focus.

EARLY PROGRESS

It is early August 2011, and I am back in Nshupu, Tanzania, this time without Gil, five months after our first visit to Precious. The Clinton Foundation has paid to send me to Swaziland, and I route myself there via Tanzania for a three-day stopover. This is not like going to Philadelphia and stopping in New York City en route. It is like stopping in Montréal on the way to Cuba, a long way, a fact I belatedly assimilate.

The plane lands in inky dark countryside with no lights below but for those on the landing strip. The huge aircraft disgorges its full flight of tourists and safarigoers, and it takes me a good forty-five minutes of anxious vigilance until my duffel bags show up in baggage claim. Somewhere during my eleven or twelve hours in the air, I had been seized by a wave of second-guessing and self-doubt. What was I doing? Who did I think I was? Did I imagine the warm welcome I had experienced some five months ago? What if that was an anomaly and I come back to studied indifference, a polite but chilly reception? What if I really don't belong at all?

These are the ghosts of travels past. As a kid, we crossed and recrossed the Atlantic in ancient military prop planes. No movies, no music, often even not enough food. I would stare out into the black night sky, watching my reflection in the window and the blinking light on the airplane wing. Untethered and unmoored, I had no idea what might be next and nursed this nameless dread silently.

Thankfully, on this night the ever-patient taxi driver Mr. Salim is there to meet me, holding my name up on a placard.

I feel the first surge of relief to see this familiar face so many time zones from home. Mr. Salim is a stick-thin older man who drives a battered white sedan. I know from our prior trips that he is an efficient and careful driver. We drive fifty minutes through the night, passing occasional clusters of bars and tiny food stalls lit by only by a few bare bulbs. Usually I sit in the front and chat with drivers in Africa. This time I plead fatigue and sit in the back. Mr. Salim has no airbags in his antique sedan, and I hope that if we hit a cow at night I at least won't go through the windshield. I recently learned that on the access road to a very nice hotel Gil and I had stayed at months ago, an SUV carrying safarigoers was held up at gunpoint en route from the airport. Any nostalgia for that nice hotel has totally evaporated with this news.

Nshupu and the Ngare Sero Lodge are reputed to be safer. The lodge owners have worked for decades to benefit the local village. The grounds are not surrounded by cut glass, locked metal gates, or barbed wire, as though to dare intruders to penetrate its defenses. Gangs with guns do not frequent this access road, I am told. Good. I will gladly accept this narrative on the risks here.

Mr. Salim takes the long access road to Ngare Sero Lodge at a snail's pace. The dirt road is impossibly rugged and littered with large rocks, which hit the car's undercarriage with loud thuds. Finally, finally, we arrive and I stagger into the lodge reception area. Rama, the Tanzanian on duty at the desk, whom I had come to know earlier, gives me a polite but careful hello. My heart sinks. But then he comes out from behind the counter. I am no longer backlit, and he sees my face under the lamp. "Susie," he calls out. "I could not see you there. *Karibu, karibu sana!*" (Welcome back!) He takes my hand and smiles warmly. I am back. I did not misremember this Tanzanian welcome. I inhale it.

That night, though spent with jet lag and fatigue, I cannot sleep. I am tuned to every night sound. The quiet movements and murmuring of the Maasai night watchmen, the steady thrumming of insects, and well before dawn, loud and random bird calls and deep-throated grunts of colobus monkeys marking their territory. Then, just before sunup, the haunting notes of the Muslim call to prayer followed by the ubiquitous African morning chorus of roosters and dogs. I thrash about in the bed listening to the noises bring us toward the light, then fall into a short deep sleep just as the world around me wakes up.

I head to breakfast seeking strong, muddy Tanzanian coffee to jump-start me. *"Kahawa na mazima moto tafadhali"* (Coffee with hot milk, please). Adam, the reservations clerk and my patient language teacher, greets me warmly and listens to me muddle through the results of his teaching from my prior visit. There are more warm welcomes (and hugs this time) from other staff. Happy, short for Happiness, is a chambermaid who could easily pass as a model in another world. Her skin is an even caramel color, her eyes bright and almond in shape, her features pleasingly symmetrical, her carriage erect and proud. She is unfailingly gracious but never obsequious. I know nothing about her life outside the lodge except that she lives in an immaculate yellow house in the village. Patricia too comes by to greet me. She has been working at the lodge her whole life, fifty-something years. In fact she was the nanny for the lodge manager, now in his thirties. She has worked so that her three children could go to school, something she never had. Her English is as sparse as my Swahili. *"Karibu sana,* Susie," she repeats over and over, her face saying much more. I long for more words so as to inquire after her health and her family as is the Tanzanian custom, but for now we will have to smile with our eyes and let that suffice.

This trip I have come with a duffel bag filled with clothing, school supplies, books, letters, and photographs for each child from their newly matched sponsor families in the US. William comes to meet me and helps me carry the gear. I am sitting on the veranda when I see him coming up the stairs from the forest. After months of communicating solely by email, it is wonderful to see him in person again. He is animated, talkative, flawlessly polite. I am after all quite old by Tanzanian standards, and my age alone earns me deference I hardly see at home. (Only recently I have bought a book called *How Not to Look Old*. The book's counsel was useless for me: tight jeans, high heels, trendy hair.) All of my efforts to deny my advancing age seem especially ridiculous once I get here.

I want to get a bit of an update before I simply show up on the scene at the orphanage, and it is important that William should handle the dispensation of the gifts, not me. "Soooosie" he pronounces my name. "How was your trip? I will escort you," he says in his careful English. I am glad for this and his scrupulous care. I cannot seem to recall the complex route to the orphanage. We leave the lodge grounds and head up the steep hill, and the path begins to throw up billows of dust. We pass one tiny house after another, small boxes with bars on the windows and dirt yards continuously swept clean.

Dirty barefoot toddlers stand and stare at the unfamiliar white lady, and a few local women wave warily in my direction. Eventually we reach the orphanage. From every direction kids come running and wrap themselves around my knees, chattering and smiling, grabbing my hands, stroking my forearms, trying to land in my lap even as I am standing. I can call them each by name now, and I wish for enough language to greet them and tease them one by one.

The orphanage is an unbelievable beehive of activity. A dozen cheerful young British volunteers are painting the dull gray exterior of the dormitory Caribbean peach. Workers are putting the finishing touches on the enormous new chicken coop. A volunteer is dipping a tiny puppy into a flea rinse. Two young mamas are scrubbing the kids' sneakers and setting them to dry on an oil can. William and I, trailing our small herd of kids, tour the tiny facility to admire all the big and small miracles five months of fund-raising have yielded: nine beds with bed nets strung atop each mattress, sheets, blankets folded neatly, desks in the formerly grim preschool room, food in the larder, two new toilets, and a chicken coop with two dozen chickens. The scene is utterly transformed. Most importantly, the kids too are transformed, their small frames now filling out and their energy high. Laughing and chattering they pose for pictures seated and grinning at their new desks. Not only will they be able to study at these desks, now they can eat their meals there as opposed to sitting in the dirt in the yard. So much has changed in so little time. I am blown away. The kids have gelled as a family and relax in the knowledge that food for them will now be a constant as is the steady affection from William and Sarah.

WE GET A HOUSE—MAYBE

After three days in Nshupu I'm still jittery with excitement about the changes at the orphanage and the anticipation of moving here for three months with Gil in January. The lodge has offered to lease us a small cottage up the hill.

At first blush this is a gift. We will be a short walk to the lodge with access to its facilities and proximity to its friendly staff. The house itself, at least from the outside, has a certain weathered charm. White stucco with a large front veranda, it has a red-tin roof (now faded to a dusty pink) and fuchsia bougainvillea spilling up and over the roofline. It is over one hundred years old, the former home of a German colonial farm manager. To the north, Mount Meru's summit is clearly etched against the skyline, its rocky promontory in relief against an impossibly blue sky.

But once I am escorted inside the house, the charm wears off. Its rooms are utterly bare and dirty. Bat droppings line the huge fireplace. There are no screens on the windows, and many of the windowpanes are broken. The kitchen has no stove, fridge, or cabinets. The bathroom has a nonfunctioning toilet, mold on the walls, and a large tub where the enamel has chipped off leaving a gray, mottled finish. But the house has high ceilings and open rafters, and light pours into the living room from two windows in the peak of the roofline. The whole place is the definition of a fixer-upper, nothing but possibility. I try to conceal my dismay at this first glimpse, but the lodge manager, Tim, assures me that they will fix it up and furnish it. It is their hope that we might lease it not for three months but for five years!

I say we will do a trial for a few months and then decide. I can't imagine that this grim spot can be made livable. But Tim and Katya from the lodge ask what they can do to help. Maybe this can work. And I won't know until Gil and I return in January. It is a leap of faith just like our entire project. In the meantime I must pack up and head south to Swaziland, where in August, winter is still the season.

In the next months I straddle the dual realities of the nascent project in Tanzania and my ongoing work for the Clinton Foundation. Increasingly the kids steal my heart and my focus.

RETURN TO TANZANIA

Four months have passed since Tim, Katya, and I discussed the changes to the house. It is Christmas Eve here in New England,

and our departure for Tanzania is only three weeks away. This feels very different from going on a short Clinton Foundation gig. We are not staying in a hotel with all the backup of the Clinton infrastructure. We will be on our own for three months, not at the lodge for ten days. I am beset with questions and concerns. Will the cottage be livable? What about window screens, locks, outlets, water? Will any portion of the punch list be finished? This is, after all, Africa. How will we set up for cooking? What about bedding, towels, lamps? What about snakes, malarial mosquitoes, mischievous monkeys? How will it really feel to be there? Will we feel safe? Will we be bored? How fast can I learn Swahili? Is this whole deal a good idea?

I have lists upon lists of what must be bought and what we must pack. We will need flashlights, antibiotics, antimalarials, antidiarrheal pills, sterile syringes, sunscreen, hats, passports, Swahili books, sandals, long skirts, adapter plugs, vitamins, shampoo, books, socks, sneakers, dental floss. The list expands by the day and in the dark hours of now-sleepless nights.

Then there is the to-do list. Turn down the heat, shut off the mail, stop the paper, suspend the cable service, pay for medical evacuation insurance, set up the caretaker, establish autopay, notify the neighbors, deliver the cat. Pray that the laptop holds up, that my guts don't go south, that my backache resolves, that my mammogram is negative, that my toothache is no big deal, that I at least arrive there intact. Don't think about what would happen if you need an appendectomy, a root canal, a blood transfusion.

Then there are the worries about those I am leaving behind. Zack seems on track to finish college, but it is not an easy road. He does not often anticipate crises and instead picks up the cell phone and calls me, expecting an instant response. I line up support from all of our extended family and hope that it will be sufficient. My father is in failing health.

I fly up to Maine for a goodbye visit with Dad and his wife, Susan. Dad is as ever articulate and consumed in his mentoring and leadership projects with others, yet at the same time his Parkinson's is advancing and he has debilitating hand pain of unknown origin. The pain saps his strength, and he speaks of having daily thoughts of suicide. We walk along the coast in the cold and my tears freeze on my face. I am mute in the face of Dad's pain. A standing joke he used to tell was this: How do you not look old? Stand up straight and walk fast. Now he can do neither. He stoops a bit and is starting to shuffle. It is crushing to see this slow collapse of his proud military bearing.

I return to Lincoln and to my obsessional packing, weighed down with sadness, awash in images I cannot now erase. Have I always spent so much time in anticipation of loss? Did this begin with my father's wartime absences, or did it metastasize after being so suddenly widowed in my early forties?

MOVING IN

Once again I'm flying south across the Sahara desert. Beneath us is wave upon wave upon wave of sand. It is an eerie and beautiful moonscape. We are held aloft here in business class, purchased with thousands and thousands of hard-earned miles spent in coach, and while we sip champagne I contemplate what life would be like in the desert. As the sun sets, we tuck into our third meal in ten hours and move over the darkened countryside of Kenya. I have done these trips to Africa many times, but never with my husband at my side. We are both weary and anxious but we are together. I do not have to save up my stories from this trip to share with him later. This has been a long time coming, and while we really have no idea how it will turn out, we are committed. Or at least we are committed to a three-month lease on a cottage in Nshupu, Tanzania.

We have spent months packing, planning, and trying to put in order all of what we have left behind at home: our son in college, our cat, our two aging Subarus, my dwindling corporate client list, my women's group at the UU church, Gil's grown kids, my sister and brother whom I rarely see, my friends who now sort into a binary list of those who get it and those who never will, my dear dad contemplating suicide, our lovely Lincoln house loaded with African masks and fabrics, Gil's growing grandchildren who by all accounts we see too little of, my Zumba class where my chronic showing-off has now resulted in a hopefully not lifelong injury to my sacroiliac, the endless news coverage of the Republican presidential primaries, the repetitive isolationist American news media, and our as-yet-undone taxes.

Being airborne and headed away from all this has us giddy and unhinged, even as we are exhausted and anxious about what the future will hold. At last we land at the always alarmingly insubstantial airport of Kilimanjaro and exit the aircraft. It is 8:30 at night. The moon is rising yellow-orange over the landscape, and it is still very warm from the day's heat. With sweet relief we are able to bypass a small mob of tourists who must wait in a convoluted, arcane, and punitive process of standing in multiple overlapping lines. Their first brush with Tanzanians will not be of the warm and welcoming kind. They will be treated to the officious and vaguely hostile manner that is the calling card of almost everyone in uniform in Africa. But with our visas still valid, we get to skirt all of that and retrieve our obscene amount of luggage. Mr. Salim, thankfully, is there to greet us. His face and broad smile materialize out of the darkness of the parking area, and I breathe a huge sigh of relief. Soon we are crawling up the impossibly rugged and rocky access road to the Ngare Sero Lodge.

Rama, short for Ramadan, is the guy on duty tonight. Rama has always struck me as someone exceedingly poorly suited for the job of hotel receptionist. He is a very dark and inordinately private man who must work hard to be friendly and extroverted. I have always sensed the effort and appreciate the cost it seems to exact. This night, overcome with relief to be safely delivered, I bypass the usual niceties and hug Rama. He smiles, surprised, seems to shake some of his impenetrable reserve, and we are home. Home to Ngare Sero, home to Tanzania, home to whatever adventures will unfold.

In the dark and quiet of the late-night lodge grounds, Maasai guards materialize from all corners and silently whisk our heavy luggage into our room. There we hunt futilely for our toothpaste and our antimalarial medication, fall into bed, and hope to sleep. Tomorrow we will see our new home.

I admit it. I did not believe that our cottage would be livable. I had heard too many horror stories about chronic delays with other projects and was braced for a series of disappointments that would have the cottage looking promising but unfinished. I was sure that we would have to spend at least a month prodding people to do what they had agreed to do, in the meantime accruing huge lodge bills. But here we are, Katya and Tim have escorted us up the hill, and we are standing on the veranda of our home in Africa.

Lodge staff and workmen are scurrying around, and both Happy and Patricia are in the house barefoot, sweeping their way out to the front door. Proudly Tim and Katya usher us inside and we are astounded. Walls inside and out have been whitewashed. Floors, beams, window casings have all been painted black. Screens have been installed, windows repaired, and all have bright *kitenge* cloth curtains. Simple chairs and sofas with colorful cushions are in the living room, and fresh flowers sit in brass vases. Six oil paintings of Maasai herdsmen grace the walls in the living room and dining room, and we have even the loan of Tim's mother's fine china. The bathroom, a grim disaster area months earlier, has been painted and cleaned. There is a new toilet, and a lovely carved wooden mirror sits over the sink. Perhaps most importantly, a backup battery inverter has been installed, and this will allow us to weather the twenty-some power outages that happen every day without them bringing us to our knees. When power cuts out, the battery will serve as a backup. So long as we are not profligate with lights and appliances, we should be good. And we must be careful. Later the indulgent purchase of a toaster turns out to be a bad bet. Simply to push down the button on one piece of toast cuts out our power altogether.

If Tim and Katya wanted us to feel welcomed, we truly do. They have gone to great effort to make this house a home, and we all know that this will increase the likelihood of our leasing it on a longer-term basis. But we must still deal with some basics. There is no stove to cook with and no fridge, and we need things like lamps, bulbs, sponges, and housewares.

Bats in the bathroom

We have been in Nshupu only five days, but the sensory overload is so profound as to crowd out the parallel reality of the world we came from. This moon-landing strangeness is huge and surprising to me. This is my twenty-first trip to Africa and my sixth trip to Tanzania. But we are not here on a short consulting stint. We are setting up house, and that changes everything. There has been a bat in the bathroom for the last two nights. I enter the bathroom, he flaps past me to roost somewhere else in the house, and then I am left with his small turds on our clean towels. Not only that, there is an enormous spider in the bathtub. I dispatch the spider while muttering to myself, "This is Africa, Susie. Don't be a wimp." There are also six geckos that cruise the rafters of our bedroom. This is good news, as they eat bugs. The bad news is that geckos poop. Yes, they poop and quite a bit. They seem to prefer the living room couch or anything that is upholstered.

Jet lag and new noises make for restless nights. Not only that, we discover that the Tanzania National Artificial Insemination center is our neighbor. You couldn't make that up. The first time we hear a roar at night it brings us bolt upright in bed. What is that? This is not a cow lowing, it is a bull roaring, and he sounds like he is ready to charge the house. Thankfully he is not, he's fifty yards away, and there is a wire fence separating us. Fortunately the roaring is intermittent and we can drift back to sleep. But Africa's wake-up calls start early and are protracted. Here's how it goes:

> 4:30 a.m. Colobus monkeys bark and growl to
> establish their treetop turf
> 4:45 a.m. An insect that sounds like a cell
> phone running low on battery starts to
> beep beep beep
> 5:00 a.m. A bird that makes a *whooeeee*
> sound begins to call
> 5:10 a.m. The village dogs start their call-and-
> response barking throughout the area
> 5:20 a.m. Local roosters take up the chorus
> 5:30 a.m. Muslim call to prayer sounds from
> down the hill
> 5:45 a.m. Serious birdlife symphony tunes up
> and gets gradually louder. Remember the
> Robert J. Lurtsema radio show? Like that,
> only louder.
> 6:00 a.m. Colobus monkeys have another
> altercation

And so it goes. By 6:00 a.m. I am totally awake and trying to discern if my husband's steady breathing comes from sleep or from a futile effort to regain it. "Did you hear that roaring?" I ask in the barest whisper. "Yes," he whispers back. Good. I am not alone now in my wakefulness. The sun is up, Africa is wide awake, and we need to follow suit.

The dust here is fine and ubiquitous. We breathe it, wear it, and daily, futilely, try to scrub it from our clothes. Unlike all the Africans in this village, we have running water. In fact we have running hot water. The hot water comes from a small firebox external to the house, and our Maasai night guard tends to that fire. Electricity is too unpredictable, propane is too expensive, so this small and efficient firebox actually works quite well. The challenge is that if the fire is made too enthusiastically, scalding water, brown from the rusty pipes, comes sputtering out of the tap. Otherwise it runs clear and we are okay. But we must never ever drink this water, wash our vegetables in it, or put our toothbrushes under it. Instead we must soak our vegetables in a bleach-like disinfectant solution if we cannot peel them. And as challenging as some of these facts of daily living are, I never for a moment forget that, relatively speaking, we are living in the utter lap of luxury, the way white people do in Africa.

DRIVING INTO ARUSHA

It is blazing hot and we are on the highway in our rented jeep on the way to Arusha to provision the house. The forty-five-minute trip is terrorizing. Tanzanians drive on the left, and Gil as the driver must sit on the right and shift gears with his left hand. The two-lane asphalt road has no shoulder but dirt and is crammed with cars, motorbikes, buses, and trucks all belching black exhaust into the blue sky. The public minibuses stop and pull out into traffic with no warning, passing us on the right and on the left. They are all emblazoned with biblical passages and references to Jesus, but this does prompt any restraint whatsoever in their kamikaze driving. Personally I would not want to ride in the van emblazoned with "Washed in the blood of Jesus." I am traveling too close to that possibility as it is.

Pedestrians, goats, children, and donkeys line the roads. Gil does not speak, as it takes every shred of his concentration to stay on top of the unfolding chaos. Cars routinely pull into our oncoming lane and play chicken with us right up until the last second. With my sweaty hands I have a death grip on my seat belt, and I am working my imaginary brake with my right foot. Each time we have yet another close call, I cannot help but squeak, much to Gil's annoyance.

We pass by the scene of a recent fatality. A dump truck loaded with cement cinder blocks crushed a motorcycle underneath it as it overturned. Another empty motorcycle lies alongside the truck. The bodies are no longer there, but this is surprising. In Arusha if you are in a traffic accident, there will be no ambulance to come to get you. With unerring speed, thieves will come and take your money and strip your car. You may pray to have some Good Samaritan pick you up and hurry your bleeding body to a clinic. Once having arrived at the clinic, you hope that there actually may be staff on-site to care for you. There will be no trauma center, no ER, no team of doctors and nurses to tend to you swiftly. I hope to die directly if I am in one of these accidents.

Everyone knows the story of the truck that rammed into a huge passenger bus on a narrow bridge over a deep ravine a few miles outside of Arusha. The truck was going so fast that it sheared off half the bus, pushing it halfway over the bridge and onto the steep cliff below. Twenty-five or thirty people died in that accident, some on impact, some as they were pushed into the ravine, and doubtless others for lack of adequate medical care. Our friend Adam was on the scene at the time and still has nightmares about pulling a woman up from the bridge by her hair.

Not much has been done to change the traffic patterns across that bridge: no widening of the lanes, no strengthening of the Jersey barrier, only the construction of a few more speed bumps on either side of the bridge. Speed bumps litter the highway from Usa River to Arusha, without demonstrable improvement in traffic sanity. Police also stop people periodically, scrutinize their papers, and extract bribes, but there is no visible consequence for driving to endanger, since everyone drives like that.

There is another feature of this part of the road that we learn about. Another factoid that falls into the category of things you need to know but wish you didn't. At night, groups of thugs wait to ambush white drivers here. The strategy is to throw a large rock at the windshield. When the driver stops to assess the damage, the car and its occupants are robbed. Tim tells us if we ever have a flat tire on that section of the road, keep driving. These are not reassuring anecdotes, but they are realities of life here. Most tourists who come this way do so only once and are inevitably in the back seat of a safari vehicle. But as we are taking up residence here and must go back and forth to town, we must be forewarned.

We have come to Arusha to buy some of the important basics we will need: sim cards for our cheap cell phones, a dongle for our computer that will allow us to access the internet via the cellular network, a stove and fridge for the kitchen, and basic household goods for cleaning and cooking. We will not use credit cards for these purchases, as most stores do not accept them, and if they do, there are huge fees attached. So first we must go to an ATM to withdraw cash. The maximum that an ATM will allow you to take out at any given time is 420,000 Tanzanian shillings, about 120 dollars.

This is never as simple as it sounds. Sometimes it takes a trip to three or four ATMs to get one to yield up the cash. When the cash is disbursed, it is in huge numbers of small bills. I skulk away from the ATM stuffing my purse with a brick of cash as though I have just robbed a bank. Sometimes the ATM does not give any cash. Instead you get a receipt telling you that the money has actually been debited from your account in the US, but the machine will not give you the cash in Africa. This takes weeks to resolve between the two banks, with both entities often behaving with complete indifference.

Arusha is a small city, but not easy to negotiate for two white *muzungu* newbies in a rented car. Like most African cities, Arusha is a hodgepodge of contradictions, a few high-rise hotels for well-heeled tourists, beat-up government-run hospitals teeming with people, huge open-air markets selling food and used clothes, the huge building complex for the Advisory on Corruption, and hundreds of small storefronts. Most of the city is paved and has sidewalks, and there are enormous warrens of commerce accessible only through narrow dirt roads where no safari vehicles ever go.

Often as we park the car, we are surrounded by street vendors selling maps, sunglasses, knockoff watches, fruit, shoes, and cheap jewelry. For the most part, a polite and broken-record response of *"Hapana asante"* is enough to wear down the persistent. But the key to that is to evince no interest at all in the products themselves. If I finger any of the proffered items, this invites a larger swarm, and it takes much longer to disentangle. This day, however, we buy some bed pillows from a wandering street vendor, four of them in fact, all wrapped in plastic. We bargained naïvely and largely ineffectively. The seller was elated. Probably his only sale for the day. Buying a stove, food, and cooking supplies is far more complex and takes several death-defying trips.

CHAPTER ELEVEN

Big Wins and Big Challenges

Now that our house is set up with the bare basics, we can come back to our reason for being here, the kids. It is 3:00 p.m. and Gil and I have set out on foot to head to the orphanage for our first visit in some time. We follow small dirt paths uphill through Nshupu village to get there. The heat, dust, and altitude have us sweating and puffing though the actual distance is not great. We pass goats, small fields of tall, dry maize plants rustling in the thin breeze, and tiny brick houses, their dirt yards swept clean. Groups of uniformed schoolchildren pass us. We greet them in Swahili; they freeze at first and then respond, saying slowly and shyly, "Good afternoon, madam" to both of us. We pass an older woman carrying an impossible load of water on her head. *"Pole mama,"* we greet her. (Sorry for your troubles.) *"Asante,"* she replies. Women here work like donkeys. They fetch water and firewood, make meals, care for children, and tend the crops while husbands gather down the hill at the local bar.

Up the hill we trudge, panting, sweating, and swigging water from our plastic bottles. Little kids, too young or too poor to go to school, run alongside the path in small packs announcing our arrival. *"Muzungu, muzungu!"* (white people) they call out to one another. In one small compound we see Christina, who does gardening work at the nearby lodge. She spots us and rushes out, calling, *"Karibu, karibu."* Unlike most lodge staff, Christina speaks no English. Her face, while stern in repose, lights up with her smile. Christina is of indeterminate age. She has an ample figure and her hair is carefully straightened and curled. Like all African women she bends to her tasks from the waist, knees locked, spine straight.

We do not know how to carry our bodies this way, those of us who spend too many hours each day seated. Christina smiles hugely and motions us to come into her house and visit, but we demur knowing the kids at the orphanage are on high alert watching for us. Christina proudly introduces us to her daughter, Mary. Mary looks about fifteen and has a baby on her hip. She stands tall and addresses us in careful, limited English. She is pretty but for her front teeth, which are stained brown. This phenomenon we see often, caused by too much fluoride in the water. Fluorosis weakens bones and tooth enamel. So many children in this small village will see their bright white smiles turn brown. Some will have neurological damage. The condition is irreversible.

We take our leave from Christina and Mary as politely as possible and continue, now having alerted the entire village to our presence. The warren of footpaths up the hill is confusing at first, but soon we spot the orphanage. Originally the buildings were all unpainted gray concrete. Now they stand out on the hillside, a cheerful Caribbean shade of peach.

We round the bend and the kids spot us. All nine run to the gate laughing, smiling, and calling out greetings. Once we are inside the gate we are mobbed. The smallest children slip their hands into ours, and the others press in, stroking our arms and our heads. We greet them each by name and their faces light up. Baraka, the oldest boy (his name means "blessings") gives us the tour of the orphanage, now so changed from the grim circumstances of only ten months ago. Although the yard is all dust and packed dirt, the dorm is impeccably clean and tidy. Once nine kids doubled up in two bunk beds. Now each child has a bed, a bed net for malaria prevention, and a blanket. Once the children shared a few clothes. Now they each have a cubby and a small stack of their own clothes. Shoes and toothbrushes are neatly stored on wall racks. There are three tiny rooms, one for the four girls, one for the five boys, and one for the two young mamas who cook and do endless loads of laundry, a Sisyphean task in the ubiquitous dust. Baraka shows us the chicken coop behind the dorm now populated by thirty some young *kuku* who have just begun to lay eggs. As the yield increases, the eggs will be sold to the lodge and will generate a small revenue.

Sponsor letters from a world away

Once Baraka has finished giving us the grand tour, we unpack individual letters for each of the nine children from their US sponsor families. The children crowd around, their faces alight with excitement. Some of the children received greeting cards with photos, some get simply penciled letters authored by the children in the sponsor families. Everyone is equally excited. I noticed this last year when I brought dresses for the girls. There were no comparisons. No jockeying for who got the best dress. No whining. I worried that the children who received a basic email instead of a fancy greeting card might be envious. I saw no shred of that. The children each clutch their letters to their chests and press in on William, waiting to hear them read aloud and translated from English to Swahili. The gaggle of children gets quiet as each letter is read and each individual recipient sits rapt, listening carefully to each word. Nora, age six, came to the orphanage after her mother died of AIDS and her father was jailed for murder. She is tiny and sits utterly erect in her dusty pink sundress. She listens to William with a huge smile and a birdlike intensity.

The first time I brought sponsor letters, the children could not really grasp the concept of strangers writing to them from half a world away. Since then they have come to understand that their clothes, their school uniforms, and their changed circumstances are a gift to each of them from the authors of these letters. William often makes this connection for them too.

The adult sponsor letters say things like, "I am so proud of how you are doing in school." The sentence is translated. The child beams and breathes in the acknowledgment. The letters from children hit a chord too. One letter describes how sleeping in the top bunk bed is like a bird's nest. And across the worlds, the metaphor works. Patrick, who sleeps each night in his bird nest, laughs and smiles. And so it goes for the afternoon, the reading, the translating, the connections knitting. I take photos of each child listening to their letters and my face hurts from smiling. These kids have been abandoned, some have been beaten, and all are bereft of birth parents who love them. There must be some scars, but I cannot discern them this day. Their hearts are open without reserve. Mine is too.

Shopping with Adam

In the meantime, at our house we are still relatively clueless. Everything here is more complex and takes infinitely more time. We got a dongle for our computer, but it took hours to get it up and running. We bought a stove but had to find a padlock so that our propane gas tank would not be stolen. We bought some vegetables but had to learn to disinfect them. We have water but must learn to filter it. We have hot water, sometimes, but the firebox must be lit and the fire not too big. Thank God for our friends at the lodge who patiently instruct us in all of these important fundamentals.

In his time off, Adam offers to take us into the Sunday market to shop for some basics, a bin for washing clothes, a thermos for filtered water, clothespins, onions, garlic, bananas, and best of all, *parachichi* (avocados). The avocados here are the size of grapefruits. The pits are huge, but the meat is perfectly ripe. The market here in Usa River takes place on Tuesday and Sunday and thankfully is smaller and less intense than the markets in Arusha. There is more room to maneuver, I do not fear as much for pickpockets, and while Gil and I stand out as the only white people here, neither of us feels the target of particular hostility. I cannot imagine how any of the food vendors make money. Everyone is selling the same things: tomatoes, carrots, onions, garlic, eggplant, cucumbers, potatoes, rice, avocados, pineapples, bananas, and plantain. In the midday heat I feel the sun frying my too-white skin and I long for anonymity I will never have here.

Like imprinted ducks, we follow in Adam's wake as he takes us from one crowded spot to the next. Adam has been our guide to all things local since that first "cultural tour" last year. His English is very good from his long tenure at the Ngare Sero Lodge, and he has been able to span the two worlds: the privileged existence of lodge guests and the enduring poverty in the town of his birth. The Usa River vendors know that he is negotiating on our behalf, so the bargaining is a bit more challenging for him with us standing by. But he is patient and persistent, and the back-and-forth is not without humor. We offer to buy more than one item and ask if there is a discount for a larger purchase. This usually opens things up a bit. Adam and the vendor arrive at a final price, which Adam translates for us. We do some fancy calculations in our heads, knowing that we still have been offered the tourist price, but that price is well below what we would have obtained on our own. We pay up and everybody is happy. We know that we must wean ourselves from Adam's care and for that we must learn Swahili. We ask William to offer us three lessons a week.

Language lessons with William

It is 9:00 a.m., time for our Swahili lessons with William. I gather the chairs around on the veranda, trying to avoid the patches of sun, which are quite hot even at this hour. I put out glasses, a thermos of filtered water, and fetch our small white-board, my notes, and my homework from the previous day's lesson. In our small language school there is me, Gil, and our friends Ann and Robert from next door. We are an earnest if rowdy group, and there is much laughter as we mangle pronunciation and struggle with some of the complex pronouns and sentence structures. William is a superb instructor for us, well prepared, energetic, and at the same time demanding. He has had many years teaching secondary school, so this group of goofy grown-ups approximates the adolescents he has learned to cope with.

I choose a patch of shade for my seat and enjoy the quiet alone before our lesson begins. I love these early mornings. The sky is clear and very blue. The outlines of Mount Meru are sharply etched in the distance, and each day I seem to notice some new flowering plant or tree in our yard. Just yesterday we discovered that we have not one but four lemon trees, filled with small green fruits as hard as golf balls.

While we enjoy a bit of space and privacy in our immediate surroundings, we can hear the village life all around us. Children playing, roosters crowing, hand tools clinking, and people calling out greetings to one another. What we don't hear, and I don't miss, is the sound of motors. We live at the end of a dirt road, and the only car that ever comes up this road is our own. There are times when we can hear horns from traffic on the road to Arusha below, but they are faint and far distant.

Our lessons begin with basic pronunciation. We learn to pronounce the vowels as they should be and how to deal with words that begin with consonants like *ng*. For example, the word for cow is *ngombe*. To pronounce it correctly, one must open the tongue in the mouth to make an *OOOmbe* sound. We know we don't have it quite right, because when we try the word out with the kids at Precious, they laugh and try to get us to say it again! The Swahili lessons are engaging and fun and much more difficult than any of us naïvely imagined. It is one thing to learn a language at age six and quite another to do it at sixty-three. But we are intent and hugely reinforced every time we try on a new phrase with our Tanzanian friends at the lodge.

Hiring a "houseboy" and a night guard

As we slowly add to our repertoire of Swahili words (*mwisho*: Is that your best price?), the lodge managers tell us that we need a "houseboy" and an *askari*, a night guard. We call Joseph our handyman, but everyone else here, Tanzanian and otherwise, refers to him as our houseboy. I flinch at this colonial reference, and yet I am the reluctant beneficiary of all of that grim early history. We live in a house that, after all, was built by a German colonial farm manager in the early 1900s. The literature written by whites describes the German plantation owners here as firm but fair. Yeah, I bet firm. Firm is what is at the end of the whiplash. The Tanzanians attempted two insurrections, neither of them successful. You don't plan insurrections if you're happy campers.

In any event we now have Joseph in our employ and he makes about four dollars a day, a generous wage by local standards. He shows up at 7:30 a.m., rakes the lawn, waters the plants, does the dishes, washes clothes in the bathtub, and scrubs the floor. Joseph was referred to us because the lodge manager knew that he was HIV-positive and correctly guessed that this would not freak me out, my having worked in the field for some years now. What did freak me out was learning that this young man had been deeply stigmatized by our friends at the lodge and by people in the village, and that he came to work for us with only the clothes on his back.

Joseph is half Maasai, which accounts for his height and build. He has a ready smile that lights up his face and a child-like curiosity and delight in all things new. When I show him photographs of the snowstorms we have left behind, he is thrilled and amazed. Laughing, he asks, What happens to your maize crop when it snows? And how can you sit on the chairs on your patio if there is snow on top of them? And what happens when you open the door of your house? Does the snow fall in? Joseph's English is basic but he is very bright, so we are able to bridge the gap. I quickly fall into the habit of sharing photos from home simply to provoke his smile and his amazement. I have never had hired helpers working in the house alongside me. I had worried about how that would work. Instead Joseph brings warmth and humor and broad knowledge of plant life. He brings cuttings, nurtures them, and they grow: aloe, lemongrass, lavender, hibiscus, agapanthus. Eventually his work is altogether outside, where his plantings create a green oasis from what was a gray wasteland.

After signing up to work for us, Joseph rents a small brick cell of a room down the hill, and we later learn that his room contains nothing but empty soda bottle crates. No bed, no mattress, no stove, no food, no cooking utensils, nothing. We also hear that Joseph is leaving us every afternoon to work another four hours at the lodge in order to be fed supper. This skinny young man, HIV-positive and still recovering from TB, is working a twelve-hour day and going home to sleep on a bare concrete floor. We are horrified.

William has become our cultural interpreter in all things Tanzanian, and at our request he reaches out to Joseph to find out if he is getting the HIV treatment that he needs. We watch from a distance as William gently does his due diligence. He walks around the back of the house where Joseph is working, introduces himself, chats a bit to Joseph in Swahili, takes him by the hand, and they walk down the hill holding hands. I am always moved by this African custom of adult male friends who hold hands. It seems so tender and unguarded.

William finds out more about Joseph's situation at the lodge. No one will touch him or allow him to use the same utensils they use. He is fed but shunned. Of course I know about stigma but I have not seen it in action close-up. The staff at the lodge have become our friends, patiently answering basic questions, reinforcing our beginners' Swahili, offering a warmth and welcome that is so sustaining. I am glad I do not know who has been so callous with Joseph. This learning is so at odds with our own experience as privileged whites. It begins to dawn on us that everyone here occupies a dual reality. There are the lovely picture postcards of Africa, its beautiful land-scape and animals. Then there is the reality of generational extreme poverty, and tribal custom and beliefs. It is as though we try to peer under the hood of the car to understand the cul-ture around us but we will never get more than a peek.

Gil and William go on excursions to buy Joseph a bed, a mattress, a stove, and enough food to last a month. We take Joseph to get some lab tests and to be put back on antiretroviral medication. We know that in three weeks we have changed this man's life prospects completely. He is deeply grateful and shows that in every possible way. His wide smile, his careful attention to all of the plants and flowers around the house. We came to support nine small orphans. And now we have another soul under our wing. Would that it could be that simple.

While hiring a handyman is optional, everyone agrees that we absolutely must have an *askari*, a nighttime guard. Our Maasai night watchman is right out of central casting. His name, we think, is Darsch, as best we can decipher. He speaks no English or Swahili, so we rely on elaborate pantomime to communicate back and forth. Like all Maasai, he is very dark, very tall, and stick thin. For clothes he wears two blankets draped around his body, one cobalt blue, the other bright red, the two colors worn by all Maasai. For shoes he wears sandals fashioned from tire tread. His ankles are braceleted with traditional beadwork, as are his wrists. Most distinctive are his earlobes. They bear two very large holes (now empty of earrings) and hang almost to his shoulders. On his face, both cheeks show subtle scarifications of round circles. Maasai mothers toughen their babies very early in life. Those scars just below the eyes are made with a hot poker. Salt tears in those new wounds are very painful, so babies learn not to cry, good preparation for a life of hardship and deprivation. Darsch's teeth are brilliant white against his blue-black skin. Traditional Maasai subsist on a diet of blood, milk, and occasional beef, so they are not exposed to sugar and refined carbohydrates. Across his waist is the scabbard for his very large knife, and in his right hand always is a large stick fashioned with a leather knob on its end, a weapon Maasai boys learn to use early in life, a *rungwa*.

We have been advised to hire Darsch so as not to be unnecessarily parted from our cameras, money, clothes, and computers in the dead of night. The whole village knows we are here, and although we are known as good guys for our work at the orphanage, we have not improved the lot of countless others who have no idea where their next meal is coming from. All over this part of Tanzania, expats and locals hire Maasai night watchmen, as they are known for their loyalty, bravery, and fearlessness. Darsch shows up at dusk, patrols the perimeter of our house until sunrise. He also tends to the small firebox that heats water for us. Maasai have been nomadic pastoralists for hundreds of years. We have been cautioned that one day Darsch is likely to simply walk off the job, restless and needing to move on. But for now he is on the case and happy to have a predictable salary to send to his wife fifty kilometers away. Darsch has few cattle, so he can afford only one wife.

Darsch's nightly arrival is always utterly silent. Suddenly I will look up and notice him on the hill staring fixedly at the house. He stands tall and erect, one leg straight and one bent like a stork's. His bare legs and buttocks stand out against his blankets. Once I get over my initial surprise, I call out a greeting to him in the only Maa word I know: *"Sopai!"* His reply is always the same: *"Epa."* A Maasai trainee at the lodge, Edward, has been trying to instruct me in a more correct and polite Maa greeting. The reply from a woman to a man is meant to be sung in a very, very loud melodic tone: *"Aaoooo! Eekwa!"* I practiced this a few times with Edward but we were alone, thank heavens. I have not yet attempted this with Darsch. As it is, my daily Swahili lessons have me nearly marooned with the more than twenty words for *this*, *that*, and *those*. I dare not try to superimpose the Maa on top of this flimsy foundation.

The Maasai come by their legendary courage and endurance in a set of cultural rituals that have been unchanged for thousands of years. Adolescent boys undergo circumcision as

a group in an ancient rite of passage. Tribal elders perform
the rite with no anesthetic. If a boy so much as whimpers or
flinches he will endure a lifetime of chagrin and censure for
his failure. After the circumcision ritual, young warriors spend
years living on their own, protecting their herds of cattle from
predators. Long ago each would-be Maasai warrior had to
kill a lion with only a club to be fully recognized as a man.
Thankfully that is no longer the custom. But Maasai men are
proud and confident. Those who stay in their rural outposts
marry in their early thirties and then take as many wives as the
size of their herds will permit. Each wife then builds her own
mud-and-dung thatched house, and those huts form a circular
boma surrounded by thorn bushes to protect livestock inside
at night.

I cannot imagine the night watchman job, with its cold
nights, staying awake in the chill, the rain, the dark, walking, sitting, patrolling, staving off sleep and boredom. Each
night when we come inside and leave Darsch outside, it seems
wrong. The night sky in Africa is breathtaking. There are no
streetlights here, no ambient light of any kind, and at this time
of year no clouds at all. This firmament is dizzying. And we
trade it nightly for a few dim light bulbs, our four walls, and
locked doors. I do not romanticize Darsch's cold and lonely
outdoor nights. But the trade-off of these night skies for our
close rooms gives me pause every time we lock ourselves in.

This evening Darsch arrives as he always does at dusk,
but he is agitated. He tugs at Gil's sleeve and pantomimes his
concerns. Men, he says, three of them, have been coming each
night to stare at our house in the dark. He points to the large
hole in the wire fencing just behind the house. And then, to
reassure us, he shows us the pile of stones he has amassed to
throw at them if they come back. All of this he acts out with
great urgency. And he wants us to know he is on the case and
will protect us. I get the gist of the story and I am scared. The

house we are living in was robbed a few years ago, and its occupant shot the intruder. And I have had too many colleagues (five this fall alone) burglarized elsewhere in Africa.

I grab my cell phone and call our Tanzanian friends at the lodge down the hill. To my relief, the call goes through, and three staff immediately march up the hill, Rama the night receptionist and two other Maasai *askari*. Rapid-fire words are exchanged in Maa and in Swahili. Calls are made, reinforcements are brought in. Now four fierce Maasai will patrol the house. We feel safe and sleep that night. Come morning, we find out the real story. There have not been three guys casing our place. There has been one night watchman from the bull farm in the abutting property walking by. The holes in our fence have not been cut by bad-guy burglars but by young boys. The grass in the fields at the bull farm is plentiful and nutritious. The young boys are sent to steal it at night so their scrawny family cows will yield more milk, their own patches of grass at home now turned to packed dirt in the dry season.

So, again, we learn the parameters of poverty here. Certainly our laptops would be a great haul, make no mistake. But these kids are simply trying to feed a few cattle.

EXISTENTIAL SURRENDER

It is 1:30 p.m. and I am lying indoors on the bed as it is simply too hot to be out on the veranda where we spend most of our time. All is quiet here at this hour. Everyone has retreated for food and quiet. I am happy to be prone and looking up at the ceiling where my daily routine is to count the number of geckos I can see at any one moment. Today I see around six running about in the high rafters.

We have been here now a full month, and it has been a time of huge change for us both. It is hard to explain what is so compelling about being here. It is a constellation of things. There is the chance to palpably change the lives of the children at the orphanage. There are also other community projects incubating that might actually come to pass. There are remarkable flowers, birds, and vistas of Mount Meru. There are the monkey acrobatics in the trees. There is the thrum of the wings of the great African hornbills. There are avocados the size of grapefruit, and mangoes lying in the road. There is the challenge of learning to speak this mellifluous Swahili and the looks of delight and amazement when we add a few more sentences to our repertoire.

But fundamentally the pull is this: in a thousand big and small interactions every day, we are shown a warmth, a welcome, a reciprocity that is stunning. We drive up and down the access road to our house in a rented Range Rover generating clouds and clouds of dust onto pedestrians, many of them carrying heavy loads on their heads. We wave and call out a greeting in Swahili, and we get two-handed waves, big smiles, and an answering greeting most every time. This generosity of spirit feeds the soul and surprises me every time. People here have so little and we have so much. If we were driving a jeep and spewing dust all over American pedestrians in most places, the hand gestures would not be as welcoming. Over time we start giving "lifties" to the women walking to market with forty to fifty pounds of fruit in baskets on their heads. They are so happy to be spared the five to ten kilometers of dusty, hot walking. We are often given a piece of fruit as a thank-you.

This is the core of it. The people connections, the greetings, and the friendships now deepening. Then there is the stuff that is hard about being here. Letting go of any expectation that anything will ever happen on time. Trying to maintain some semblance of predictability when all things technological are hanging on by a thread. For just this reason, I don't set up a lot of Skype calls with clients. But I set up three one day, and I am unable to complete them or politely cancel them either. This is the kind of thing that drives me buggy. I try to remind myself that only a few years ago when I came to Africa, I was *in* Africa and not expected to span the two worlds. But now having had just enough reinforcement that in fact we can send emails from time to time, I got bold.

Being here is this ongoing lesson in existential surrender. Absolutely nothing happens the way it is supposed to, by Western standards, and virtually never in the timeline that we have planned for. We negotiated what we thought was an excellent three-month car rental. And in the space of one month we have had to turn in the car for repairs at least four times. The car would not lock, the brake lights would not work, and the inspection sticker expired. And because Gil has become friendly with the owners of the car-rental agency, he is not screeching for a refund. Now he is coming home after having had a major breakdown the other side of Arusha. The car overheated, the engine nearly melted, and then the guy who was sent to fetch him had a blowout. If Gil is further delayed then he will have to drive the gauntlet past the crooks at Tengeru. I am jittery until I hear his car coughing and sputtering up the hill toward home. Because Peter's death years ago had been so sudden, when Gil is delayed I rehearse losing him too. Who would I call? Would we bury him here as is his wish? This line of thinking can unspool quite a distance before I can wrench myself out of this useless ruminating. So just in case we missed today's lesson on letting go of expectations, here comes another lesson from Mother Africa.

I almost hope this lesson will persist, as it is chipping away at my type-A chronic impatience. At home I cannot bear to sit at a red light, to be stuck in traffic, to wait a full ten seconds for my computer to turn on, or to be kept waiting more than ten minutes for any given rendezvous. I expect the world to be on time like me. Here, that is beyond ridiculous. And so I feel myself relaxing, almost, into that reality.

I have been here only a little over a month this trip, but I feel irretrievably pulled away from my realities at home. Yes, I seem to be able to maintain some vestige of email contact, but as each day passes I am less and less capable of explaining or trying to bridge the gap between this world and the one we have left.

The best antidote to my disconnect is work, and there is plenty to be done.

A Fast Track for Nshupu?

William has heard about my HIV/AIDS prevention work in other parts of Africa and is anxious to try the same method to see if more education and awareness might stem the contagion of AIDS in the area. At his urging I have put together a preliminary Fast Track plan that is wildly optimistic. The next step is to train William and a few facilitators. And, crucially, we must run a meeting with local elders to make sure they are supportive.

The meeting of eighteen senior local Tanzanian community leaders was to have started at 2:00 p.m. It is now 2:45 and only three have shown up. Our fledgling team of newly minted Fast Track facilitators are anxiously pacing the perimeter and calling the no-shows on their cell phones. I am dressed in my African *kitenge* outfit and trying to make myself useful and invisible all at once. This African scene is deeply familiar to me. The meeting will start when it starts, when some unacknowledged critical mass of the truly senior people arrive, and not before.

Eventually the important people enter in a chattering flurry, everyone is seated, and a pastor is asked to provide an opening prayer. The most senior Pentecostal female pastor stands to address the room. Mama Abigail is very brown and very round. She is swaddled in colorful purple *kitenge* with a matching head scarf. Her face exudes a gentle warmth, a maternal sweetness. I wish I could get closer, settle under her wing, hold her hand, inhale her acceptance. Little do I know how much I will need it.

This meeting set-up, the format and the endless waiting, I have seen these before. But this is not a Clinton Foundation–sponsored affair. This is Gil and me working without a net, not employed or legitimized by an NGO. Just showing up at the encouragement of a few longtime resident Tanzanians who think this idea can help address challenges related to HIV awareness and treatment access.

The meeting of "big shots" is the kind of cross section we always like to see: doctors, village headmen, church leaders, influential businessmen, and partner NGOs. So far so good. Then Dr. Masawi kicks off the meeting and he does so in English, clearly for Gil's and my benefit. We urge him to proceed in Swahili, but he demurs, saying that he is sure all can understand English. This tilts the meeting at its outset in the wrong direction, as if wholly sponsored and run by these two white people. The English doesn't last long, however, as the planning team goes to their project overview in Swahili, with accompanying flip charts in Swahili as well. Tanzanians are polite to a fault, so they let him talk through all seven flip charts without interruption. When new facilitator Chris stops and asks for questions and comments, there is even a careful hiatus.

Then suddenly the meeting erupts into passionate debate in such rapid-fire Swahili that we can only discern a few words. But several stand out and give us a clue as to how the discussion is going: *maji* (water), *malaria, root cause, clinic.* Initially the most intense input comes from a man people refer to as "the professor." The guy surely looks the part: tortoiseshell glasses, corduroy coat with elbow patches, bow tie, economics textbook in hand, and a facial expression that starts out dour, then goes to even more grim disapproval, his mouth turned down. We remain silent, figuring that the usual initial debate is happening. What is the most important problem to solve here? Is it HIV or is it access to water? Treatment for malaria? The construction of a dispensary? Road improvements?

All around the table, people weigh in and with much passion. The village headmen speak, the woman from a local AIDS clinic, the man from a local counseling center. The professor has fallen silent, glowering in the middle of the group. Gil and I scribble a note to one another: "We can always pull the plug if no buy-in." This idea begins to have substantial primitive appeal as the debate rages on all around us.

It is only the day after that we learn fully what has gone on. Regrettably some assembled thought that this effort was sponsored by the Clinton Foundation. Word spread along with fantasies of large sums of foundation money to be disbursed. Water projects could be funded, roads repaired, dispensaries built. Bonanza! The truth of course is that we have only a shoestring budget for things like food and flip charts. Why would the Clinton Foundation be so cheap as to only focus on AIDS when all of these other issues are so pressing? No one here understands that I have not one shilling of Foundation funding to disburse.

Remarkably the meeting ended in consensus, a truce really, that the project should move ahead. William, followed by Dr. Masawi, gave a last-ditch pitch that kind of went like this: Susie and Gil came to Nshupu and offered this Fast Track to us as a resource. Susie is a PhD and has a lot of experience in Africa. Maybe we can tackle water projects or roads someday. There is no budget for these items today. Right now this is a pro bono offer and this is an important issue, so let's do it.

So, net net, we got an okay. Not quite in an ideal fashion. Now we have to yield results.

The Nshupu Fast Track meeting

After our lukewarm endorsement we must galvanize to attend to a myriad of details. Here Gil and I must play all the roles: mentors, trainers, sponsors, and gofers.

In most Fast Tracks it takes four to six weeks to put all of this together. But our other efforts didn't include William Modest, a man on a mission. He has never done this before, but he is determined to make it work as we are suddenly under enormous scrutiny. The overall HIV prevalence rate in Tanzania at this point is about 12.6 percent. William knows intuitively that it is much higher in Nshupu. For example, condom use is almost unheard of, and those few condoms get reused. Too many people in the village have already died from AIDS.

Remarkably, two weeks after our meeting with the village elders we are ready to go. A hotel in Usa River has offered us the use of their covered back patio, we rent one hundred plastic Coca-Cola chairs, and set up the flip charts. Sarah Modest organizes a bevy of women to cook for the gathering. The prospect of a hot meal rouses participation like nothing else. This I know from many other African events.

The meeting begins as all these gatherings do, with a long-winded prayer. I too am praying to any and all gods that we can pull this off. Dr. Masawi welcomes the participants, and our ambitious goals are delineated. Within ninety days, the teams are challenged to bring AIDS education to over five hundred people and to enlist three hundred into testing.

The teams work with great energy and enthusiasm to draft a plan for recruiting and for building awareness. One of the most innovative solutions proposed is the use of football (soccer) heroes as role models.

Football heroes urge HIV testing

I have never been much of a sports fan, much to Gil's dismay. I just didn't get that gene, the part that has me able to concentrate on arcane rules and get wildly jubilant when a group of guys gets a ball from one end of a space to another. But today's game is different. It is the final playoff game in a series brought to fruition as part of the Fast Track plan. A local HIV/AIDS clinic was persuaded to bring nurses and a mobile testing unit to the big playoff. All the participating team members agreed to be tested, and they in turn urged their peers to do the same, publicly! By the end of this football final, 481 people have had HIV testing, and forty have tested positive. Now those forty will be referred to extensive free care. To ensure that those forty get into treatment, they are visited door-to-door (at home) by a Fast Track team of volunteers and one of the nurses from the Care and Treatment Center (CTC). We know that 50 percent of Tanzanians who get into HIV treatment stop actively participating for a number of reasons and are lost to follow-up, but that won't happen here. Peer pressure and support will see to that. What our small team has set in motion is truly extraordinary, and this football final is no typical local game.

The game starts late, of course. First the fans arrive packed into cars and trucks with ten and twelve people whooping and sounding their plastic horns. They then proceed to do donuts in the middle of the dust bowl that is the football field, spewing up huge clouds of dirt. Finally the teams arrive. Handsome in their brightly colored uniforms of red and blue, they are tall, slim, and very agile as they do their warm-ups. The mobile clinic has been set up, and the players make a show of going inside to be tested.

The nurses and the doctors from the CTC pose for pictures with the players. Opening speeches by visiting dignitaries stress the importance of HIV testing and treatment. It is a classic case of bringing the care to the people rather than expecting them to go to the treatment. It has worked magnificently in Swaziland and it's working here too. I am so proud of our facilitators and of the results they've achieved with the community teams.

By the time the match begins an hour later, some four hundred people are watching the game and all the goings-on. The game itself is aggressive, physical, and hugely athletic. The dirt field is unleveled and full of potholes, just to make things more challenging. At times the dust is so thick you can't see the ball or some of the players.

By the conclusion of the game an even higher echelon of government officials is in attendance. When we began this effort, the support was reluctant and sparse. Now it is being covered by national TV and three local radio stations! The best part of all of this is that these ideas are not from white folks. They have been wholly generated by the grassroots teams.

Next will be the choir competition, an even more idiosyncratically unique phenomenon in Africa. Church on Sunday in Tanzania is almost an all-day affair. Simultaneously serving the purposes of community building, support, and celebration, the services are a chance to dress up, dance, sing, and have an exuberant party without benefit of food or alcohol. Choirs in Africa don't just sing. Elaborate choreography accompanies every musical piece, and huge amplifiers crank out backup music. It is an honor to be a member of a choir, and there is an informal kind of competition between them as to which ones get the best soloists.

Our Fast Track teams are taking advantage of this and will use a choir competition to increase awareness and uptake into HIV testing and treatment. Each choir group that competes will be asked to compose and perform a special musical number that encourages healthy self-care and HIV testing. The relevant pastors don't need extensive persuasion, as they have seen so many of their congregants die from the disease.

KINDERGARTEN UNIFORMS

While working on Fast Track activities, we are also seeing to the newly expanded kindergarten at Precious Orphanage. Now thirty children from the poorest families come every day from 7:30 to noon while the older kids are in school. We hike up to take photographs and see the class in action. We pass some children clearly unable to attend primary school. Schooling in Tanzania is technically free, but children must be able to come to school wearing shoes and uniforms. They must bring their own water, pay a security fee, and provide their own desks. The desk fees persist year over year, long past the actual need for the furniture. But the fees exist still, and someone at the school pockets the forty dollars per child.

So the haves are distinguished from the have-nots in this very clear way, a uniform or not. One young boy of seven or eight walks the path in front of us carrying a load of grass easily twice his size on top of his head. In five months, the lot of people on this hillside looks to be largely unchanged. Their small subsistence yards look as sparse and unyielding as ever, though this is springtime and there should be rain for planting. John, the ancient gardener next door, says he prays to God every day for rain with as yet no response. He might do better to pray to the developed world to care more deeply about climate change.

From a distance we can hear the singing and clapping in the classroom. It is loud, rhythmic, and joyous, as though the walls themselves are pulsating. We poke our heads inside and see thirty very small children standing near their desks singing in English and clapping. "I am clapping, I am clapping. I am laughing, I am laughing. Look at me. Look at me!"

The room was once a grim, gray, concrete room with a dirt floor and nothing but a blanket and an antique chalkboard. Now with plaster, paint, desks, and wall hangings, the room starts to resemble a schoolroom. The children do a few more rounds of singing in English, the days of the week, the parts of the body, the numbers. We pick up our cameras and start to film. One young boy in the front row looks at us. He is wide-eyed, terrified, and soon dissolves, sobbing loudly. He has probably never seen white people before, certainly never this close, and surely he has never been photographed. Chagrined, we put down our cameras, he is comforted by his teacher, and Gil starts a little high-five game with him. Soon he begins to laugh, smile, and initiate the game himself.

Next we have been asked to present each child with his or her brand-new school uniform. The uniforms have been created on a shoestring with inexpensive material and the donated services of a local seamstress. The girls have red-checked dresses with red Peter Pan collars. The boys have red shorts and tiny button-up red-checked shirts with red collars and a placket over a small pocket. Each child is called by name and is presented with what is no doubt the nicest piece of clothing they own. They light up, run out the door, and get some help changing into their new uniforms in the kids' dorm next door. They assemble outside in the bright sun and resume their group singing and clapping. It was at the insistence of the government regulators that these uniforms be provided. No child in Tanzania is permitted to go to school without a uniform. We were rather more preoccupied with getting them

some predictable food, and clearly we will have to figure out
how to make that happen.

THANKSGIVING GENEROSITY

November in Tanzania is springtime in full flower as we are
just below the equator. The jacaranda trees are huge in their
purple profusion, the weather is mild, and the birdlife is
more vocal and more numerous than ever. We have missed
New England's fall colors, but we know that as Thanksgiving
approaches, our yard at home will be a sodden mess of brown
leaves. Our emails begin to fill with anticipatory avalanches of
Thanksgiving ads, recipes for pumpkin pie, and previews for
early Christmas shopping. At home the commercialization of
this excess is already too much. Here it is particularly jarring.
But it gives us a brainstorm.

What if we capitalize on this dissonance and can share
it with our friends and donors? We all know that we eat too
much, have too much, buy too much in this season. What if
we did a Thanksgiving appeal to see if we can get donors to
sign up for what we will call a "Breakfast Club"? With some
predictable funds earmarked for food, we can give all the kindergarten children a high-protein porridge.

I send an email to a huge list citing our small-scale food
crisis and asking for support. The appeal does it. Within four
hours we have four months spoken for, and within eighteen
hours we have pledges from twenty-two people. The speed of
their response seems almost miraculous, proof for William,
who says, "God is working through us." We notice too that it is
the same donors who come back each time. They have a connection with us now, and they dig deep. It is not the wealthiest
people on our list who sign up so quickly. It is people who live
well but modestly. I can't wait to send them photographs of

kids with porridge in hand. We are jubilant, and every time we get a new batch of pledges I call William to crow about it. His response is always the same. He whoops with laughter and delight.

After the pledges are all in, William announces to the kids that they will be having porridge every morning. They clap wildly. Gil and I feel like heroes. This lasts for a few weeks, then the yo-yo of existence in Africa catches up with us.

CHAPTER TWELVE

Heartaches and Resilience

FIRE AT PRECIOUS

It is May of 2013 and we have returned from Africa just one month ago. Each morning I log on, eager for news of William, Sarah, and the kids. And today I open my mail to this heart-stopping news:

> Hi susie,
> Today fire broatke out at precious at arround 11 am.it was in the boys dometry. we are lucky no any child got burnt but many things like 2 beds plus 4 matresses,sheets,blankets,home clothes,schoolshoes,home shoes,-school bags.
> These is only for the boys room. Fire was put down using fire extinguishers by us and our neighbors.

Sarah was in the class with the teacher and
the mamas were in the kitchen cooking for
sure it is a big loss at the orphanage.
      fire was caused by baraka who was play-
ing in the room a match box after the mattress
cought fire plus a mosquito net the boy ran out
to call the mamas and sarah but it was too late
to put it off.
      I will still get you informed
      william

Many Skype calls later, we confirm no children were hurt but
Baraka lit the fire deliberately. He told Nickson and Innocent
that night that he wanted a break from school. He offered them
some matches but, terrified, they refused, and they hoped he
had given up the idea. But just before dawn Baraka lit the mosquito netting, and fire spread fast after that. Tanzania has no
fire-retardant bedding. It is a miracle that no children were
killed or injured.

      We are scared and sobered now. Baraka, the oldest boy,
has always baffled us. In virtually every group photograph we
take he is in the back row glowering. Mostly we don't notice as
the rest of the kids are so ebullient and animated. But there he
is, this enigmatic presence. Baraka came to the orphanage at
the age of eight and is nine now. His single mother abandoned
him as an infant before she later died of AIDS. William offers
Baraka additional responsibilities as the oldest boy. He is the
one who handles the offering money for Sunday school and
organizes the little kids for meals, for prayers, for photographs.
He is praised for these duties and beams when he is acknowledged. My favorite photograph is one of him grinning, gently
holding an egg from our chicken coop.

      William tells us he has managed to avert a court case
because there were no injuries, thus preventing Baraka from

being remanded to a juvenile facility. Here in the US these facilities are beyond grim. We can only imagine what they must be like in Tanzania.

All of us are chastened by this close call. We have a fundraiser next week. Thinking we had the nine kids "squared away" we are sprinting to do more for more kids and to plan a model farm and new home. The truth is that we have no idea how the children will fare as they cruise into adolescence, what scars they bear from their early losses and neglect. We keep our fears to ourselves as we prepare our upbeat pitch for more donor money.

HOUSEHOLD HASSLES AND CONCERN FOR JOSEPH

Our return trip four months later has more challenges in store. Our water tap functions only every other day, frequent electrical outages persist, and we have endless problems with a car that has been reincarnated from stray parts. Sometimes I am sanguine about these various issues, knowing that these are, relatively speaking, problems of abundance. I tell my friends that Africa is a cure for whining. But today I feel like whining.

The weather has begun to change markedly, with fewer blue skies and huge thunderstorms that take out power and internet and rattle the house. Gil took the car into Arusha to shop and, when an unexpected downpour materialized, found that the windshield wipers don't work. After his second stop he put the key in the ignition and it broke off. Fortunately Harold, the accountant for the lodge, had a brother in the vicinity who was able to get a new key made. Then Gil tried to get home and ran into standstill traffic jams. A simple trip to the grocery store had become a day-long epic. Exhausting.

And on the home front, we have worrisome discoveries about the health, well-being, and judgment of our handyman Joseph. We have already had countless difficult discussions with him about going AWOL and not doing the work that was agreed to. Because these were stern talks, we decided not to muddy the waters and ask about his health. But yesterday he had to go to the hospital fearing that he had malaria. He is not taking his HIV medicine, and more importantly he is not obtaining the necessary nutrition to keep him from wasting away. I asked William to look into it and found that there is absolutely no food left in his house. As is the African custom, he must share what he has, and so his already scanty food has been shared with a steady stream of visiting Maasai friends. Then too his mother is far away and in poor health.

I give him some of our food stash, but this cannot be a weekly occurrence. He seems to be using his salary to pay off a bunch of loans and has nothing left for food. At the same time, he is refusing to go to the CTC, where they provide HIV patients with free medication and a monthly allocation of cooking oil, rice, and maize. Perhaps he is too proud, but right in front of our eyes he is wasting away. This is painful to see. Short-term handouts of food or money will not stand him in good stead over the long haul. This illustrates the statistic that 50 percent of Tanzanians on antiretroviral medicine are lost to follow-up. I have spent almost a decade working on this issue of HIV testing and treatment adherence. And here's a small cameo right under our noses of why this is so difficult.

Finally we get Joseph to agree to go to the CTC. He was to have gone for an 8:00 a.m. appointment but lingers around here until at least 9:00 a.m. and then rides his motorcycle right in front of the police wearing no helmet. The police confiscate his bike, and instead of going to the CTC center next door, he walked all the way home dejected. I give him money and send him back down the hill to go to the CTC and that was at noon. It is five o'clock now, and there is no sign of him.

Even with in-depth conversations, we don't know what Joseph is really thinking. What we do know is that he cannot seem to make good decisions regarding his own health or show up reliably for this job even when he knows it's on the line. Maybe there's some Maasai pride and tradition that we are trampling on. I'm afraid that this young man we really care for will lose his job. And with no job, no money, no food, and no family support of any kind, how will he live?

Ironically, while we cannot get the young man in our employ to go for treatment, the AIDS prevention work we have started with our local Fast Track seems to be going extremely well. The volunteer teams are energized with their recent successes, and many more locals are coming to the CTC for testing and treatment. Donors too are excited to hear progress and sign up to do more.

SAFARI WITH THE KIDS

Generous visitors and sponsors are eager to pull off a fun outing for the kids. Very few Africans ever see the abundance of wildlife that draws visitors from all over the world. It is simply beyond their means to get a vehicle, gas it up, travel that far, and afford even the very reduced park fees offered to Tanzanian nationals.

It 8:00 a.m. and we are waiting near the road to meet up with the minibus and the kids. Suddenly we see the kids come tearing across the field. They are wearing their new giraffe T-shirts and their very best Sunday school skirts, pants, and pink polka-dot socks. They are running, grinning, waving, vibrating with excitement. We pose them for photographs in front of the minibus and then pile in. The kids are wide-eyed and fascinated with everything they see out the window: zany traffic, huge open-air markets, and all the chaos of commerce in the city. As we leave Arusha and begin the long drive toward the park, the landscape becomes empty but for scattered Maasai *bomas*, herds of cattle, and, of course, the Maasai men and boys who tend them, draped in red or blue blankets.

Bahati and Tumaini are especially alert. They are Maasai by birth and this landscape is deeply familiar. Both of their parents are dead, and the girls were left with no one to care for them. Their destiny was stamped by tradition now centuries old. The elders in the Maasai tribe would have ordered female "circumcision" before selling them into polygamous marriages for a goodly number of cows. Girls are a valuable commodity in these tribes. One who is bright or pretty may fetch twenty or thirty cows, and cows are the key to all wealth and status for Maasai. When Bahati and Tumaini arrived at the orphanage, they could only speak Maa. Now two years later they speak fluent Swahili and have a beginning foundation in English. But when they left their birthplace, the girls were five and six years old, certainly old enough to remember shards of what they left behind. Both stare out the windows, intensely focused, pointing out each new tribal encampment and waving intensely at the Maasai children whose parents send them to the edge of the tarmac to beg for handouts. Our Swahili will never be good enough to find out what the girls feel now, and what is happening to them may even be beyond simple words anyhow.

Only minutes beyond the park entrance, we begin spotting animals: elephants, warthogs, giraffes, ostriches, baboons, waterbuck, gazelles, and in a remarkable stroke of luck, a female lion posing atop a large rock as though waiting to be photographed. Each new discovery is greeted with hoots of delight. The children clamber over one another to get to the windows, eyes wide, at last seeing animals from their world of picture books and classroom posters.

At 1:00 we stop at the park's designated picnic spot and bring our box lunches to a table under a tree. This particular picnic spot is infamous for its vervet monkeys, who will snatch a sandwich right out of your hand, and if thwarted, run up the tree over your picnic table and pee on you. These monkeys are small and unremarkable but for their fluorescent turquoise testicles. The picnic area is already alive with monkey antics, tourists photographing them, and clueless others feeding them and encouraging their misbehavior. But our kids have been handed the biggest lunch they have ever seen, and they are way more interested in this abundance of food than in the monkeys. So the adults try to keep the furry bandits at bay while the kids eat. Our kids are oblivious, focused on the largesse of their lunch. Each lunch contains a juice box, a large piece of fried chicken, a samosa, a meat pie, a doughnut, a crepe, and a package of shortbread cookies. We adults can barely make a dent in our lunches but the kids eat theirs as though there will never be another one. Undeterred by monkey antics, the kids wolf down their lunches with quiet concentration, then run back to the bus grinning and clutching their packages of shortbread cookies.

The afternoon unfolds with more wondrous animal sightings, big skies with distant thunderheads, huge baobab trees, their bark stripped by elephants, and many more antelope and giraffes. After all the excitement, we head home through an enormous thundershower. Drivers in Tanzania go at top speed, whether on a remote desert road or a packed city street. Our driver is no exception. After we go through two small villages at 50 miles an hour on slick roads while he leans on the horn, in a quiet shriek I hope others cannot hear, I call out, *"Pole, pole, tafadahle"* (Slowly, slowly, please). To my relief, the bus slows and my heart goes from my throat back to its usual place.

As the kids start to droop, the old camp counselor skills come into play for us American grown-ups. So we teach them our ancient summer-camp songs: "Make new friends but keep the old; one is silver and the other gold." "If you're happy and you know it, clap your hands." The kids are quick studies, and pretty soon the bus is rocking with songs and clapping. We have been so close all day, on laps, arms around small bodies, holding hands, making silly faces, playing peekaboo between the seats; the simple pleasures that connect adults and kids everywhere in the world. As we round the bend in Usa River and move from the tarmac up our impossibly rutted dirt road, three quarters of the kids are asleep. William too.

HOME

The safari was wonderful but the fire at Precious and its aftermath has dented our wild optimism. There are more challenges in the offing.

One morning a few weeks after the safari outing, I awoke to a very long string of alarmed emails from my siblings. My dad has been experiencing dizzy spells so severe that he does not feel safe walking. They write too that there was some discussion of last wishes and memorial plans, but perhaps he now has once again walked away from that precipice. It is certainly hard to tell from this distance. I know we will lose him this year. It would be no easier being closer to ground zero, but hearing this news from this distance makes me unbearably sad.

I worship my dad and have spent my life trying to live up to his largely unspoken expectations of me, that I live a life of simplicity, sacrifice, and service. The simplicity I never manage.

He lives in a Maine house with no dishwasher and heated with wood. I like my appliances and central heat. The houses that I live in he thinks are too big, too grand. But this work in Africa does give me points for sacrifice and service. I am not living in a mud hut, but living here has its challenges, and we are here for the sole purpose of being of service. Dad has never been lavish with praise, but his recent birthday card I savor and post on my bulletin board. In handwriting now crabbed and shrunken from Parkinson's, he scribbled, "I so respect you for your work in Africa." This is enough to lift my spirits for days, this midlife affirmation. This work in Africa has brought me back to my roots as a social worker. And this time, my dad understands.

I am not really ready to go back to the cold, to the endless Christmas catalogs and commercial frenzy, to the ever-escalating bills for Zack's long-ago bike accident, and to whatever other unpleasant surprises await us in the tower of mail. For better for worse, life is much simpler here. The basics take a lot of planning and organizing, there is no possible overload from the internet, and there is no TV, no football games or media drumbeat about the Republican backlash to the Obama election. Head in sand has been a good place to be. Instead of TV, we have our nightly bush baby viewings.

Here in Nshupu the dirt path below the house is lavender with blossoms. The flame trees too are blooming, and when the red flowers drop from the trees, before they are flattened by foot traffic, each blossom looks like a perfect red orchid. And we are still beset with the usual hassles. This morning Gil had a flat tire. The toilet continues to leak inexplicably. And just a few days ago the firebox at the back of the house exploded, and Joseph had to hose it down. So much for hot water. We have enjoyed electricity, internet access, and running water, though rarely all in the same day. This is frustrating but it is business as usual, and we are here to make stuff happen.

The next dream is bigger and bolder now for Precious: That we leave the rented site, buy land, and build. Build a large and comfortable home for William, his family, and all the orphans. Build a primary school. Have livestock. Plant a garden. A big vision that has taken hold now that we have all nine children so well provided for. The money needed to pull off something like this is far beyond what we have managed to obtain thus far. Amazingly, two close friends offer $15,000 toward the purchase of the land, others match it, and so now William can move ahead to look for it. He is ebullient, we're mildly terrified, and now we open a new chapter.

HOME FOR THE HOLIDAYS

We arrived home in the midst of an early snowstorm, the heat was off in the house, and both of us were very sick with shigella, a type of dysentery that comes with high fever and severe diarrhea. So even as we are home, we are relegated to the house until the Cipro kicks in. I am in my flannel pajamas night and day.

But at least the two of us suffer together and together experience the crash-landing that is each return from Africa. Though certainly I am grateful to see my friends, it is as though each time we come home, a vital sense of purpose seems to leach out from within me, leaving me adrift and dispirited.

We will spend this hiatus seeing family, getting our teeth cleaned, eating a lot of rich dinners with a few close friends, then we will pack up and go back to Africa again before I can sort out what it is I am meant to do when I am home. Clearly there is a certain amount of administrative follow-up to be done to keep the fund-raising machine going and to sort out our own affairs here. In the meantime, I overeat, overshop, and overthink.

The email news from Precious is that thieves have cut the fencing at the orphanage to try to steal food stashes. Apparently the rates of theft and burglary are much higher near the Christmas holidays. Families too poor to feed themselves decide to even the score from other, unsuspecting households. Fortunately the food stores were under lock and key. It is pointless to call the police, as they will not investigate without a bribe.

The US is a hard place to be now. Twenty children in Newtown, Connecticut, were murdered by a guy with a gun, and the NRA is saying it wouldn't have happened had more good guys been carrying guns. The debate is beyond bizarre, and we are saturated with media coverage. But who knows? If the robbers at the orphanage had guns, then Precious would have definitely given up its food stores, a horrific scene to imagine. This point-counterpoint comparison suffuses all of our days at home. We are now beyond idealizing Africa. We have seen enough corruption, theft, and petty malice in our small village. We are no longer visitors. We have kids to feed and care for, and we are in it for the long haul. For we now have pledges of enough money to go ahead and buy land for a new home, an exciting and terrifying prospect.

THE LAND SCAM

Four months later we have put together the funds. William wastes no time and finds a beautiful two-acre piece of land for a new orphanage that is down the hill from our rented site and faces east toward Mount Kilimanjaro. We know this land, and it is exquisite by any measure, but the price is $30,000. This must surely be the white-people's price. William says we won't be able to do better. He wants to set the deal in motion and we reluctantly concur.

In rural Tanzania, land transactions don't involve banks and mortgages. It works like this: Only age peers can approach one another with an offer to buy land. Since this land is being sold by an elder, an elder must make the approach, in this case William's father-in-law, Gerald. So Gerald conducts the negotiations on William's behalf, and once a price is agreed to, the village chairman convenes the land committee. Their job is to interview all of the abutters to make sure there are no objections to the sale. Furthermore, they must pace out the property, as surveyors are not hired and land boundaries are ancient and approximate.

If the property is in excess of the quoted two acres, then the property will be sold at the original quoted price. If the property is less than the quoted two acres, then the seller has to lower the price. Furthermore, all of the family members of the seller need to be assembled to agree in person to the sale of the property. All of this, we are told, has taken place. The seller mama is paid the princely sum of $30,000, and the land is ours, or so we think. The sale is duly executed and recorded and workmen begin digging posts for a fence. A man appears, waving his fist and shouting. "What are you doing on my land?" he bellows. "This land is mine!"

Apparently there is one son who did not show up in front of the land committee, saying that he was ill. He had already sold the land without telling his mother, we learn. Impossibly, the land has been sold twice. William, chagrined, tells us in a Skype call that the land we are busy fund-raising to build on is no longer ours. We are flabbergasted. On the eve of our next big fund-raiser, we look like fools. Gil is furious. I am sick at heart and wondering how this will unfold. But another two and a quarter acres is located, and William writes that this new parcel of land is far superior to the first one. It abuts a large old-growth forest that can never be built on, and better still, it is next to a mountain spring with potable fresh water.

The property is lined with fruit trees, something which did not characterize our previous parcel. The only zinger, and there always is one, is that we must fork over even more money for this new piece of property. Soon the prodigal son returns his ill-gotten gains to his mother and we are reimbursed. And still I marvel, Are we complete dupes? This is one of those experiences where we feel our otherness so acutely. It is not the stuff of cheery newsletters home. It is the downside of the roller coaster and a bitter pill indeed. William is ebullient. But the new plot is very steep, and an engineer at the lodge pronounces our rudimentary building sketches unworkable. We cannot hang onto our worries and our outrage long. There is simply too much to do, and we need to be in Tanzania to do it. We are in the US in a white catacomb of snow, chafing to return.

Five more days before we head back to Tanzania. The winter landscape here in Lincoln is crisp, white, stark, and lovely. Day after day of blue skies and winter light that tinges the bare trees pale pink in the early morning. I am glad for this glimpse of snow and for the sunlight that pours into the house at midday. Mostly I am glad to be leaving again, as winter here is unending. We have all but put away the Christmas decorations. Zack has returned to college. I dream every night of Africa, the kids at Precious, the heat, the color, and the work. Although we have made it a point to connect with friends and family, I feel oddly invisible here now. Our two months at home has been filled with unpacking, sorting, and then repacking and sorting. We have never really been here, in some fundamental way.

As I get the inevitable predeparture anxiety, it feels as though I am continually trading one malaise for another. First there is the malaise of reentry, coming home to Black Friday and children gunned down in elementary school. Now there is the malaise of leaving. I know Zack would like to have us here. He is flooded with anxiety about his final senior term project and trying to craft an independent life for himself on the other end of college. I worry I am not being the supportive parent that he needs.

And then there is my dear father. He is eighty-seven now and seems to have come to some truce with his horrifically declining physical condition. He tells me that it takes five minutes for him to put on one sock. What a crushing lesson in humility for my Green Beret dad. I pray for my sake that he will be here when I return, and I pray for his sake that when he chooses to exit he can do so as peaceably as possible.

I seem to be continually trying to solidify some predictable plan for my life at this stage. I want to have it all, roots, the warm embrace of longtime friends, and wild adventures perched on the edge. I settle for this oscillation between safety and predictability, never quite settling into either reality, this restlessness long stamped into the family DNA.

WHAT JUST HAPPENED?

Once back in Tanzania we must pick up the pieces, figure out what happened with the land scam, salve our bruised egos, and get the ball rolling. Eventually we must make peace with what we will never know. People in this village are descendants of tribes that are centuries old. Our arrival here and inevitable departure will be a mere blip on the page.

Things are in full bloom here now. The enormous yellow flowers Joseph planted continue to produce blossoms year-round. The jacaranda trees that were lavender when we were here in November are now fully leafed out. The guava tree just to the edge of the veranda has now generated hundreds of white blossoms. The lemon trees are producing again. And the casual planting of some lemongrass and ginger has yielded quite substantial plants. Our compost bin is cooking nicely, and soon we will produce beans and arugula. Too, the bush babies are back. It took only one night for them to realize that the gravy train had returned. So we will resume our evening bush-baby-watching detail. We sit by candlelight on the veranda, waiting for their arrival as dusk turns to dark. First you can hear them leaping from tree to tree, and then these small primates come right up to the edge of the veranda to feast on banana slices we have put out. As they stare into the beam of our flashlight, their eyes are an unearthly orange-red. It is our substitute for TV, media, and news, and it is endlessly fascinating.

But our nightly entertainment has its price. In the middle our first night back, we are awakened bolt upright by a crash on the roof. In our jet-lagged disorientation, we have no idea what has caused the noise, and at the same time we know that Darsch is on the case and that we are safe. It is only after we wake up in the morning that we learn it was an avocado. We have three avocado trees, and they are dropping fruit quite regularly. It is our bush babies who eat the collar of each fruit so it will drop to the ground. Troublemakers!

After a wakeful night, we are up with the sun and unpacking our hundred pounds of gear, clothing for the kids, the mamas, and Joseph. Included in our luggage was Gil's Christmas gift to me, a small set of speakers that would allow us to have music in the house via our iPhones. I plug in the device, and soon the house is reverberating with American rock 'n' roll. Joseph is drawn by the music and runs into the house barefoot and grinning. And in a split second we are dancing and laughing, hands held high, spinning and moving to the music. Joseph does some amazing footwork, and we laugh some more. It is 8:00 a.m. and I am woozy with jet lag and the alchemy of surprise, connection, and delight that happens here.

Our delight extends to the post-Christmas reunion with the children. We hike up to the home with duffel bags filled with clothes, jump ropes, footballs, underwear, and socks. The underpants are quintessentially American, dense with images of Star Wars, superheroes, cars and trucks, flowers and fairies. We hand them out one by one to shrieks of delight. The kids have no guile, no embarrassment. They are simply thrilled to receive whatever it is we bring. Their English is starting to bud, and our Swahili is incrementally better, so there is more chance for conversation. But always there is the sheer tactile pleasure of kids in laps, sandwiched between us on the bench, small brown fingers stroking my hair, Gil's furry forearms, and the stubble on his bald head.

BUILDING THE NEW HOME

At last we are ready to start construction on the new orphanage and school. Building here bears slim resemblance to a construction project in the US. First we must create a written contract, with no precedent here. We have no architectural renderings, simply a crude crayon rendition of a box on a hill surrounded by small green blobs to represent trees, a child's image of what the home will look like, missing only a bright yellow orb of sun. Our contractor, Obede, is a small handsome man who has built other schools and homes. Having a written contract is a new concept for him, but as we write it, he realizes there are some built-in protections for him as well.

Once the contract is typed up, we take it to the attorney general's office, where a lawyer makes it official. When we ask for a receipt, however, she demurs. If you want a receipt, she says, it will cost you three times as much. It dawns on us that she will pocket the money herself right under the nose of the attorney general. We have brought only the requisite cash and, dumbfounded, we hand it over, realizing that we too now are complicit in corruption. But we have a contract in hand, and within days Obede has hired local workers to get busy clearing the steep hillside.

A motley crew of guys in flip-flops shows up every morning at 7:00 sharp. The entire project happens without benefit of a single power tool. Huge rocks are dug and moved by hand, homemade bricks are fired in village backyards, and a crew of eight women carries five-gallon buckets of water up the hill on their heads all day long for five cents a bucket. During their breaks they sit in the dirt on the steep hillside, braiding one another's hair, laughing, and telling stories. They are very happy to have this work and grin for us when we take their photographs. Six days a week the steep hillside is a beehive of activity. Cell phones play reggae music and guys in dreadlocks boogie as they work, a sweet hint of marijuana wafting over the site. The atmosphere is upbeat, exuberant. Many told us that building on this grade would not be possible. But here we are beating the odds and doing it at breakneck speed.

But it's not all hard work and fun. William must accompany Obede to purchase and count every last nail and bag of cement. A night guard patrols the fenced site so that building materials don't disappear. We are on a tight budget with donor money so we are grateful for vigilance we would not have been savvy enough to install. There are also inevitable only-in-Africa type challenges. Somehow a septic tank was omitted in the price tag and plans! So too the wiring for electricity. But William's God provides, and a donor steps forward to offer enough funds for the overrun, the drilling of a well, and ultimately the electrification of the entire property! We watch, incredulous, as this huge and beautiful home with its bright-blue roof is completed in six months. Kids dance in the empty rooms, their laughter echoing. We have enough space now to take on six new children.

Dedication of the new home

I started to dread the opening ceremony for the new home. I figured that it would start hours late, there would be endless stultifying speeches, it would either rain or be blazing hot, and basically be an all-around tedious affair. Finally the day arrives. It is three o'clock in the afternoon, and because we cannot help but be on time, we are the first guests to arrive. About two hundred plastic chairs have been planted in rows under three beat-up blue tarps. An enormous buffet table has been set up, and a bevy of women have been cooking on-site all day. I am wearing lipstick, my best *kitenge* dress, and my clunky rubber Tevas. Gil is wearing his snazzy Hawaiian shirt from Costco, but he has shaved for the event and is looking very dapper.

Just after we pull up in our dung-brown Range Rover, a big taxi delivers the three pastors from William's Pentecostal church. They are all seriously dressed up, and Mama Abigail is exuding palpable delight. Her support both spiritual and practical has buoyed William and Sarah from the early days when they had no idea where the next meal was coming from. She has from the very outset told them that God would provide, and she is deeply happy to see her predictions come true.

As we greet them, Gil and I are thrilled to see the Precious logo on the right-hand side of the gate. And then, stunned, we find a quote on the other: "Never doubt that a small group of committed people can change the world. For indeed it is the only thing that ever has." The words of my hero, Margaret Mead, borrowed by William unbeknownst to me to represent all our hard work.

Guests begin arriving. There is a fancy car full of the big shots, the village chairman, the ward councilor, and other men traveling in the wake of the most senior person, Mr. Kishongo. Kishongo speaks good English and he begins politely grilling me. How many children will we house? Where are we getting our water? Are we using rainwater collection? What else is in our plans? His questions are penetrating and his interest seems genuine. In his speech perhaps he will claim this project as his own.

Over a hundred men and women flood the gates all at once and promptly seat themselves in the plastic chairs under the tarp. The women are dressed in their Sunday best, bright ruffled long dresses and headdresses. You show respect at church, at funerals, and at events like this by turning yourself out like a wild and exotic bird. I feel personally honored with the effort that everyone has taken to dress up and walk so far. But this event is the biggest deal in town today. And there will be food, lots of it!

Agnes, our kindergarten teacher, is a stunning woman any day in a T-shirt. In her gold-and-green ruffled long dress with a gold choker, she is gorgeous. Margrethe, our live-in mama who works tirelessly doing laundry and cooking, has dressed in her best too. Margrethe has terrible fluorosis, which has turned her front teeth a dull brown. So when she smiles she hangs her head to hide her teeth. Today she is equally shy, but her dress is fabulous. It is cobalt blue and gold, hugs her fanny, and flares out in layers of bows and ruffles. She is also wearing a wig. I barely recognize her at first.

Tanzanians from the Kilimanjaro Film Institute are there putting together a film about this event, and so they hold all the children in abeyance on the other side of the gate so that they can be filmed coming in as a group. I see them there being gently herded by their teachers. Our orphanage kids seem to tower above the kindergartners and the wannabe kindergartners. When the cameras are ready, the gates open, and the kids rush in. Some look solemn and a bit scared. Some come at a dead run. There are easily a hundred kids. Our nine are dressed in their Christmas best. Many others are in their kindergarten red-checked uniforms, likely the nicest piece of clothing they own. Some are in their pajamas. I stand there with the kids running and swirling around my knees and my eyes fill up. There are a few moments like this when I feel absolutely grounded, glad to be in my own skin, and glad to be doing what I am doing. This is one of these moments, fierce and true. I had not expected this, not at all.

The kids settle under the tarps and sit absolutely quiet through lengthy speeches. One such speech is my own, delivered in Swahili. I never expected the response I got, applause after every single line! The audience was clearly thrilled by the effort to address them in Swahili as much as by the predictable content. But each time I look up from my notes, a sea of faces is beaming. Gil too offers a short speech in Swahili and presents William with a surprise brass plaque to honor the memory of his mother. William is visibly moved, stopped in his tracks for a moment.

After all the speeches, the prayers, and a hymn dedicated to us sung in English, we all troop up the hill for the ribbon-cutting. I know the kids are hungry, eyeing the buffet. A huge pink ribbon has been strung across the threshold, and Mr. Kishongo cuts it. The doors are flung open, and people pour into the common room. The women all ululate, their voices loud and joyous. The sound bounces and echoes in the empty room and somehow bestows a blessing on us all. The room is dark, as there is no electricity yet and no furniture. But we have built this beautiful home and we are here together to celebrate.

Early in the day, a cow was slaughtered, and women have been cooking since dawn. There are vats of rice, pilau, meat, bananas, chickpeas, tomatoes, watermelon. There are crates of every conceivable kind of soda. Gil and I and the big shots must serve ourselves first, then the adults, then the kids. I wish it were the other way around but this is the custom. By the time the big shots at our table are picking their teeth with toothpicks, kids are still thirty or forty deep, waiting patiently in line, each small body pressed close to the one just ahead.

A very old Wameru man shows up in the buffet line. His earlobes had been crudely cut open in his youth, and now they drag toward his shoulders. He is wearing large Wellington boots and a suit so ancient, so dirty, it looks like he has been wearing it for decades. On his head is an antique wool hat, and he is followed by his dog, who looks better fed than he does. He fills his plate with a towering pile, takes a Coca-Cola, and seats himself alone at a remove on his plastic chair. Women graciously tend to him, and his plate is filled three times. I think he has not eaten for many moons.

The kids too pile their plates and eat so much their little bellies are distended. But the food energizes them and they begin running and playing. The borrowed amplifier from the church is now cranking out African dance music, and I begin to sway to the sound. It takes no time for me to be joined by a crowd of African women all grinning, laughing, moving fluidly to the rhythm. It is very dusty where we are dancing, and we kick up clouds of dirt. My feet have turned brown as has the hem of my long dress, and I don't care. Soon we are joined by the kids, and they dance with their own singular concentration and abandon.

This is the scene I will never forget: the women in their brightly colored dresses smiling and dancing with me, the small children all moving to the music, the long shadows in the late afternoon light, the simple scene shot through with grace.

We have not raised enough money to furnish the home except with beds. We don't yet have electricity or a predictable source of water. But this home belongs wholly to the kids and the Tanzanian NGO. It sits high on the hill with a stunning view one hundred miles south. This was nothing we ever could have dared dream about, and it has happened. For the time being, we rest on our laurels and breathe in the windfall.

CHAPTER THIRTEEN

Corruption Up Close

LOST TO FOLLOW-UP

As we make progress with Precious, I am still eager to continue the public-health work that was my initial entrée to Africa. In my eagerness to move along, I schedule a meeting with the AIDS Control Office of one of the largest hospitals in Arusha. I make the horrific hour-long journey into the heart of Arusha to continue conversations begun months ago. The staff there have a real interest in a pilot Fast Track to address the issue of the 50 percent of Tanzanians who are lost to follow-up once they start treatment for HIV. If they cannot reverse this trend, their funding from USAID will be at risk.

The meeting was billed as a quiet conversation with two senior staff. When I get there, twelve people are waiting for a formal presentation. This kind of "lost in translation" event happens frequently in Africa. I wing it without my presentation, hoping that the quiet and polite looks are not masking a complete lack of understanding of my English. Remarkably, however, we agree to move ahead with the pilot, and I will return next week to start planning in earnest. I hope we can get results.

I am certainly no public-health expert, but six years working with the Clinton Foundation on AIDS prevention and treatment taught me a bit. The mantra all over the developing world is test and treat, test and treat. This is been the focus of all my efforts in multiple countries. But what often doesn't get discussed is the lost-to-follow-up problem that continues to haunt Tanzanian public health. This is a depressing statistic and one that seems replicated over and over across sub-Saharan Africa. Study after study surfaces the same set of precipitating factors: stigma, lack of food and therefore inability to tolerate the medicine, poverty so great that bus fare to get to a clinic is an impossibility, and always the lure of local herbal remedies.

Here in Nshupu, 40 out of the 481 that we convinced to go for HIV testing came out positive and have begun treatment. What we have learned from our team is that they start off with quite a bit of support from the clinic: counseling, home visits, extra food, and a plethora of information about how important it is to maintain balanced nutrition and stay on the medication. But that support lapses after a month or two, and the difficulties of daily living then set in. ARV patients need 30 percent more nutrition than others, as the virus simply speeds up their metabolism and chews through the food they eat. People who are already living on the edge, not knowing where their next meal is coming from, should suddenly have balanced nutrition? No wonder people drop out when they feel better, when the local herbalists offer an illusory solution, when their families don't support or know about their condition.

A casual review of the literature shows many studies documenting the phenomenon and relatively little on what to do to encourage retention and treatment adherence. The Clinton Foundation found that in Mozambique, groups of six

HIV-positive peers could assist one another by taking turns to make the difficult and expensive trip to get medication refills. Partners in Health set up a program in several countries called the *"accompaneur* arrangement." This entails training lay counselors to understand the disease, and, on a one-on-one basis, support a patient in their village in staying on treatment.

This high rate of lost to follow-up across sub-Saharan Africa fuels my discussions with the AIDS Control Office. These conversations all have a familiar feel. I am invited to give a presentation, and in this setting (remarkably) they tell me they have the set-up to project a PowerPoint slideshow. I arrive early, they arrive late, and it takes four people twenty minutes to screw in the cable to the computer and get ready for my pitch. I have worked to make this presentation quite simple and free of jargon. But I had in mind an audience whose understanding of English was at least basic. Not so. I am speaking with a room of twenty people, many of whom are community volunteers, and their presence means that every single bullet on every single slide must be translated into Swahili.

This takes forever and it is a leap of faith that my translator is hitting the mark. Then during the question and discussion there needs to be ample time for people to speak among themselves without necessarily translating for me. I listen, nodding my head as though I understand a fraction of what is being discussed, when in truth all I have mastered is a few words like *lakini* (but) and *qua sababu* (because) when what I need to understand is what follows the *but* and what precedes the *because*. The discussion unfolds with great heat and animation, and then periodically people remember to translate a bit of what is being said. I'm used to this phenomenon. It is important that anyone who's going to participate in a large-scale effort really buys in.

I have collectively spent hundreds of hours listening to conversations in various African languages that I can only guess the content of from body language. It's not about me. The participants need to bat the ideas back and forth, and I only hope that they have the basic facts with which to do that. This day the conversation is so intense and the sense of urgency so great that we work through the morning and well into the afternoon heat without so much as a glass of water or a bite to eat. I am beginning to feel a bit woozy and finally mention this as politely as possible. We take the conversation down to the hospital cafeteria, pull tables together, and tuck into enormous plates of rice and beans.

I manage to convince the group that we cannot tackle increasing HIV testing uptake, lost to follow-up, and preventing mother-to-child transmission of AIDS all in one intervention. This is a guarantee of failure. Eventually we pare down the challenge we plan to tackle to something that is still ambitious but potentially doable, and we begin to talk about the budget. I had sent an earlier email to the group specifying what the costs would be, but it is only now that reality sets in. This just about stops everyone in their tracks. The fact is that this effort has not been budgeted and may indeed not be affordable. As politely as possible, I decide to let the team do their own laborious calculations of what it costs to buy food, flip charts, markers, and so on. They will wrestle with the funding issue, and I will try to get out of town before rush hour. I am in a posture of surrender, long cultivated through many such meetings in Africa. We will do this intervention this spring while I am here, or perhaps it will need to wait until next fall when I return. Things in Tanzania unfold *pole pole* (pronounced "polay"), slowly slowly.

After the three-month lead-up, the networking meetings, the outreach, the presentations in translation, the two-day training, and an endless stream of preparatory emails repeated many, many times, we are on-site at the AIDS Control Office and ready to roll.

We are ensconced in the building that is the heart of the hospice program for the AIDS Control Office. This extensive hospice program has at any given time almost four thousand patients in treatment, 75 percent of whom are dying from AIDS. The room we are in has high ceilings, big windows, and a view of a manicured and tranquil garden, all this after a dreadful drive uphill through two miles of slums, tin shacks, open sewers, warrens of tiny shops with their dusty wares. But for the sounds of children laughing at the Bible school nearby, we might be anywhere but Arusha in this verdant oasis.

Eventually everyone arrives, the flip charts in Swahili are posted, attendees begin singing hymns a cappella. The sound is warm and sweet and the acoustics lovely in this high-ceilinged room. Our senior sponsor arrives, and at last we kick off the meeting formally with the usual extensive prayers. This being a Lutheran Church hospital handsomely endowed by donors the world around, the religiosity factor is higher than normal. At one point after tea, a participant leaps up with his Bible and gives a lengthy Scripture reading. I roll my eyes covertly with one of our local facilitators who knows that this is costing us precious time. But by midmorning the teams are starting their brainstorming in earnest. Thank heavens that William is here working the crowd with me, as it turns out we are sitting on a powder keg and it takes all of our aggregate experience to manage it.

This Fast Track has been divided into two teams. The first will try to retrieve and reenroll 33 percent or 603 lost to follow-up patients from 2012. Their task is pretty straightforward. It will mean some detective work, some phoning, some door-to-door visits with the power of persuasion. The second team has a more important task. They are looking to prevent lost to follow-up to begin with, and they are to come up with proposals that will reduce it within the next twelve months by a factor of 20 percent. The group is divided again into subgroups; one subgroup is senior medical staff, and the other on-the-ground volunteers. Many of these volunteers are called VACs, voluntary adherence counselors. Most of these VACs are themselves HIV-positive, and it has been their mission to support and give comfort and counseling to patients like themselves. Because of their local knowledge and their open HIV status, they are absolutely wired in to the realities for other ARV patients. They are paid nothing except money for transport to get to their patients.

Still others are HBCs, home-based care volunteers. They visit and care for people too ill and too poor to get to treatment. There are about twenty-five people in this team, a mix of VACs and HBCs, all dressed up in their go-to-church *kitenges* for the occasion. William convenes his team, goes over the problem statement, and the room erupts. "We don't need ninety days," they say, "to get back six hundred and three patients. If you fix some of the problems that cause them to leave to begin with, we guarantee we can get them all back in thirty days!" Then they begin venting all at once, an exorcism of long-held helplessness and outrage.

THE FACTS COME OUT

Here is what they tell us. Although this hospital is the most well-endowed within hundreds of miles and blessed with pristine state-of-the-art facilities and visiting doctors from around the globe, it is rife with corruption and patient abuse. The abuse takes many forms. Volunteers tell of an elderly Muslim woman who was told to remove her head covering. The security guards who determine off-hours access to the hospital routinely turn away African patients on foot, demanding a bribe, but grant instant access to whites, Indians, and people in cars.

At rural and urban clinics, very ill patients stand in line for hours waiting to be treated. The waiting area may house 150 patients and only six chairs. Furthermore, they say that the two most notorious bribe takers are actually in our session. One is in the next room talking about how to retrieve patients lost to follow-up, and one is a very senior nurse just behind an adjacent closed door. There are only two in our meeting today, but the practice is well embedded. If you pay a bribe, then you will see a doctor. If not, you can wait all day in the heat and then go home as sick as when you came. If you are so lucky as to get inside to be seen, you will be treated with disdain and disrespect from the receptionist right on through the hierarchy of the medical team. This is why patients are lost to follow-up. They simply choose to walk away and look for some measure of care and compassion as they struggle with the stigma and the complexities of lifelong ARV treatment.

Suddenly now, this meeting has become much more complex. We had thought we might uncover some poor work processes and some harried indifference to patient suffering, but this discovery is too big to ignore and too loaded to handle in the large plenary session. We wonder how our sponsor will handle this, and we know we cannot spring it on him in front of seventy-five people and hospital senior management tomorrow. We arrange for a private meeting first with him and then with the entire team that has surfaced these issues.

When our senior sponsor arrives early the next morning, we lock ourselves and our small team into a tiny office for private conversation. He is an extremely dark black man, but I can almost see him blanch at what he hears. It is news to him, I can tell. This, in and of itself, is reassuring. He says he wishes to do a proper investigation of the allegations of bribery but that he wants to have the discussions of patient abuse writ large and discussed openly in front of the director of the hospital. He listens intently, takes copious notes, thanks the team for their candor, and when the hospital big shots show up, he quotes from the team's disclosures chapter and verse. I can see in the faces of the team that they feel heard and taken seriously for the first time. The fix for these issues of course does not fit into our ninety-day format. Its roots go deep into Tanzanian culture. Indeed I have heard these stories throughout Africa: medical staff disparaging the dirty clothes of a poor villager, burned-out nurses screaming at women in labor to shut up, on-call doctors who no-show with no message. The list goes on. The discussion of this pervasive patient abuse is lengthy, and you can hear a pin drop in the room of seventy-five people.

The deputy hospital director is there, and he too takes copious notes. The teams present their plans, and after some nickel-and-diming about their sparse budgets, the plans are accepted. What we don't know is whether there is the will and the wherewithal to address these deeper problems. To change a whole organizational culture is a massive undertaking and requires tenacious, focused leadership at all levels.

It seems to my relatively untutored eye that the root cause for this is a combination of gross burnout and overwork, lack of training, and lack of role models. Perhaps too it comes from seeing corruption everywhere, in the police and at all levels of government. Nothing gets done without it. I imagine that inertia will set in after some attempts. I wish I could feel more hopeful. Indeed, coming home after these two days I am spent in a way that I never have been. I feel freighted with sadness. I feel naïve about trying to do anything to begin with. I am glad to get home to my husband, my hot supper, the comfort of knowing that for the most part I will never be treated this way in a medical institution. I may get handled with some amount of bureaucratic indifference, but by the time I am behind closed doors with a doctor I will feel tended to. And if not, I can always choose to go elsewhere, to file a complaint, to make known my right to be treated with care and professionalism. That is what makes my heart heavy this evening.

CHAPTER FOURTEEN

A Season of Loss

LOSING DAD

It is September now in Maine. I have been back from Tanzania for five months and I am ticketed to return in October. Dad has come to the end of his life, the end of the line, the end of his ability to tolerate the indignity of multiple disabilities. He remains as crisp and emotionally present as ever, but if the blanket slips off his body at night while he's sleeping, he doesn't have the strength to pull it back. So now with help from his hospice doctor he can make the choice to exit on his own terms. I am overcome with grief, suffused with flashbacks of my mother's difficult passage and now anticipation of losing Dad.

It is the day after the start of the autumnal equinox, a perfect sparkling September day in Lincoln. I speak with Dad briefly by phone to check in. I tell him I am getting short in my plans for Africa, and he said he too was getting short. He says that he is past being ready to shed his body, that he's not afraid of dying, but he is tired of living now. I try not to weep on the

call, as he was never one for extravagant emotional displays. I
tell him I will miss him. He says that we have our memories
to savor and comfort ourselves. I tell him again I love him. I
am doubled over holding the phone. He tells me again that he
respects and admires the person that I am and the work I'm
doing. In his better days, Dad was never much for long phone
calls. So we keep it short. Later I can wail alone in the house.
Afterward I write him emails telling him the things that I
remember, the things that I would say, the thank-yous that he
should hear while he is alive.

My friends cannot fathom that my father is this close to
death and that I choose nonetheless to go to Africa. This only
increases my isolation and my self-doubt. There is no one right
way to handle this. Daily I waffle about our decision to go even
as we are packing and confirming our flights. Dad does not
want another visit. He is adamant. He is pulling in and retreat-
ing into a space of silence and readiness. Instead, in our last
phone call he urges me to go back to Africa. "Go, go, go," he
said. "Go in peace. Go with God. Live your life."

Not forty-eight hours after Gil and I return to Tanzania,
across the miles and buried among 367 junk-mail messages
comes the subject line "his spirit has separated from his body."
I thought I was ready for this news, but it has come too soon.
Numbly I walk up from the lodge to our house and find William
waiting on the veranda. I tell him and he wraps me in a bear
hug. *"Pole sana,"* he says. While I am going to try to proceed
with the day's planned activities, he demurs and gives us an
explanation of how things happen in Nshupu when someone
important dies.

First of all, schools and businesses in the village are closed
to honor the dead. A small team of village leaders fans out and
gathers condolence contributions from everyone, even those
who can only afford five or ten cents. The money is pooled and
preparations are made for the funeral, which must happen

within three days of the death. If it is a parent who has died, the village buys a bull and it is slaughtered for the funeral feast. Mourners may number in the hundreds and come from great distances. Dishes and utensils, chairs and tables all are found and put to use. The casket is built, young men dig a grave in the family's backyard, and everyone shoulders some of the burden so that the bereaved family does not have to. The burial takes place, then a feast is prepared in a loaves-and-fishes miracle repeated with each death.

William went on to say that although my father's burial would be in the US, it was incumbent upon us to follow local custom in honoring his death. First we stand together holding hands on the veranda while William sends up a prayer in rapid-fire Swahili for the safe passing of my father's spirit. Our activities for the day are postponed, the young man working in the garden is sent home, William closes our kindergarten and keeps the older kids home from school. He is quite firm about these decisions. I am glad for his resolve.

Once William leaves, I am left with no activities to anchor my day. My stomach hurts. I wander from room to room in our small house clutching a wad of tissues then retreat to the bed in a fetal position. I am the eldest. I should be there organizing travel, writing the eulogy, spreading the news. Although Dad urged me to go, I am marooned. What was I thinking? What mistaken views of my own self-importance brought me to Africa, even as I know that the memorial service is a good month away? No amount of preparation for Dad's death cushions the blow of his actual passing.

William asks us to show up two days later at the orphanage but to forestall bringing any gifts for the children, though we had footballs and brand-new clothes we were eager to dispense. The next day we see the children for the first time in months. Just up from naps in the heat, they are all subdued. *"Pole sana,"* they all greet me. "We are so sorry." And then we take part in an extraordinary ritual, the moral equivalent of the condolence offerings. The two mamas and Agnes the kindergarten teacher have pooled their scarce money to buy me a gift, a brightly colored *kanga* cloth emblazoned with a Swahili proverb. In brilliant turquoise and navy blue the material reads *Pole mwenzabu. Yote ya mungu* (I am sorry for you my friend. Give it all up to God). Two of the women wrap me up in this bright bolt of cloth, holding me in their embrace on either side.

The children too have a condolence gift to offer: twenty-four fresh eggs culled from the chicken coop over a period of three days. Shyly I am presented with the eggs in a plastic container, some of them still stuck with feathers. William looks on proudly. He and Sarah are raising the children to give back and to abide by village customs.

Sunday morning I go to William's Pentecostal church. The service generally goes for about three and a half hours, but I come for just one hour. As soon as I arrive, a bit disheveled in my African garb, William pops up and asks the church's best singer to offer a hymn totally in English. He tells the congregation that my father has died and asks them to pray for my family and for my father's departed spirit. A chorus of murmured recognition greets his announcement. Death is no stranger here. Mama Abigail beckons me to join her at the front of the church and holds my sweaty hand while the congregation offers prayers. Each person is praying their own separate entreaty, a cacophony of sound. In the heat and the noise and the embrace of strangers I am miles away from Maine. I will see my father's memorial service on videotape, but right now this is where I am, this is what I have chosen, and while some of my friends may not understand my choice, I know that he did. There is some comfort in that.

Dad's passing swamps me. Just as I begin to slowly move toward acceptance there are more tough lessons to take on board.

CRIME AND LOCAL JUSTICE

In ten years and twenty-six trips to Africa, many discoveries have been difficult to metabolize: nurses who beat women in labor who yell too loud, passersby who rob car-accident victims while they lie bleeding, police who refuse to investigate crimes without being bribed, schoolgirls who are told they must sell sexual favors to pay for school uniforms, generations of women who perpetuate female genital mutilation on their own daughters, men who rape young children so as to be cleansed of the AIDS virus. Unspeakable events that are repeated and documented. But they are stories of people I do not know, not descriptions of my neighbors.

Here in Nshupu it is different. I did not grow up in a small town where kindnesses and betrayals are remembered and held across generations. Here, resentments, disappointments, and slights are retained, embellished, and calcified over the years. I don't know how this works and how to hold onto the ensuing set of contradictions: the kindness of the lodge staff and their cruel shunning of Joseph, the genial village chairman who collects and then pockets money designated for the World Bank water project, our friend Mohammed who converted to Christianity and his weekly alcoholic binges that sap his family's finances, and gracious Jeffrey who likely orchestrated the attempted burglary at our house.

But it is Alice who makes me heartsore. She is beautiful. At twenty-two she stands almost six feet with impeccable posture, caramel skin, and a broad white smile only partially diminished by the slight brown scarring of fluorosis on her two front teeth. She calls me Mama Susie and kisses me on the cheek three times in the manner of the French. But Alice does not dress the required part in Tanzania. Her hair is in dreadlocks draped over her right cheek, and a silver pin pierces her left eyebrow. Her uniform is skintight blue jeans, ballet flats, and a colorful blouse, while all Tanzanian women past the age of sixteen must be in long skirts. She is the beloved adopted daughter/employee of our two friends from Chicago who started the NGO of which we now are part. Alice administers their programs, manages and disburses money, writes reports, and is named their successor.

She is the postcard of modern Africa, a young woman with good looks, great potential, good English, and charm to spare. She looks forward to a trip to the US, and the NGO pays handsome tuition fees to send her on for additional schooling. It takes a while for the organization to reconcile some anomalies. Suddenly she is driving a new white car. The staff at the home for teenage boys complain that their larder is empty. It takes a while to penetrate the collective denial, but Alice has been on the take and for a long time. Her sponsors are heartbroken, and she is fired from her job. She comes repeatedly up the hill to talk to us on the veranda. At first she seems genuinely confused and distraught, and I think that perhaps it has not been made clear to her. Then we realize it is all part of the scam. I don't know how much money she took, but it was money intended for orphaned kids and single moms. She has taken the money to buy a car and a seedy little bar on the dirt road up from Usa River. In one month she goes from NGO heir apparent to bar owner.

It gets worse. She is not unique in her family, a family of "respected elders" in the village. Her father has been fired after thirty years for misappropriation of funds, one brother is dealing drugs, and the other has lied about passing the national exams. If this is the family of a respected elder, no wonder our land deal fell through.

These learnings chip away at my portrait of the Tanzanians as unfailingly generous and kind, a broad-brush stereotype stunning in its naïveté. After all this time, I too cannot seem to look at Africa except through this polarized lens. What else have I not figured out? And how will my ignorance corrode the impact that we hope our good works will have? I thought that some longevity here might protect us from *muzungu* mistakes. It won't. We must rely wholly on William to be our cultural translator, and I am more than twice his age. He seems up to the task and certainly takes it upon himself to give us blunt guidance when we miss the point. But he is only one man, and this village protects its own.

We make it clear to Alice that she is not welcome at the home with the kids. I miss her, or more accurately, I miss the young woman I thought she was. She stops asking us for explanations as to why she was fired, and I think somehow we are at a truce with these realities. But that is before the robberies and the rape.

It has been a while since there have been robberies on this little stretch of dirt road where we live, but shortly before he was to leave Tanzania, our neighbor Robert was robbed. He left his computer notebook on his dining room table behind a locked door with a night guard standing watch. But the computer disappeared together with a couple of bottles of liquor, and Robert never found out whether his guard was complicit or merely asleep. The police demanded money for gas to arrive at the scene to interrogate Robert's guard. But nothing was concluded, no one was charged. Business as usual.

Shortly thereafter, fleeing the hard rains to come, we flew home, leaving our house as a sublet to a lovely Welsh couple, Molly and Ollie. Our man Darsch was on the case and they were happy to have him there. Once the rains come, the noise on the tin roof is deafening. They never heard the two guys who slithered through the office window and stole their cameras, computers, cell phones, and wallets, all while they slept in the room next door. The police, of course, do nothing, find nothing, and punish no one. Whoever has fenced the stolen goods has probably lined their pockets as well.

Darsch too was sleeping, in the back seat of our car, so did not do his job to interrupt the robbery in progress. He was fired the next day. There was no other option. Once a night guard has had a lapse like that he cannot be kept on. It sends the wrong message. We are relieved that our friends were not hurt and sick at heart that Darsch will not be there upon our return. We know too that we are not altogether innocent in this outcome. From time to time we found the back door of our car not quite closed in the morning. Gil surmised that Darsch slept there off and on. We never confronted him, enamored as we were of his archetypal bearing and presence. Once, when presented with the gift of some wool socks for the cold nights in his tire-tread sandals, Darsch expressed his thanks by jumping. Maasai men celebrate by propelling themselves vertically to enormous heights. With Darsch on duty we lived out our fantasy of how it is meant to be here in Africa. When we return, our new night guard is not so colorful. He is from the local Meru tribe, wears street clothes, scolds us for our flawed Swahili, and does not appear to be thrilled to come to work at dusk each night. I don't think we will ever see Darsch again. He has returned to his wife's village fifty kilometers away and will not come back to the scene of his humiliation.

Extra bars are placed on each window of our house, and the doors are reinforced with additional locks. Gil puts a machete on the floor on his side of the bed. With all our new precautions I am not prepared when I interrupt a burglary in process in broad daylight not thirty-six hours after we return to Tanzania.

It is a sunny Sunday afternoon and the house has been left locked and vacant for only an hour while Gil and I access the internet down the hill at the lodge. I come back up the hill solo, spot a man on the veranda and call out, thinking he is a visitor. He hears me, pivots, and streaks off through the bull farm fence hole behind the house. By the time I call the lodge staff and they speed up the hill, he is long gone. But one lodge staff member's behavior is suspicious. Told to remain at his desk while Adam investigates, instead RL outruns everyone up the hill and skirts around the perimeter of the house.

I am in tears, jittery with jet lag, and terrified at the prospect of the scenarios that could have happened. The installation of further deadbolts and crossbars does nothing for my sense of safety. It takes so long now to lock and unlock the house that I worry that if there were a fire we would be immolated before we could get out of our self-imposed fortress.

We will never know who orchestrated the attempted burglary but RL is certainly a candidate. We learn that he has stolen from the lodge on three different occasions, gets fired, returns contrite, and is rehired. The guests like him. He is handsome, his English is good, and he is unctuously attentive to their every need. Adam thinks that he is in cahoots with a convicted burglar who lives a scant quarter mile from the house. The hypothesized scenario is that they work together, one as a lookout and one as the doer. Whoever has orchestrated the burglaries, they are no doubt known to the village and live here. Protected? Tolerated? Feared? Part of the fabric of the village. It is us *muzungu* who will always be profound outsiders. Yes, we speak rudimentary Swahili, we are doing good works in the village, but not every family is the beneficiary of our efforts, and we do not live here on the edge. We live here but not really. We come and go, spend obscene sums of money on airfare, carry the latest high-tech gadgets. If we get really sick we can be evacuated to some fancy hospital. We cannot have it both ways. This awareness settles in my gut like a lead weight. My early morning hikes in the village still offer cool air and friendly greetings from most of the people I meet. But I feel a hint of menace. Am I walking by the home of the burglar? Is this the part of town where he lives? At some point my anxious vigilance ebbs a bit. The kids and the project are the antidote to resignation, and life goes on. It is the gang rape down the road and its aftermath that truly takes us off our moorings.

The land surrounding our house is surrounded by cobwebs of small footpaths winding through the old-growth forest, the maize fields, and the far reaches of the village. One such path I have taken many times is shaded with old-growth trees, cool and green. It skirts the lodge property, crosses the road, and dumps out on the road not far from Alice's bar.

William phones us right after breakfast and asks to meet us, and soon we see his broad outlines striding up the path to the house. He is out of breath and clearly agitated. We get him some water to drink and he sits down heavily on the veranda chair. There was a rape last night just down the road, he tells us. A seventeen-year-old waitress at Alice's bar was accosted on that path by four men at 2:00 a.m. as she walked home from her shift. Three of them raped her repeatedly while the fourth, a younger boy, looked on and handed out condoms. The older three fled the scene, and, terrified, the younger boy confessed and identified everyone. There is no anonymity for a crime like this in a village this small. The girl knows who raped her, and the whole village knows by daybreak.

One is Adam's ne'er-do-well cousin, Mathew, another is his distant cousin, James, and the third is Luca, longtime beneficiary of housing, schooling, and generous handouts from Ann and Robert's NGO. Heartbreak enough to go around. Alice spends the next day ferrying the woman to the police and to the hospital, and charges are filed. She believes that Luca was instrumental in getting her fired so she is especially anxious to see him put in jail.

In Africa most gender violence goes unreported and certainly unpunished. But the magistrates for a rape case are all women, and they routinely recommend thirty years of hard labor for rape without exception. There is no lengthy trial and presentation of evidence. Only two weeks may go by from the date of the crime to conviction and imprisonment. William argues while we sit stone-faced that thirty years of hard labor would be the end of life for these three young men. Instead William recommends the community try to resolve the matter "at home" the way this has been handled for centuries. The elders of the community and all of the family members of the perpetrators go to the victim, offer their profound apologies and compensation in the form of sugar or money. The victim in turn drops the charges and the case is over. Perhaps the boys in question get some form of a caning from their family but there is no court case. The police must then be paid a bribe for them to officially withdraw the charges and close the books.

Numbly we listen to William's proposed course of action. We have always asked him to explain to us local customs. This dénouement is not up to us to decide, but William hopes for our support as his elders and benefactors. I struggle, overcome with images of the rape and the lifelong trauma for this woman I do not know. Would a prison sentence of thirty years alleviate her pain? Probably not. But she would not have to live alongside her tormentors in this bell jar of a village. This I need not have worried about, as the boys never return. They go the way of countless other criminals on the run. Dar es Salaam is a favorite destination, a huge city teeming with pickpockets and burglars who pack guns.

The elders convene, Adam hands over 1.4 million shillings to the victim, and she accedes to dropping the charges. The next day, Alice demands 750,000 shillings of that for herself. She says she has closed her bar for two nights and that this is the profit she lost and furthermore that she should be compensated for the fuel involved in taking the woman to the hospital and to the police. This sad tale comes full circle once again to Alice's supreme selfishness. Or is it sociopathy? That is my armchair clinical diagnosis. But if she is a sociopath then how many others in the village would I tar with that same brush?

The burglars who tried to steal food from the orphanage at Christmas? The families that steal laundry from neighbors' clotheslines? Or is this mere desperation born of poverty and lifelong role models of corruption? Round and round I go trying to make sense of what I see here, warmth, generosity, and callous disregard. If we are to stay here and do good over the long haul, I must learn to withhold this facile judgment. It is cheap and puts me right in the company of the colonialists who once occupied our house. It is time to bear down on the task at hand and see to it that the kids we have pulled back from the precipice can actually get an education and live a good life. Yet these are not the only crimes to cloud our idealism. When Patrick is wrenched from our care we are stunned and again brought up short.

Patrick is taken from us

From the very start, six-year-old Patrick Edward won us over. He was an imp, irrepressible, a grin from ear to ear with dimples. Even more than most he liked to be hugged. My first photograph of him in 2011 shows him leaning into me though we had only met the day before. What psychologists describe as "indiscriminate friendliness" is often a hallmark of neglect. We did not know that then but we surely know it now.

When we first met William and Sarah, all the children in their care were described to us as orphans. Maybe that was the most effective way to gain our sympathy and support. It certainly worked, though we did not need persuading, so magnetic were the kids themselves. Energetic, affectionate, playful, and eager for simple tactile connection. As the years unfolded we began to learn that not all the children were technically orphans. Some parents had disappeared, some had abandoned their children, some were in jail or mentally ill. These disclosures came slowly, randomly, and only when we got savvy enough to ask directly, Is there a living parent?

It was Patrick's story that taught us to ask. Here's how it happened. For the first four years we knew Patrick, he thrived. When he had three meals a day his small frame filled out and he ran with the pack, flourishing with the orphanage's blend of love and structure. At public school, however, he was a restless jumping bean, and for that he was regularly caned. As soon as we could get enough donor funds we sent him to private school, where corporal punishment was forbidden. We talked about vocational school being the right destination for him in the long haul. If he were in America he would surely have been put on Ritalin. But we did not fret about Patrick's long-term prospects. William and Sarah were intent on a model that would support the children well into adulthood. They would help him find a vocation and he would have a good life. That was the plan, our fond hope echoed by his enthusiastic US sponsors.

In March of 2014 we were getting ready to leave Tanzania. The hard rains were on their way, and we had been there for three months. I was past ready for a change of scene, a haircut, and some creature comforts. By now we were accustomed to a stream of last-minute requests for money, crutches for a crippled son, funeral expenses for a young boy, tin sheets for a roof leak soon to be a deluge. Usually the petitioners would stop us on the path below the house. But often they came right up to the veranda, took a seat, and waited for us to show up.

These visits were usually daytime affairs, so we were surprised at the dinner table when our night guard, John, told us we had a visitor on the veranda. A beautiful young woman wreathed in bright colors sat just under the outside light. She introduced herself to us as Patrick's mother. Stunned, we knew in an instant that she was telling the truth, so closely did she resemble her handsome son.

With John as our translator she then went on to make some outrageous assertions. Her son Patrick was not being fed at the orphanage, he was being beaten there, and she wanted to go to the village office to lodge a complaint. Was this a veiled request for money? What did she really want? And where had she been all these years?

We met with William early the next morning to tell him of this unwelcome surprise. Not only did we worry for Patrick, we felt like dupes ourselves. How come we never knew that he had a living parent three minutes from the orphanage? How many of the other kids are not really orphans? What else did we not know?

Gradually we got Patrick's story. Four years ago Patrick was seen wandering the village hungry and dirty. His mother had eight children by seven different fathers and had banished him to the street. His grandmother brought him to the orphanage. In the four years that Patrick was under William and Sarah's care, his mother never once walked up the hill to see him. His grandmother did come by twice, but that was the extent of it.

So now what did Patrick's mother want? A meeting was set for the village chairman's office but we were not included. This confrontation had to happen in unfettered Swahili. Patrick's mother repeated her accusations about the quality of care at Precious. The village office was unimpressed, as they knew better. Patrick himself was interviewed and asked what he wanted. He cried, saying he wanted to stay in school and at the home with his friends. His mother then announced that she wanted to remove her son from the Precious Home. William and Sarah had no recourse. Patrick had never been legally remanded to Precious, and the Tanzanian government was on a campaign for biological parents to keep their children.

William and Sarah brought us this heartbreaking news. I wept to hear of our impotence and our impending loss. Mostly I wept for Patrick. His mother had agreed to send him to public school, but we knew it would not go well and he would not be supported to go forward into vocational school. We labored over our emails to his US sponsors, trying to explain some realities that we ourselves could barely understand.

Patrick's mother came the next day to remove her son from Precious. There was no time for goodbyes. She wanted to leave quickly with him and refused to take his backpack of clothing and school supplies. We left Africa before we saw him again and it was some months before we had a sighting. I was headed up the dirt path on a walk one morning and suddenly Patrick emerged from behind some hanging laundry and ran pell-mell to wrap his arms around me. Skinny and dirty, he still gave me one of those inimitable grins.

After that day I saw Patrick often on my morning walks, still skinny and dirty. Often I invited him home for a big plate of scrambled eggs. But that was all we could do. Emissaries of elder village women could not budge his mother to return him to school. Nor could an elder uncle who also made a case. We began to resign ourselves to seeing him in a future life of petty crime. Would our sweet Patrick be robbing our house in another five years?

And yet somehow the tide turned. A neighbor offered to pay school fees for a year of vocational school, and we guaranteed the rest. Off he went to learn auto mechanics. When I see him now at age sixteen, he stands tall and proud. He earned a salary in his fieldwork placement and used that money to buy a goat, some chickens, and a rabbit, all the beginnings of a self-sufficient and responsible life of his own. Our hearts are full.

Making their own way

Self-sufficiency is our ultimate goal, for the kids, for the village, and in particular the women who have been invited to join our women's empowerment group.

Women's empowerment is a term used a lot in Africa, and it has interchangeable meanings: eradicating gender violence, building self-confidence, skills training, civil liberties, community building. When I heard such a group had taken shape at Precious, I envisioned something like the women's support groups I had been involved with all my life, heavy on the emotional support and Kleenex, light on business and money issues.

Then I visited the group and had my stereotypes upended. The group capped its membership at thirty-two women, with a focus on widows and single parents, those who would never be able to have a real bank account. Prospective members were vetted by consensus, and the group established a chairperson, a secretary, a treasurer, and a disciplinarian. Yes, a disciplinarian, as the rules that were set down and agreed to in the first meeting are quite strict. Here they are: Weekly meeting attendance is required. If you show up late you pay a fee of 200 shillings or 8 cents. This requirement is especially stunning here in Africa where no one wears a wristwatch and time is always an approximation. It is also a meaningful incentive since 200 shillings is what many people here earn in a day. If you miss the meeting you must pay 500 shillings (22 cents). Every week each member must contribute 500 shillings to a community fund, which is used to support families who have a death, an illness, or a crisis. (In the event of hospitalization or a funeral, all the women from the group show up to provide cooking and family support.) This financial contribution is assumed. They must also purchase a minimum of one share at each meeting, which costs 1,000 shillings. They may purchase up to five shares at 5,000 shillings ($2.20).

The meeting begins as all meetings do here in Tanzania, with a prayer. Then careful attendance is taken, and the first installment of basic community funds are collected. This goes on for an hour, during which the gathering is utterly quiet. There is no small talk, no laughing, no storytelling. A small baby is passed around, but quietly. At the head table, the chairwoman, secretary, treasurer, and disciplinarian carefully enter by hand and calculate the funds obtained, checking and rechecking to ensure an accurate count of the many small dirty bills. Loans are repaid and carefully logged. The interest rate on each loan is 10 percent. No exceptions to the rule. This is how the women will make money for one another. No sad stories (and this village is awash in them) will change this calculus. I watch this unfold mildly stupefied. Each of the women here assembled has weathered suffering that would long ago have put any of us under. No therapy, no Prozac. Most of the fathers of their babies are distant memories, they've had infants dead before they could crawl, clothes drying on a line stolen by others even more desperate, no jobs, no money for school fees, the verte-brae in their necks forever compressed by loads of water and firewood, and not much food to put on those hard-won fires. Malaria, typhoid, TB, dysentery, HIV are all a regular part of life. But these women are not here to tell their sad stories. They are here to yank themselves up and out of poverty, and with discipline they will do this. They mean business. By the end of the proceedings, the group has $122, a remarkable number given that they began with such nominal sums. Several small startup businesses have already been funded (e.g., brooms and soap). And by year end a few more will have been incubated.

Our vision for Precious is that it would be much more than a home and a kindergarten. We want to be a community resource to those in the village who have the very least. This group will have clones. And we are glad for that.

This group gave itself a name: Wanawake Wanaweza, "A Woman Can."

DEBORAH COMES TO PRECIOUS

Extreme poverty in a country with no safety net forces families to make choices inconceivable to us affluent expats. Five-year-old Deborah came to us because of her mother's desperation and the hope that we could provide her with what her family cannot: a bed to sleep in, food, an education. In short, a future beyond her mother's lot.

When her mother came to speak with us, the younger kids were shooed indoors so their raucous laughter would not interrupt the solemn proceedings on the veranda. Deborah was dressed in her best, a jacket over a blue chiffon dress with tears in the fabric and dirt on the hem. Her pigtails had been lopped off, her head shaved so she would be in compliance with typical Tanzanian school requirements. At first I did not recognize her but for her shy smile. Deborah's mother was dressed traditionally, probably her best *kitenge*, shawl, and head covering. There are only five chairs for six of us. I impulsively lift Deborah into my lap, wondering as I hold up her small body, Was this presumptuous? But her mother seemed almost collapsed into herself, covered in layers of fabric and sitting with preternatural stillness. She made no move to hold her daughter. Deborah mirrored her mother's stillness. She never moved on my lap, keenly attuned to the adult conversation happening around and about her. Her small brown fingers are lightly placed in my hand, but I cannot see her face.

William runs a delicate, carefully translated meeting in which he explains our role as benefactors and details the care and schooling Deborah will have at Precious. He makes it clear that mother and daughter can visit but that going forward her new family and home is here. Deborah speaks in a near whisper, and Gil and I try to offer reassurances that we hope would mitigate the pain of this separation now impending. The air is thick, and one by one all six of us begin to weep. Gil and William wipe their eyes on their sleeves, and Deborah's mother uses her shawl. Deborah's eyes fill too as the enormity of the occasion began to register.

Deborah's mother asks if she could offer the prayer. Of course, we murmur. She stands up and prays at great length in Swahili. The further along in the prayer, the more she seems to gather strength and timbre to her voice, her words a consecration of this leave-taking, this baptism into our home. Mostly, we later learn, this is a prayer of thanks to God and to us for making a miracle happen this day. We take a mother-daughter portrait, and the photograph says it all. The mother's face is set in a posture of strength and resignation. Little Deborah has a small smile on her face. There it is digitally recorded, the sadness, the letting go, and the hope.

Once the prayers and the family portraits are complete, Deborah's mother, Mary, visibly relaxes. It is done. She has relinquished her daughter, something she has prayed about and advocated for two years now. William gently inquires after her current living circumstances. With some visible embarrassment she tells us that she is not a widow as she had formerly claimed. Her husband simply fled two years ago never to be seen again, leaving six children, their mother, and no visible means of support. Mary works as an occasional field hand cutting hay for livestock, earning ten cents a day. The family lives in a rented cinder block square with mud floors, a door but no windows. Is there a bed for the family? William quietly asks. No, they sleep on flattened cardboard boxes. This latest disclosure sobers us all. We are taking Deborah under our wing. She will have three meals a day and will sleep on her own bed with clean sheets, a blanket, and mosquito netting.

William is now visibly agitated and reflexively turns to us. Will we buy a bed for this family? Of course, we say, then William thinks better of it. I have a bed, he says, and abruptly goes next door to his home. Within minutes he emerges, grinning, hefting a battered wooden frame and a large foam mattress now gray with use. We muscle the bed onto the top of our antique Range Rover and batten it down with string. Deborah is ushered inside the home by the older girls, their arms wrapped around her birdlike frame. While she has a bed designated for her, it will be weeks before she sleeps in it alone. The older girls will see to that, holding her close each night against the bad dreams and missing her mom.

William, Gil, Mary, and I pile into the car and set out, holding fast to the mattress with our arms so that it does not fly off into the dusty road. Mary's rented "house," a bumpy three kilometers away on the other side of the village, is hidden in a banana grove. The cinder block square is twenty feet by twenty feet, a windowless gray box. We arrive, unload the bed, and prop it against the building. I am curious, but we are not invited in to see its grim interior. Instead we pose William, Mary, and the bed for another photograph. William and Mary are both beaming in this freeze-frame. Mary has loved her daughter enough to give her a second chance. And in the bargain she gets a bed for herself and the five boys who will stay behind. It does not seem a fair trade, but my life has always insulated me from this kind of impossible choice. Living here we see up close what it is to live on the edge. We never get used to it. And daily we learn more and more what hardships these villagers must face.

MAMA BEATRICE

Over the last year, Mama Beatrice has become an emblem for what we are trying to do here. She has two granddaughters on full scholarship in our school, and for many years she cared for Baraka, abandoned into her care as an infant. A year ago William took us to visit her so that we would understand directly what poverty looks like from the inside. It worked. Mama Beatrice lives in a one-room brick house with mud floors and bars on the windows but no glass. During the rainy season there is nothing to prevent torrential rain from soaking her tiny sitting room. Miraculously her wall posters of a strawberry-blond Jesus seem to endure from one year to the next. The home has no interior latrine or kitchen. There are two small brick huts in the back of her well-swept dirt yard for that.

In a distant way, Mama Beatrice reminds me of my own paternal grandmother. Short in stature and with a generous bosom, she wears bright, knee-length polyester dresses and sensible shoes. She is like so many older African women of indeterminate age, her posture erect from years of carrying water on her head, her skin unlined, her teeth stained brown. She walks a bit stiff legged, teetering from side to side but never faltering.

The other reason William took us to meet Beatrice is her wildly vocal gratitude for the help she has received. When we were first introduced, she tried to get to her knees on our veranda to thank us. Horrified I scooped her up and plunked her down on the sofa next to me, whereupon she grabbed my forearm, stroking it as she thanked us and God profusely. Beatrice cares that we understand her Swahili, and so she slows her delivery and pantomimes a lot of what we may not get at first blush. She will repeat a sentence three or four times with great animation until light dawns and we get the gist.

Beatrice has two adult sons who live next door on either side together with their wives and her four grandchildren. There was a husband at one time, but no one speaks of him now. Thirteen years ago she woke up one morning hearing an infant's cries. There on her mud floor was baby Baraka, screaming and bleeding from a head wound. She never knew who dropped him off that night, and she took over his care as best she could. When Precious Orphanage opened its doors in 2010 she brought five-year-old Baraka to live with William and Sarah. He stayed in their care for four years until he lit the fire that burned down half of the orphanage. At that point the village elders insisted that Baraka be remanded back to Mama Beatrice's care.

She took up his care once again, sending him to public school, and Precious paid those school fees. The food was up to her to figure out as she always has: watercress from the nearby lake, bananas and maize when she could get work as a field hand.

This winter it was time to update the video on our website to continue our endless trolling for more funds. We wanted to show our donors vividly how hard life is in this village, and so it was without a moment's thought that we asked Mama Beatrice to be the star of our short film.

She agreed right away, and we spent a day at her home. The three young Tanzanian filmmakers spent hours shooting her as she swept the dirt yard, fed her goat, and extolled the virtues of our project against the ubiquitous African soundtrack of children crying and roosters crowing. The short film was a success, and we returned to thank her with bags of rice, sugar, tea, and coffee. Grandchildren piled into her tiny house and shrieked with delight as they saw themselves on the silver screen of Gil's laptop.

A few days later Mama Beatrice came walking up from the path below. She said she was exhausted and feeling sick. Would we take her to the hospital the next morning? Nonplussed, we agreed and set a time for the trip. By the time we were scheduled to leave, our car was once again on the fritz in the garage, and so we gave Mama Beatrice 30,000 shillings ($13) to pay for transport and medical care. At 5:30 that night that she reappeared on the veranda, this time collapsing onto the floor in exhaustion.

She had been diagnosed with diabetes, high blood pressure, and some bacterial infection for which she was prescribed antibiotics. So now Mama Beatrice is not only a poster child for poverty but also the poster child for a new pandemic in Africa: noncontagious lifelong chronic disease. The diet here of almost exclusively corn products, white flour, and sugar is the set-up. Poor women who have not enough to eat are still grossly overweight by Western standards. I never thought about it much before now.

Diabetes alone will kill more people here than AIDS and malaria combined. It is the leading cause of blindness in the continent and goes undetected for many years until a crushing fatigue begins to catch up with its victims. Mama Beatrice at fifty-nine (she looks to be in her midseventies) is two years over Tanzania's life expectancy of fifty-seven. In our video she says she hopes to live to see her daughter become a leader in the village. Odds don't look too great for that.

And there are others in our extended Precious family who are suffering too.

GABRIEL'S SORROW

I have been looking for Gabriel since I heard his news. I finally saw him yesterday at Precious School. Gabriel is a teacher of English and history for third and fourth grade. He genuinely likes the kids he teaches, and they soak it in and put out their best efforts for him in turn. Gabriel comes to work every day in big, billowing, bright shirts cut from wildly colorful African *kitenge* cloth. I can always see him coming. His body is short and round, his smile easy, and his face an open book. His colleagues on the teaching staff say that coming to work is a helpful distraction now.

I spot him walking toward his classroom and call his name. He stops, pivots, and comes rapidly toward me. I take his hand, not to shake it but to hold it, and begin by saying *"Pole sana."* I am so very sorry. He nods, his eyes fill up, and we stand there for some time holding hands. I tell him we have been thinking of him every day and praying for him and his family. He replies that he is so grateful for our support. "This has been a very difficult time" he says. "Of course," I say. "The death of your son, now your worry about your wife, almost too much to bear." He said that he was able to work and function because of the love he felt surrounding him. Indeed the entire Precious community has rallied around him, showing up en masse for the son's burial and the care of his wife. When you are in the hospital in Tanzania, there is no food service to be had. Family and neighbors set up camp behind the hospital and cook your meals on an open wood fire. Women who have backbreaking jobs show up after work and cook so that the patient gets food.

A month ago Gabriel's wife went to the local government Tengeru Hospital for a scheduled cesarean section. Her first child had been born via C-section and so it was assumed that she would need a second one. Piecing together many accounts, I learned that Gabriel's wife, Christine, gave birth via C-section to a son. Afterward she and her newborn were not thriving. Her son sustained injuries from the equipment used in the C-section itself and lived only eight days. She was hemorrhaging seriously. The hospital figured out that some piece of equipment or cloth had been left inside her after the surgery. She was operated on again to remove the offending item. Because she was still too sick and too weak, her family decided to spare her the news of her son's death. They would wait until a group of elder women from the village could come to her bedside to help her endure this news. As Christine lay in her hospital bed barely conscious, the entire Precious staff of thirty-five attended the burial: teachers, administrators, cooks, farmworkers. First Gil drove them to the morgue to retrieve the infant and his casket. The morgue was doing a brisk business, and the tiny pine casket for Gabriel's son had been given to another family. The teachers waited stolidly while a second casket was constructed. Then the teachers caravanned to the cemetery with Gil and Gabriel. The pastor who was scheduled to preside over the interment was three hours late. More waiting. And as they wait the women sing a cappella, one hymn after another. It passes the time, and it helps heal the heart. As the sun lowers in the sky and the blistering heat begins to abate, two nursing mothers have to leave before the actual interment, and Gil takes them home. The dead infant's name was Miracle, in a stroke of irony somehow uniquely African.

For days Christine remained unresponsive and in pain. The doctors did a second and third surgery to diagnose the issue. No luck. She was closed up once again and released from the hospital. Now she has a partially open wound for which she gets daily care at a local clinic. She was told about the death of her baby boy. Now her husband waits to see if the wound treatment will resolve any infection. Gabriel is back at work and glad for the support and the distraction the teaching provides.

Simultaneous to Gabriel's unfolding crisis, our lovely young secretary, twenty-three-year-old Mariel has been through her own kind of hell. She has become the backbone of the administrative team, churning out reams of mandated paperwork for intrusive government officials. After weeks of pain and bleeding, Mariel was diagnosed with a large uterine fibroid tumor. I resort to Google, cruising for information about how fibroids should be treated.

One headline that kept reappearing was that surgery was the very last choice, particularly in a woman of childbearing age. But Mariel's mother, Mary, took Mariel to the same clinic where six years ago the doctor had given Mary a hysterectomy under local anesthetic. Mary nearly died. This doctor does a brisk weekend business in hysterectomies, though it is said that these surgeries are medically unnecessary. But it is not the custom here to seek second opinions or ask doctors penetrating questions. It was determined that Mariel would have surgery, and when I heard the details of the procedure I had to have it repeated to me several times. Apparently the doctor pulled her uterus out vaginally, removed the fibroid, and then put the uterus back inside her body. She was home recuperating in substantial pain for some time and is now back at work. Mariel is a young woman in a culture that values childbearing very highly. I cannot imagine that she would not want children at some point. She still seems to believe that is possible, but I see her face in repose. Her gaze takes her into some middle distance, a mask of resignation.

Then too there is the saga of Mama Rose, her life a tableau of deprivation and loss.

MAMA ROSE

In our early years at Precious I often wrote articles that described how hard it was for me to reenter my affluent US world, how dire the realities of disease, poverty, and desperation are in Africa, all documented with stunning self-absorption. It was all about me, how adventuresome and brave I was to be here, our challenging day-to-day life, how we flirt with the odds to do good. Friends and donors amplified that self-image, cheering us on from afar.

On our website we told stories about the kids we had rescued, the families that were struggling, and the grace shown by so many living so close to the edge. We omitted mention of the gang rape down the street, the robberies at our house, and the six deadbolts on our front door. And with time, our paranoia began to ebb. We stopped taking antimalarials and invested in insecticide. We aped the nonchalance of the forty-something expats we knew, the ones who were paragliding off Mount Kilimanjaro, camping among rhinos, smoking dope by the lodge pool on Sunday afternoons, and speaking an inimitable patois of Swahili and English.

One particular woman we profiled on our website exemplified dignity, perseverance and the support our project was trying to offer. Mama Rose was tall, thin, handsome, and moved with liquid grace in her long skirts. For a solid year she cooked porridge in what was our old cement chicken coop, stooping to tend the fire in the close heat. Mama Rose was happy to have the job. Her teenage daughter had recently given birth on the mud floor of their hut, and there were four other mouths to feed, too. We learned that for years Mama Rose had been beaten viciously by her husband. At one point she was so injured that the government stepped in and forced him to leave. She must have been near death for this to happen, as domestic violence is so common here, so embedded.

Mama Rose rebuilt her life, or so we thought. When we opened our school and its cheerful new kitchen, Mama Rose was hired to do the cooking, and one of her young children got a full scholarship. In huge vats she prepared porridge and stews of maize and vegetables for 130 kids. Her colleague in the kitchen, cheerful and strong Max, was caught systematically stealing food from the storage room. He was summarily fired. Then Mama Rose was found to be stealing also. She was summoned to a meeting with the administration but collapsed. A trip to the nearby clinic left her with a diagnosis of advanced AIDS, her husband's last remembrance.

We met with William and Sarah to discuss next steps. Firing Max was a no-brainer, important to send the right message, etc., etc. To fire Mama Rose was more complex. With no job and no food she would be dead within months, orphaning her children. The four of us wrestled with the implications of this moral dilemma for over an hour. In a shared insight we knew it was time to convene the entire Precious community. Everyone knew by now that Mama Rose was seriously sick and knew as well that she had been caught stealing.

The next day the teachers, administrators, security guards, farmhands, and cleaning crew all took their seats in the third-grade classroom, squeezing into the children's small desks. Someone said a prayer to open the meeting, and everyone was invited to speak and offer their perspective on what should happen with Mama Rose. As is the custom in traditional classrooms, each attendee stood next to his or her desk to speak. Unanimously the staff urged that she be forgiven and offered a different job with less risk of theft. The meeting lasted an hour with impassioned talk about what it means to be a family and how important it is that we all live by the same rules.

While the staff debated disciplinary action for Mama Rose, her situation deteriorated medically. Sarah brought her to the clinic unable to wash or feed herself. Now with full-blown AIDS, her situation was precarious. The local HIV clinic has no beds, so someone as sick as Mama Rose must be cared for at home.

She was given medication and sent home. The Precious community swung into action. Food was delivered and cooked, her children looked after, and Mama Rose was given a paid medical leave, a rare practice in Tanzania. Her colleagues at Precious knew that the kindness they extended to Mama Rose would come full circle. When we left Nshupu in March, we thought we would never see her again. And yet remarkably she has come back from the brink with aggressive medical treatment and will be able to return to work by the time we return next fall.

One year later and we are in a whiplash of surprise and regret, when we finally have to fire Mama Rose after much discussion with William and Sarah. Her debts totaled 3.6 million shillings, about $1,500, an enormous sum of money by any standard, with a portion owed to everyone she knew: Rama's wife, the teachers' savings group, her local women's empowerment group, and a broad swath of abutting neighbors. She had so many debts that the police showed up at Precious School with a warrant, telling school administrators that if the loans were not repaid she would go to jail. Since her line of credit at Rama's store involved the purchase of Konyagi (a cheap local gin substitute) it was a good hypothesis that this money had been used for alcohol, but $1,500! It takes a long time and a lot of booze to amount to that much, especially here where it can be had so cheaply.

Mama Rose had been brought back from the brink of terminal AIDS, and now we discover she is also a full-blown alcoholic. There will be no more second chances for her at Precious. There is too much at stake, and our reputation must be upheld. Collectively there is a sigh of relief even though Mama Rose will still live just up the road, and one of her daughters will continue to receive a full scholarship at the school. Our bleeding hearts have hardened a bit now. We make this decision rapidly with William and Sarah and move on to other business at hand. There is another painful firing to come.

We fire Joseph

Like watching a car crash in slow motion, we knew that ultimately Joseph could not keep his handyman job with us. He disappeared too often, sometimes for months at a time when we were out of the country, leaving our house unattended and at risk. And although his own HIV treatment was spotty at best, he told us he had taken a girlfriend and wanted to have a family. He was ebullient, grinning, and handsome.

The tiny house we had built for him on our property was more and more often a gathering place for large numbers of Maasai. Joseph fed his guests all the food he had while he remained spectrally thin. We had many serious sit-down talks on the veranda, with Adam translating. Gil patiently spelled out the job duties and his dismay at Joseph's failure to do the basics. I sat on the periphery weeping quietly.

A few weeks later Joseph brought home his girlfriend and proudly announced that she was pregnant. Our hearts sank. Though he did not say it overtly, we knew that he was planning to raise his family in that tiny house. It was not going to work. The lodge property owners would never tolerate that arrangement. We hardened our hearts and told Joseph that he could not raise his family there. When the baby came they would have to find another place to live.

Finally, inevitably, Joseph again disappeared when he was meant to be on duty, and Gil fired him, giving him three months' pay but making it clear that Joseph's young family needed to leave the house before Christmas. During the meeting I cried inside the house.

For the next weeks, Joseph lobbied me privately when Gil was out doing errands. "Jesus makes mistakes," he said. "Why can't I make mistakes too?" I had no ready answers for this line of inquiry. Awash with sadness I would offer up a lame excuse and absent myself.

Two years later Joseph came to visit us. He has two children now, named after us with some inventive spelling. He shows us the birth certificates: Gillbat for Gilbert and Sussie for me. He seems healthy, though his wife and he have separated. He grins and I am in thrall again. He has come to give back some of the money he borrowed from Gil. All is not lost for Joseph. He has his health and his burgeoning family. He is not here for a handout, quite the reverse. Beaming, he shows us his laminated certificate as an installer for solar panels. Joseph has turned his life around and we are thrilled. Sometimes here the reversals of fortune defy the odds and our own grim predictions. Happy's marriage is another such sweet surprise.

A WEDDING FOR HAPPY

Happy, short for Happiness, has been a chambermaid at the lodge nearby for many years. While other staff came and went, she endured and seemed to float above the dramas, the firings, the leave-takings, and the vitriolic criticisms from the newly installed mistress of the house.

Happy was lovely to look at, with caramel-colored skin, carefully braided hair, exquisite posture, even after years bent over scrubbing floors for white people. In the early days her demeanor echoed her name, but as time passed her smiles thinned as her body thickened. At twenty-nine her diminished options in life aged her quickly.

I always thought that Happy would pass her remaining years in the lodge's employ and would be unceremoniously retired without pension when she became too frail to continue. That is what happened to her longtime companion Patricia, whose untreated diabetes left her winded as she tried to keep up with the demands of cleaning. But Happy fell in love at thirty with a man named Ezekiel, and we were invited to her wedding.

Clutching our wedding card stuffed with cash and gussied up for the occasion, we traipsed through billowing clouds of dust to arrive at the scene. There, two cinder block houses were covered with tenting fabric in yellow, hot pink, green, and red. Innumerable five-foot sprays of roses and marigolds fronted a dais. Huge amplifiers boomed dance music, six hundred seriously dressed-up guests were already seated in rows of plastic chairs, and to our surprise, we were escorted to the front row to await the appearance of bride and groom.

We did not have to wait long in the heat for Happy and Ezekiel to show up. The crowd went wild. Happy was wreathed in yards of sequined tulle, and her husband wore a black suit with a hot pink tie. Weddings are an all-day affair in Tanzania, and the two appeared mildly dazed and stunned six hours into the day's events, with as many more to go. All of the important guests had to be welcomed and acknowledged, and as each group stood up, the women ululated. Each wing of the family was attired in matching outfits sewn specifically for this occasion in neon turquoise, bright red, or hot pink. The only alcohol at this wedding showed up in three bottles of sparkling wine, which were exuberantly shaken by dancing ushers before they were used to spray the guests.

After countless speeches and cake cutting, the pièce de résistance arrived: two roasted goats on pallets, heads and hooves intact, mouths stuffed with rosemary. The goats were partially carved while ushers fanned off flies and dignitaries were served tidbits on toothpicks. All of this was punctuated by bursts of dance music, during which a group of young women in neon blue leapt out in front for a few bars of wild and rhythmic dancing. An overamplified emcee in a red satin shirt cut short their exuberant outbursts, much to my dismay.

The receiving line came next. First the men came forward in a long line, shook the hand of bride and groom, then deposited their gift of cash or coins in a basket. Some came with more lavish gifts. A young cow and five goats were led by the nose through the queue. Then came the women dancing in a conga line. Finally four men hefted the new marital bed on their shoulders and paraded in front of the bride and groom. The mattress, still wrapped in plastic, slipped and nearly crashed into the table of assembled pastors.

We slipped out not long after that; we did not have the stamina to stand in a buffet line with seven hundred guests, and after all this excitement a quiet cocktail on our veranda seemed like a good idea.

CHAPTER FIFTEEN

The Roller Coaster

Quite unlike many NGO projects in Africa, Precious is growing at warp speed. We started in a grim concrete rental building with no electricity or running water and not a blade of grass. Six years later our new home sits high up on a hill with hundred-mile views to the south. We no longer call it an orphanage; it has earned the moniker of "home." Surrounded by organic gardens, its fruit trees are now maturing. Just next door we now have a brightly painted ten-room two-story primary school, an enormous community center and dining hall, a library, and freestanding bathrooms with flush toilets. The pull-chain toilets were so thrilling for our youngest children they made many trips just to see the waterfall. Teachers realized what was happening when they would hear the toilets flush and then the gales of laughter, an everyday miracle.

Everything is brightly painted, and it looks as though it was all planned from the start. It wasn't. We leapfrogged from one donation to the next. As funds arrived, William got projects going overnight. The home was built in four months and the school in six. Literally and figuratively we have huge visibility now. This brings a steady stream of supplicants and applicants. Parents are hoping for a spot for their children, others are hoping for a job.

No private school in the US would have gone from diagrams on a napkin to one hundred children in a building in the space of six months! We were still interviewing for staff the month before school first opened. William, Gil, and I quickly devised a team interview process, keeping careful notes and asking serious applicants to run a live teaching unit for observation. Simultaneously William designed an admissions process. This is easier said than done when less than 10 percent of kids under five have birth certificates. We decided to accept the bulk of our new students in the "baby class" to ensure careful teaching of the basics, all in English.

At first we were surprised by the volume of teaching applicants and the years of experience they brought. They were attracted by our beautiful "campus" and more importantly to the promise of actually being paid. Most private schools in Tanzania are profit-making enterprises. When business lags they stop paying their teachers. Once our staff and teachers realize that their salaries come like clockwork, their loyalty and commitment deepens.

In the US, schools have a measure of independence. Not here. Tanzania clings to teaching methods that have resulted in some of the worst educational outcomes in sub-Saharan Africa. The Ministry of Education mandates the national curriculum, lesson plans, textbooks, and exams. Almost annually, new textbooks are produced. They bear no improvements over previous editions. Riddled with spelling and grammatical errors, they add more expense to schools teetering this side of insolvency. It takes us months to learn all these things. I nurse a chronic simmering level of outrage. If Uganda and Kenya can figure these things out, why not Tanzania? Educational inspectors are ubiquitous and dictatorial. President Magufuli orders them to leave their offices and get out into the field. This means that on any given day, without preamble, inspectors may show up to sit in on classes, inspect lesson plans, grill teachers, review student reports and teachers' credentials. Often they are trolling for bribes. William has learned the fine art of deflecting and diverting, always gracious, always tactful.

But the president of the country has a well-earned nickname, the Bulldozer. This is the role model for these agents. One day, two of them swoop in threatening to take our visiting US volunteer to jail because he was working without volunteer papers. The crisis is resolved, hands are greased, unnecessary papers are bought. The crisis is fixed, and we wait for the next encounter.

Visiting agents also threaten to shut the school on their next visit unless we fire one of our best teachers. Quietly, we had hired a Kenyan and a Ugandan teacher. These two adjacent countries produce excellent teachers who speak much better English than Tanzanians do. But Tanzania's scarce jobs must be reserved for Tanzanians. Judith has been with us since we opened the school, and her English is impeccable. Her calm and competent aura is quite contagious, and her classrooms are focused and productive. William is matter-of-fact about the loss. I feel like weeping and gnashing my teeth. My life in America has not taught me how to yield gracefully to bullies. Everyone here learns this early in life.

The net net for us is that we have to play by the rules, teach to the test, satisfy the steady stream of inspectors, and still try to run a school that goes beyond rote repetition. Skilled master teachers offer workshops, videos, and individual coaching. Tech-savvy volunteers introduce well-designed educational programs on iPads. If you visit a classroom now it is more likely you will see students problem-solving in small groups than reciting words from a blackboard.

Remarkably our school places first in the entire Arusha district in the national exam. This is unheard of so early in a school's existence. We are teaching kids how to think and how to take exams, both. Now we must be careful that the government will not force us to enlarge our classrooms, as we want to hold the line at twenty-five kids.

Teaching ESL to our teachers

While we are in Tanzania we work with William and Sarah as their cofounders, mentors, and supporters. This means planning budgets and strategy, interviewing and assessing potential staff, running teacher workshops, supporting women's empowerment group efforts, hosting potential donors and partners, and brainstorming sustainable methods for day-to-day simple farming. We sponsor William to attend a permaculture and sustainability course, and he got religion there. Now we can tout our gray-water irrigation, biogas, rainwater collection, organic farming methods, and sack gardening, all strategies we can model and teach.

Precious Primary School is known as an "English Medium" school. Everyone here has been saturated in these British terms and techniques. For years I did not know what the "medium" part meant. It means that English is the medium through which educational content is delivered. The catch is that students are learning English from teachers whose English is limited and heavily accented. The English Medium designation only applies to some schools that are funded and run privately, not to the mediocre public schools millions of Tanzanians are relegated to. There they are not introduced to English as a second language until secondary school, thus skipping the prime ages for language acquisition.

Public-secondary-school students in Tanzania have to simultaneously master complex academic content and learn a foreign language, a daunting task in small, well-funded schools, near impossible with crowded classrooms and no teaching aids. Kids must learn science with no science labs, and for their computer classes they are shown a blackboard picture of a keyboard and a mouse. This is a mouse. This is a keyboard. Can you say keyboard? Keyboard. This is a picture of the cord and plug. Please copy from the blackboard.

A visit to a Tanzanian classroom anywhere in the country is predictable. As soon as your face comes through the doorway chairs screech as students stand up from their desks at attention. "Good morning, madam. Good morning, sah," they intone at top volume. "How are you? (pronounced "yuuuuu") I am fine too." For many that is the extent of their English mastery. In our school English is more advanced, but this routine of standing up and reciting for visitors seems fixed. It is the way it is done here even as we chafe at the disruption we cause.

Once acknowledged, the kids sit back down and return to their lessons. The classrooms reverberate with the rhythmic chanting and repetition of phrases, a way to keep a gang of kids engaged but hardly an aid to critical thinking. I once observed a third-grade class studying a unit on environmental degradation. The teacher drilled them on the spelling and pronunciation of the two words, but no one left that classroom understanding what either word meant, why it mattered, and what was to be done about it. Right outside the classroom window was evidence aplenty of degradation, as Chinese road builders blasted rock adjacent to the school.

Since the teachers at Precious School were taken from the ranks of people who had been schooled in traditional ways, introducing new methods had to be experiential. At the same time, our teachers' English was so poor that kids were learning words, not sentences, duplicating a pronunciation so accented that Gil and I could barely understand what was being said.

Our first teacher workshops were designed to do two things: model and use participative teaching methods and improve English fluency and pronunciation. We scoured the internet, deemed ourselves instant ESL experts, and ran classes three days a week after school.

Here's the scene.

It is Tuesday afternoon at 3:45. The heat of the sun has not helped to dissipate the fog of chalk dust that greets us in the fifth-grade classroom where we will teach. The kids on the playground have been released and they stream out at a dead run for home. It is somewhere between 85 and 90 degrees, but these kids have been told never never to remove their school sweaters. Too easy for sweaters to be cast aside and irretrievably lost. So here, as in the rest of the country, kids run walk and play with long-sleeved sweaters on.

Our twelve teachers straggle into the classroom and slump heavily into the smaller chairs and desks. There is Christian, who has a lazy eye but a penetrating intelligence and sense of humor. There is Resituta, pint-size in her Day-Glo orange outfit, her hair a curly nimbus around her head. As soon as she enters the room she shakes hands with us and holds our gaze as if we are the most important beings on the planet. Her persona works magic with her twenty-two wriggling, jiggling kindergartners as well. She never raises her voice. It is as though she hypnotizes them all.

There is Lightness, an ironic name for a heavyset woman with linebacker shoulders. Lightness has been teaching for a long time, a confident exemplar of old-school methods. In my first classroom observation she was drilling first graders on how to copy a picture of a flower on the chalkboard. "Write nice like teacher," she instructed her class as I wince in the back of the room. But she is a trouper, and Precious schools one of her children for free, so politely and willingly she comes to learn new methods.

Mr. Ben strides into the room and stuffs his lanky frame into a child's desk, mugging and hamming it up like an overgrown adolescent. The kids love him. He is inventive and outrageous, an energetic pied piper. Later he will steal a laptop from the school, lie about it, and tell others he is on the verge of starting his own business. All of us will be dumbfounded and hurt. In fact, in the space of fourteen months William will have to fire four staff members for theft. Our accountant is skimming bus fares, and food stores are filched. The thefts are not big ones in monetary terms, so these staff are trading good jobs with benefits for what has perhaps become habitual. We don't know and we can't surmise, but there are no second chances. Ben was an enthusiastic adopter of all the new teaching methods. I wonder what has become of him now, his teaching career in the trash bin.

After setting up some class ground rules we start with a vocabulary relay race. We have three teams, and each team is to write three words on the board that start with A and then run and pass the chalk to the next person on the team. The second team generates words that start with B, and so forth. Soon people are running, squealing, grabbing the chalk from one another, and then vociferously debating the accuracy of our scoring.

Everyone engages and we try to keep things lively, setting up debating teams, running for office as president of Tanzania, storytelling, spelling bees, skits, flashcards, anything that would keep them moving, laughing, working together, and engaged. In one class we bring a bag full of implements: kitchen tools, carpentry tools, hats, costume jewelry. We split the classroom into teams of two, and each team, eyes closed, picks two objects from the bag, then plans and performs a short skit using the objects.

Despite heat and fatigue, the teachers gamely show up for our sessions. Several months later we learn that some of the methods we've introduced have been modified and are in use in our school classrooms. That was the impetus, and we are thrilled. The kids are still singsonging their classroom greetings, but more subtle changes are incubating in the school. Who says you can't teach an old dog? We are old dogs too, and we are learning by the day.

A SOCIAL WORKER JOINS PRECIOUS

Strategic penny-pinching has allowed us to do what we have long hoped for: hire a social worker for the school. We now have 216 children in the elementary school. Sixty-eight of those are on scholarship because their families are too poor to pay for something so basic as a pair of socks. Many come from single-parent families and live in grim rented rooms. To call these places homes is a stretch. Some are one-room brick structures with tin roofs, an exterior firepit, and outdoor latrines. At night the houses are lit by kerosene, a health risk far worse than cigarette smoke. Children who live in the Precious Home have a well-established after-school ritual. They have no long walk home. They simply go next door where they are remanded to their rooms for a rest period. After the rest comes supper, then homework, then bedtime in a real bed. Their peers run home wearing their long-sleeve sweaters, often covering more than a mile. When they arrive they are put to work gathering firewood, fetching water, helping their mothers now exhausted from day labor as field hands. By the time supper is over (if there is one) it is time for homework. But with no tables and chairs and poor lighting, it is at best difficult. In addition, many parents are illiterate and not able to encourage study habits. But it is the omnipresence of child abuse that worries us the most. We know that it exists in a significant percentage of the families we support. But we have not figured out how to intervene.

Irene at twenty-two is diminutive, with a round, open face and an easy smile. When I arrive, she greets me warmly and gently dismisses the very small boy who was sitting at her desk working at his composition book. This is midmorning and time for chai or tea. One of the kitchen workers drops off a thermos and four slices of what looks like Wonder Bread. Most Tanzanians have no other breakfast but this sparse serving of empty carbohydrates. At least the children are getting hot porridge laced with ground nuts and milk.

Irene has responsibility for the care and counseling of all of the students and their families. When I was twenty-two, I was a veteran of my first year of social-work school, patently unready to take on anything close to this level of responsibility. I introduce myself and offer guidance. "What kind of help would you most like?" I ask. "Everything," she says, grinning, her smile open and unguarded. She then launches into her own history. Her father died when she was four, and her mother died when she was in secondary school. I listen, quietly murmuring acknowledgment of her painful story. Unbidden she goes through many details of her progressive series of losses. Her eyes shining, it is clear she is still grieving her mother. She describes her attempt to find relatives in Kenya. Eventually she learns that the two sides of her family were in conflict. No one remembers her or them.

To be untethered from extended family in Africa is to be vulnerable. Here family provides the social safety net, a sense of generational tribal identity, an assumed welcome for all the holidays, and a source of emotional and financial assistance. Here the smallest landowner will carve up the family *shamba* or backyard farm to build a home for progeny. This is assumed. In the US it is a badge of courage for young people to separate from family and to wander the world, often building adult lives thousands of miles from their family of origin. In Tanzania it is a lifelong heartache and stigma to be without family.

While Irene tells me that her identity as an orphan makes it easier for her to connect with so many of our children, I am struck by both her spunk and her fragility. I know that last year she was an understudy to a senior social worker in a larger school. But her supervisor, Walter, is gone now and so too the umbrella of emotional protection he offered her. Now she has a very big job, a job she has herself configured with outsize expectations. No one here knows how to offer her supportive supervision, and she is one of a kind in this school. Her own social-work plan for 2018 has thirteen complex items, including these:

To make individual canceling to a child: child who has individual problems that can lead a child do not performing well in the class, unhappy, urinate at night on bed, discipline issue. After discover a problem of a child I will communicate with manager so we can help a child.

To doing home visit; purpose of looking more relatives and gathering more information concerning about a child. Also how a child doing during holiday, to looking up true of information they have been given us. How child be during holiday in terms of discipline, participate in home activities. Also individual counseling with families.

I read through Irene's plan while she sits expectantly across the desk. It is not the tortured English that bothers me. It is the scope of what this young woman is putting out as her goals for the year, with no one here to really support her and help her refine her plan and talk through difficult cases (and they are all difficult). If I so much as posit myself as the answer to this dilemma I will amplify her long history of loss. But I can offer her intermittent support when I am in Tanzania. We agree to meet twice weekly, and our first task together will be to plan the second workshop in a series I have been running.

TEACHING CHILD PSYCHOLOGY

Today is the second teacher workshop on child psychology. Many of our kids are showing signs of abuse or neglect, and training might help teachers spot and respond to kids at risk. I have agreed to teach these workshops somewhat against my better judgment. The teachers have asked for the equivalent of four years of graduate training in three ninety-minute workshops. But they press on and I cave, flattered by their insistence and the implication that I am so gifted I will impart all of what they need in three inoculations.

At the end of a long day, sixteen teachers straggle into the seventh-grade classroom limp with fatigue. Below us on the playground the kids are just the opposite. As school is dismissed, 220 kids explode from the building, running at top speed. Their energy is electric. Seen from the balcony they look like popcorn in a hot skillet, running running running in their beige pullover sweaters.

Our schoolroom looks as recycled as we feel. The air is thick with chalk dust, the surfaces of the desks dusty white and the blackboard itself a pale gray. Backpacks are strewn into the corners, and the desks are positioned every which way. Tall windows are closed and eclipsed with school charts. We scurry to open them wider for better ventilation only to discover that drumming practice will take place just nearby. This is not traditional African hand drumming. These are marching band drums, and the kids hit them so hard they often break the drumsticks. It is deafening. When a donor gave funds to support a music program, Gil and I were thrilled.

We weren't fantasizing about huge amplifiers and electric gui-
tars, but rather traditional drums and woodwinds. This was
another point at which we simply had to keep our counsel. It
is a Tanzanian school and this is how they want to run it, we
remind ourselves. Another chance to trade in the picture postcard for what is real. Like the Maasai herders with cell phones.

As the teachers come into the classroom, they shake hands
with me one by one, Editruda, Boaz, Resituta, Peniel, Kafuba,
Mungure. I greet them by name, proud of the correct pronunciation I have worked to achieve. Everyone shakes hands on
any occasion here, everyone: walking down the street, leaning
out of car windows, greeting total strangers. Every hour or so
I reach into my African carrying bag and surreptitiously give
my hands a squeeze of sanitizer. Resituta shook my hand at
the door and then told me she had the flu. She looks wan and
washed out. I then try to be subtle with my sanitizer appli-
cation. If it gives any benefit to me it is more likely a placebo
effect, as I get so sick so often in Africa.

Prior to the workshop, the assistant headmaster asked
what they would like to learn. I read the list and my heart sinks
a bit.

- *Understanding with the children behavior and
  how to deal with them*
- *Psychological ways of helping the pupils with
  stress*
- *Assistance in understanding emotionally dis-
  turbed pupils*
- *Psychological torture*
- *Pupils with disorder*
- *Psychological understanding of everybody as a
  community*
- *Inferiority complex*
- *Physical impairments*

With a list like this almost anything I do fits somewhere in this universe of possibilities. I begin by asking the room as a whole if anybody can remember some key points from the workshop we had together in the fall. Silence. I try again. Does anybody remember anything we talked about in the first session? The silence of the damned. Irene can't help because she doesn't know the material at all.

What was I thinking when I signed up to do this workshop? I take a swig of water from my bottle and soldier on, now leading the witnesses a bit. Does anybody remember the ACE study (I am half yelling as the drumming is now at top volume), the adverse childhood experiences research? I see a glimmer of recognition in some faces. I go over the research again, pointing to various body parts, heart, brain. I ask the class what feelings they have when they have just escaped a near collision. Tick tick tick. Finally Sarah pats her chest, pantomiming her heart beating fast. I do my best to make the analogy between the physiological stress response and its damage to brain health and development. I explain that feelings don't just happen and then go away. Some feelings of fear stay in the body and create a chronic "fight or flight" response.

I begin to realize that people do understand the list of possible health consequences but that no one knows what the word *adverse* means. And certainly no one will tell me they don't know the word. We give up on that word and use the more basic synonyms: negative, harmful, painful, bad. The children we teach at Precious have lives pockmarked by adverse events, emotional and physical abuse, parental separation, addiction, mental health issues in the home, emotional and physical neglect. Now we are talking. The teachers have seen these life events among their young charges, and they want to know how to help. We talk about how neglect is even worse than abuse in terms of long-term outcomes. If a parent beats a child, the child at least knows that he or she is seen. The instances of neglect are more chilling.

This is the time just before the short rains when there is work in the fields. Poor women are eager for work. It is back-breaking. For their babies they dig a hole in the dirt and leave the child in the hole so he or she cannot crawl out. The babies scream and cry, baking in the hot sun, but the mothers cannot come to their comfort. Getting paid fifty cents for a day's work is too important. Otherwise there will be another night without food. Each time I hear of this practice I feel a hollow ache in my gut. This very early neglect sows the seeds of attachment disorders, an inability to form trusting relationships with others. There it is in living color, a fact of life incomprehensible to most safari tourists.

I think of our Baraka. How is it that we never really noticed his angry scowl, so stark against the wildly exuberant faces of the younger kids? Maybe we did not want to see it, enamored as we were of kids who still wanted to sit on our laps and delight in simple patty-cake games.

For a while it seemed as though Baraka might blossom with increasing leadership responsibilities. When offered praise he would grin shyly and soak it up. But as he got older the early damage began to show up in dangerous ways, starting with arson. Then at age twelve he began stealing from small shop-keepers. At first it was only small candies, later larger items. A village meeting of elders was convened, and he was asked to leave the orphanage. Once again, remarkably, Mama Beatrice took him in and sent him back to public school. Not long after that he began drinking, smoking marijuana, and hanging out with boys who were trouble. Now this year the most crushing disappointment: he has been convicted of rape and awaits sentencing in the jail at Usa River. Baraka is not featured in our cheery newsletters to donors. He is our first failure, a shock that cauterized some of our early rescue fantasies.

In our third teacher workshop it is time for us to talk about children we have in our care who may be at risk and install a simple framework for teachers and administrators to share information. We go over the concept of confidentiality, understood but not practiced in these villages where rumors have a shelf life of generations. But our teachers get it when I mention the concept of preserving the dignity of the children. Somehow this concept resonates hugely. When these teachers were in school themselves, kids were routinely shamed and caned in front of crowded classrooms of their peers. Their work now gives them a chance to reverse that sad legacy.

We set up a case conference right in the center of the classroom, in two concentric circles. Headmistress Mme. Deborah, her assistant, Mr. Kafuba, and the teachers who have the most contact with the child to be discussed sit in the center. The other teachers observe from the periphery. I lay out a very simple three-part framework to guide us as we discuss children of concern.

1. FACTS: What behavior have we personally observed? What is the child telling us? What facts do we have that tell us a little bit about the situation?

2. POSSIBILITIES: What might be going on here? What possible cause and effect linkages can we make? What interventions might be helpful? What other data do we need?

3. NEXT STEPS: Is this the time for a home visit? A parent conference? Should Social Welfare be involved? What is the best plan of action knowing what we know?

Two groups of teachers convene to agree on the short list of children they are concerned about. The teachers for the older children make up the larger group of ten. They stand and huddle closely the way Africans do, arms slung over one another, bodies pressed close. Here there is no prescribed "social distance." Once I had an Ethiopian priest fall asleep on my lap in an airplane, and when I gently suggested that I wanted my lap to myself, he was surprised and offended.

Once the attendees are selected and seated, Mme. Deborah (with me dropping quiet hints) convenes the meeting and asks who has the most data on the student in question, James. Six-year-old James is almost a cipher in the first grade. Quiet and isolated, he is often absent. He lives with his mother, who is described by all in the village as mentally unstable. This being a rather vague term, we ask for specifics. Apparently her troubles began when her husband abandoned the family. She spent three months in a mental institution in Moshi but has been released and is apparently not medicated or supervised. She carries a huge panga knife hidden in her long skirts and threatens to slice or kill anyone who intervenes and tries to take her son to school. She hides his exercise books and his school clothes and threatens to poison him and any relatives who get overinvolved. Often she takes James by the hand and walks alongside the highway, machete in hand. The room falls absolutely silent as the total picture emerges. The mother has upped the ante by locking James in an empty room and setting fire to his schoolbooks.

It is obvious that this child is at risk, and we escalate the problem to the program directors, William and Sarah. In William's office, he and Sarah listen intently, adding other information they have gleaned from the village. William steps in and authoritatively outlines a plan. First he will gather the appropriate elders and family members for a village meeting. He hopes that someone from the extended family will step in and take James under their care. If this does not transpire, Social Welfare will be contacted, with the likely scenario that James would be legally remanded to Precious for care. There is no foster care system, no Child Protective Services, and no fifty-two-page Individual Education Program document. But with skillful enlistment of the wisest elders and with the very real compassion of the Precious staff, we will do the right thing for this boy.

The plan works, the family declines to take James on for fear of the mother's violence, and Social Welfare designates Precious as legal guardian. James is immediately moved into the home. There the boys put together the clothes he will need from their own stashes. Seamlessly he is welcomed into their games. We see him smile for the first time.

HEALTH EDUCATION FOR WOMEN

As part of our plan to offer education for adults as well as young people, we discover an NGO out of Canada sponsoring health education for women and sign up for a pilot session.

A hundred women show up to our event in March 2017. The dirt roads are swampy with mud, small huts now soaked inside too. But the women come, lifting their skirts and sliding in silently, sitting close together on the children's benches. Something unprecedented is happening this morning. Women are gathered together to talk about what is never talked about: their own bodies, how their bodies work, and in particular how to better handle menstruation for themselves and for their daughters.

Tanzania has one of the worst secondary-school completion rates for women in sub-Saharan Africa. One of the most frequent reasons for school dropouts is the onset of menstruation. Toilet facilities are primitive, and poor girls have no money to buy sanitary supplies. Some make do with rags, and many simply stay home burning with shame when their uniforms are stained with blood. Some try to stanch the blood with leaves and mud, leading to infections. Many stay home from school for the duration of their periods, and some do not have the heart to return at all. Still others trade sex for money to buy sanitary pads.

No caring conversations with their mothers have prepared them for growing up. Menstruation, pregnancy, sex, all of these topics are taboo, especially here among the Meru tribe, where female circumcision and polygamy persist in some communities.

This morning we flaunt these taboos and talk. The five trainers are hard to miss in their unconventional outfits. Wearing tight blue jeans and bright red T-shirts, these young women command the room with flip charts, stories, and an irrepressible insouciance. The project director's given name is Very Nice and she speaks good English. When I murmur how very nice it was to meet her, we laugh. This must happen all the time.

I am seated on the periphery of the meeting hall with one of our schoolteachers, who has agreed to be my translator for the morning. My Swahili gives me a few phrases but nothing close enough to grasp the rapid-fire discussions now unfolding. We sit close together the way Africans do. Judith, still on staff at the time, leans into me a bit and puts her hand on my forearm. Her skin is as dark as burnt charcoal and flawless, my own mottled and pale.

The trainers put up their flip charts, faded diagrams of ovaries, fallopian tubes, and the uterus. Then too the odd angle of female anatomy never quite seen or understood, the view from below, the view none of us can ever see short of squatting over a mirror. Then they lay out the guidelines for our meeting: respect, candor, confidentiality, and *kujikubali* (accept yourself as you are). An elusive task for women with bodies etched in hardship.

The trainers collect written questions from those too timid to raise a hand, and the session unfolds: this is the trajectory of the egg through the fallopian tube, and this is how and why menstruation happens. I remember sitting at the blue Formica kitchen table with my mother getting this same story at the age of ten. She did a good job, only turning skittish when I asked how the sperm actually got into place to meet the egg.

From basic anatomy, the class now turns to the topic of virginity: What exactly is it? There is no word in Swahili for the hymen, and so it is taught that a hymen can be broken with vigorous play and is therefore not the ironclad hallmark it is made out to be. Furthermore, the trainers counsel, a carrot should not be used to break the hymen. A carrot? This is a new one. The facilitators clarify that virginity is lost when intercourse happens and that once lost it cannot be recovered even by placing an onion in one's vagina. This assortment of putative vegetable solutions leaves me breathless. I am glad we are doing this education; clearly we need to do more.

The session was billed as a ninety-minute undertaking. It runs for three hours. There are more questions, more stories, more laughter, more acceptance. *Kujikubali.* At the conclusion of the session each attendee receives a pink linen bag. Inside is a bar of soap, a washcloth, a small metal basin, a well-designed washable and reusable pad, and best of all a tulip cup. State-of-the-art in Europe and Canada but barely known in America, these cups can last up to ten years and are the very stuff of liberation. The women are elated, grinning and holding aloft their beautiful pink bags.

And for our second act, I think, lots more diagrams and teaching about how the sperm meets the egg and how to arrange it so that this rendezvous happens less often!

CHAPTER SIXTEEN

The Future

We have been at this now since 2011. We started with nine kids in a rented cement bunker. Now we have a "campus" with bright-blue-roofed buildings on a hilltop with long views to the south. Our original nine kids are now age eleven and up and often no longer want to sit in our laps. Happily for us, seven newcomer younger children are quite willing to snuggle.

Our primary school has 250 children, most of whom are under the age of seven, 68 on scholarship. When we show up, sweet chaos ensues, with kids streaming out of the classrooms, running to greet us, grabbing for our hands, eddying around our legs. Once there was only William and Sarah and two young mamas. Now there are twelve teachers, two school administrators, an accountant, two cleaners, a cook, a farmhand, two night guards, and two mamas for the home. Sarah wears long dresses every day, and William greets big-shot visitors in his office. Skilled volunteers come to design curriculum, and kids use small, sturdy iPads. A former school principal mentors and teaches new methods. The staff are eager learners, and the classrooms are vibrant.

In our dining hall and community center the staff dish out two hot meals a day, and in the off hours, literacy groups and women's empowerment groups convene in the huge open-air space. So many dreams have come true so fast. We are proud and we are weary too. Our operating expenses have ballooned, and so too has the fund-raising burden. We hire a senior development director who helps us launch multiple campaigns for large sums. I miss the days when an email could solicit enough cash to buy nine mosquito nets.

We still take two long trips a year to Tanzania but with a reduced roller coaster of predeparture anxiety and reentry malaise. Coming home from Africa was more complex in the early years. While we exulted in drinking potable water from the tap, we had episodes of paralysis in the produce section of our grocery store, too much abundance to choose from. At dinner tables we extolled the virtues of the African welcome and mused aloud about America's love affair with one-click shopping.

At holiday meals we still overeat and talk too much about the grinding poverty we have temporarily left behind. Eventually I can discern when people want to hear about Africa and when they do not. Belatedly I realize that our running negative commentary about Western values is wearing thin for those who choose a life here, with no compunction to do good in the developing world. It is a choice we have made that has not been without consequence. Friends and family weather illness and loss, and we are not home to comfort them. We have always prized the notion of showing up, and email can never suffice. Yet somehow kids, grandkids, and close friends of thirty-five years forgive us our hubris and our absences.

We pick up the thread of long-standing conversations, tiptoeing tactfully around the birthdays, the hospitalizations, the life crises we have missed altogether. I pine for these connections when I am in Africa. We have made new friends there, but they are twenty to thirty years younger, the Tanzanians and the expats. I can confide in Gil about most anything and yet I know that my wish for extended self-disclosure regularly outruns his. He keeps his own counsel and happily posts on Facebook. I use my journal to siphon off some of what I know to be broken-record complaints. Occasionally I set up Skype calls with my women friends while in Africa, but the technology erodes all spontaneity. I can't just pick up the phone. A date must be negotiated across eight hours' time difference. By the time the call happens, whatever acute need prompted the outreach has subsided.

In Lincoln we put on parkas and wool socks to walk the trail behind our house among the trees bare in a landscape of brown and gray. Passersby avert their gaze or mutter a quick hello. This lack of connection, New England's chilly distance, is always a slap in the face, yet now less of a surprise. This sepia palette is where I have come from, the old stone walls, fields gone fallow for the winter, the tall white spire of the first parish church, the belted Galloway cows now furry for winter. I walk through our neighborhood where everyone is indoors behind double-glazed windows. On the road we wave at each other behind car windows, too busy to disembark and chat. New England has always been the foot of the compass in my life, though I find her winters increasingly difficult to bear.

Reentry from Africa is different now, with less existential dissonance. Instead I return home and fall in love again with my appliances. In the dark chill of my early-morning kitchen I smile as I turn on bright lights, NPR, the electric kettle, the coffee grinder, and the dishwasher, as the washing machine produces load after load of pristine clean clothes down the hall. Even as I exult in my push-button life, I see Cecelia washing clothes in our Tanzania shower. Gracefully she bends at the waist, her back straight, her knees locked. She does almost a full load of washing without straightening, then hangs the clothes out on the line to dry in the blowing dust. My American euphoria fades as I am flooded with images of Africa, the people, the heat, the color. Soon I will trade in our luxuries and return once more.

Gil and I must look now in earnest for a successor who will manage the day-to-day of our project in the US, orchestrate the now complex fund-raising machine we must have, and someday succeed the two of us. We know that a health issue for either of us could permanently suspend our time in Tanzania. We are not getting any younger. We cannot imagine coloring ourselves gone, and it would be irresponsible not to have some kind of plan.

Running the US operation now entails a blizzard of administrative decisions and details that pull on a set of skills we have never really developed. We now pay others to run this complex back-office operation. This succession process is not easy. Experienced NGO executives make big salaries, and we balk at the overhead we must fund-raise for. In turn, sophisticated applicants inquire tactfully but relentlessly to discern whether or not Gil and I have Founders Syndrome, that inability to give up control and truly hand over the reins.

Of course we have Founders Syndrome! This project has our fingerprints all over it. Every aspect of it has been discussed and planned and obsessed about and fund-raised for with William and Sarah and our US board and staff. We have been patient mutual teachers. They teach us about Tanzanian culture and values, and we teach them planning, budgeting, and managing. Our progress has come from hours and hours of sitting together on the veranda. There we plan and problem-solve and daydream. We have endured theft and delays and disappointments, some with one another. And yet we always figure it out and come back to the bedrock of respect and mutual affection that animates our lives together. So of course we have Founders Syndrome. It will be through an effort of will that we diminish and ultimately release our central role in this project. We have changed the lives of many kids and families for the better. And we have infused our own lives with a deep sense of purpose. We cannot fathom letting that purpose leach out of our beings. We pray that we have a good long honeymoon with our successor before it is time for us to take a back seat.

And we know we will never take the back seat with the kids or with William and Sarah. They offer us the same reverence that is the gift to all elders in Africa. When I turned sixty-five, William sent me an email birthday greeting. His salutation read "May you live so long that all your teeth fall out!" Not exactly my fond wish.

Still I inhale their affections and their vocal prayers. I know that those of us who do live long are treated universally with respect and deference. Africans cannot understand why Westerners complain about their parents, put them into nursing homes, and pay others to care for them. Tanzanian children are taught that when parents visit, children must run to greet them to show respect and to instantly shoulder whatever they may be carrying. When Gil and I arrive at the home, all the kids come running. We saunter up the hill empty-handed while the smallest kids stagger along carrying half their body weight in our duffel bags. We know that we will be greeted in this fashion as long as we draw breath. This comforts us even as we know we must replace ourselves in due time. We only hope we can do this with grace when the moment comes.

PHOTOS

Robert Jr., Susie, and Michele, West Point 1958

A 1968 snapshot of the Rheault family in Okinawa

My father, Robert B. Rheault

Zack and Susie with a lion cub in Zimbabwe

Swaziland MP and his staff

A Fast Track team brainstorming in Tanzania

The original Precious home

The first Kindergarten in 2011

Susie and Darsch, our night Maasai guard

The Precious cofounders: Gil, Susie, Sarah and William Modest

Our rented cottage in Tanzania

Precious new home for orphaned children

Gil and the kids

Five children after school

Precious Primary School

Precious campus with Mount Meru in the distance

Photos provided by Susanne Rheault and Ina Ghaznavi

ACKNOWLEDGMENTS

First I would like to offer my profound gratitude for the late Mary Oliver. Her poems have always been an inspiration, and in particular the last two lines of her poem "The Summer Day." She asks the reader "Tell me, what is it you plan to do / with your one wild and precious life?" I have often used that quote to push me out of creeping complacency, to try something new, to try to be bolder, braver.

Next I would like to thank Carol Burnes for her pivotal early coaching. Carol, you helped me see that indeed I did have a story to tell and a book to write. You were the early midwife for this project, urging me to move from travelogue to in-depth memoir. I am forever indebted to you for that.

Shannon O'Neill, my developmental editor. You were a vital partner and guide. You gave me enough authentic affirmation that I could then easily take on board the many useful suggestions that you offered. I cannot imagine completing this book without your steady tutelage.

To Bill Bean and Ed Wood, my heartfelt thanks for getting me to Africa to begin with and then believing in me enough that I could expand and continue my work there. Without your encouragement and your support, there would have been no work in Africa and I would have missed the most important chapter of my life.

And to Carol Peacock, my long-lost and dear friend, you threw yourself into my book project as though it were your own. I will be forever grateful for your enthusiasm and wise counsel. Somehow we have managed to show up for one another for almost forty years now!

William and Sarah Modest, you are the heart and soul of Precious Project in Tanzania. Without your dedication and love there would be no Precious Project, and three hundred children would be the worse for it. You have taught us about Tanzanian culture and customs. You have forgiven us for our naïve blunders and you have taken us into your confidence in the most crucial decisions for how to move ahead.

Elliot Kronstein and May Baldwin, you first came to visit us with a suitcase of toothbrushes. Then you came back and brought your generous hearts to work. Without your steady dedication we would be nowhere near where we are today. You are leaving a lasting legacy.

To my friends and family, this book was years in the making. You were tolerant of my broken-record obsessing about how long this would take and could I really do it. Many of you read excerpts and urged me to keep going. Bruce Boley, you said I was writing a page-turner and that feedback fueled me for weeks.

Lastly, I want to thank you, Gil Williams, my dear husband. You have listened to me read aloud every word and every page of this book as it evolved. At first you were the cheerleader from abroad and now indeed you are my partner in crime, stitched at the hip in this project that has now come to define our later years. From the beginning of our life together you have encouraged me to follow my dreams, and now look at where this has taken us! I have seen a level of courage, commitment and kindness in you in these years in Africa that I deeply admire.

Some of the proceeds of this book will go to the Precious Project. For more information about the project, please visit our website www.preciousproject.org.

ABOUT THE AUTHOR

A PhD psychologist, Susanne Rheault has worked for over ten years in sub-Saharan Africa, serving as a special advisor to the Clinton Foundation Health Access Initiative. As the cofounder of the Precious Project, a school and home for vulnerable children in rural Tanzania, Susie serves as a key advisor and advocate for the organization, working alongside her husband and two Tanzanian cofounders, William and Sarah Modest. *My Wild and Precious Life* is her first book.

70976777R00171

Made in the USA
Columbia, SC
23 August 2019